To Dick,

With best wishes.

Jim

PURSUIT OF POWER

PURSUIT

Edited and translated
by James C. Davis

◀ HARPER TORCHBOOKS
Harper & Row, Publishers

OF POWER

Venetian Ambassadors' Reports
on Spain, Turkey, and France
in the Age of Philip II, 1560-1600

New York, Evanston, and London

PURSUIT OF POWER

English translation copyright © 1970 by James C. Davis.

First HARPER TORCHBOOK edition published 1970

LIBRARY OF CONGRESS CATALOG CARD NUMBER: 70–134281

To my father and mother

Contents

Illustrations

PURSUIT OF POWER

INTRODUCTION:
THE VIEWERS AND THE VIEWED

"The reports of the Venetian ambassadors." For generations these words have held a certain fascination for historians of early modern Europe. The authors of these
reports were those clear-eyed and politically seasoned
gentlemen who represented one of Europe's most admired
governments at Rome, Paris, Madrid, Vienna, and Constantinople, and the reports contain their observations on
the European civilization they knew. This book aims to
introduce the general reader to these celebrated documents[1]
and to draw from them a political and social portrait of
Europe in the age of Philip II as it was seen and understood by some of the period's most skilled and experienced
observers. It is, then, a kind of reconstruction by means of
selection and abridgment, an epitome, a distillation of the
ambassadors' understanding of their world. The Venetian
ambassadors were interested chiefly in the way power was
held and used by the great European monarchies and
empires; the pursuit of power therefore looms large in this
reconstruction of the way the ambassadors viewed Europe in their time.

To know what to make of these reports, to understand
what their picture of Europe in the latter sixteenth century

1. The Italian historian Luigi Firpo is editing a photo-offset re-
printing of the best editions of all Venetian ambassadors' reports that
have ever appeared in print.

has to say to the world in the latter twentieth century, one must first know some things about the reports' authors. To put it another way, before considering what was viewed one must first know the men who did the viewing. The ambassadors came from that cluster of sand dunes in the north Adriatic Sea whose settlement and transformation during earlier centuries into a vibrant city-state serves as one of the most impressive demonstrations of human adaptability. Undoubtedly the ancestors of most of the ambassadors, like the other early citizens of Venice, had moved out to the sandy Adriatic islands in the sixth and seventh centuries, a time when the Lombards and other barbarians were raiding and conquering the towns of the mainland. Very little is known about the early leaders of the island settlements. Perhaps they were provincial Roman nobles, as their descendants would later claim, or perhaps they were merely the more successful of the fishermen and petty traders of the lagoon islands. In any case, there seems to have developed in the dimly known early medieval period a group of men who were both the rulers of the islands and the chief traders of the region. When Venice later emerged as a great midpoint of trade between Europe and the East, the men of these families were the prosperous middlemen of this exchange, and some of them built great fortunes on the trade in slaves and silks, woolens and damask, sugar and wheat, malmsey and muscatel wines, copper and frankincense.

Before long these great merchant statesmen were referred to as "nobles." At the end of the thirteenth century the nobles passed new rules about their Great Council which had the effect of transforming the loosely organized patriciate into a rigidly exclusive ruling class, a textbook example of an aristocratic republic. These exclusive merchant rulers ran an efficient city-state government, fought wars, and put together a far-flung empire of Mediterranean islands and north Italian plains. The Venetian ambassadors of the age of Philip II of Spain were the descendants of these settlers, merchant princes, admirals, and empire builders.

The government for which the ambassadors worked was,

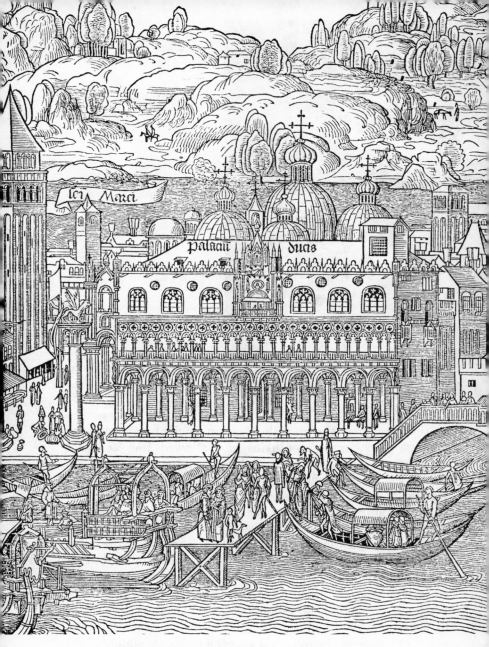

1. Ducal Palace, Venice, as Seen from the Landing.

(Detail of panorama in von Breydenbach, Peregrinationes, *1486. Library of Congress, Washington, D.C.)*

2. Doge Andrea Gritti, by Titian.
(National Gallery of Art, Washington, D.C., Samuel H. Kress Collection.)

as the foregoing sketch indicates, an ancient one, and the passage of so many centuries had allowed the Venetian ruling class to develop remarkably stable governmental institutions. (The Venetians would probably have said that it was the genius of their institutions that permitted their city-state to endure for so many centuries.) The reader needs to know a little about three of these institutions with which the ambassadors customarily had dealings. The first is the doge, who stood at the apex of the pyramid of government, but by the sixteenth century was largely a ceremonial figure. Because the doge presided over the Senate, where they read their reports, the ambassadors occasionally address remarks in these reports to him, calling him "Your Serenity." Beneath the doge in the pyramid was the Collegio, which might be considered the executive body. It was the Collegio that usually read the ambassadors' dispatches from foreign courts and shaped policy on the basis of them.[2] Beneath the Collegio was the Senate, which comprised the Collegio and nearly three hundred other men. The Senate was responsible for deciding major questions of commerce and foreign policy, usually after the Collegio had formulated the proposals that it debated and decided. The Senate elected the ambassadors, and it was to this body that the ambassadors read their reports.

Surveying Venice's diverse group of government institutions—the doge, the Great Council, the Collegio, the Council of Ten, the Senate, and others—people said that its government was "rich and consolatory like its treacle, being compounded nicely of all the other forms—a grain of monarchy, a scruple of democracy, a drachm of oligarchy, and an ounce of aristocracy."[3] But clearly aristocracy was the chief ingredient. For century after century the doges, admirals, generals, ambassadors, governors, and officials of the state were chosen from the same group of families. Small wonder then that they developed an almost religious loyalty to their state and a high level of competence in all aspects of government.

One of these aspects was the conduct of foreign relations. Most historians agree that European diplomacy first developed in Italy. In the fifteenth century, Italy anticipated on a small scale what western Europe as a whole would later resemble: a collection of fiercely competitive states constantly engaged in struggles for survival. To meet this challenge these governments responded in the ways all modern governments have since learned to do. That is, they found ways to raise large sums of money in crises, they raised armies not of feudal knights but of career soldiers,

2. As with the reports, the ambassadors often address remarks in the dispatches to "Your Serenity," because the doge presided over Collegio meetings. Some dispatches were sent to the Council of Ten instead of the Collegio.

3. Hester L. Piozzi, *Observations and Reflections Made in the Course of a Journey Through France, Italy, and Germany* (Ann Arbor, Mich., 1967), p. 102. Writing in the eighteenth century, Mrs. Piozzi called this "not an ill saying, though an old one perhaps."

they developed competent and professional bureaucracies, and they began the use of resident ambassadors—men sent to live for considerable periods in other states and represent the home government there.[4] The Venetians played a leading role in developing all of these institutions, but in none more than diplomacy. By the latter Middle Ages they had done much to shape the job of ambassador and had also acquired a high reputation for the skill with which they carried out this work. Perhaps they were aided by the fact that they were a hereditary ruling class; it was easy and natural for fathers to train their sons in the diplomatic arts when they were confident that the young men would eventually put this training to use.

By the latter sixteenth century—the period with which this book deals—many of the statecraft techniques developed in Italy had already appeared in northern Europe. They may have appeared spontaneously, as reactions to the same conditions that prompted their development in Italy, or they may have appeared as a result of imitation—what Arnold Toynbee has called "the political Italianization" of Europe. In any case diplomacy as practiced by Venetians was no longer different in form from that of other western European countries. But there were certainly differences in quality. Probably more than any other state, Venice had men who had been born into a tradition of diplomacy, who had traveled with their fathers or uncles on missions and thus absorbed the arts they saw practiced, who had heard oral reports delivered to their governments by returning ambassadors, and who had read confidential diplomatic dispatches while serving in high government offices. Thus despite its smallness Venice probably had a larger body of ambassadorial talent on which to call than any other state. The perceptiveness and general accuracy of Venetian am-

4. For an admirable discussion of the beginnings of European diplomacy see Garrett Mattingly, *Renaissance Diplomacy* (Boston, 1955). Chapter III of Donald E. Queller's recent book, *The Office of Ambassador in the Middle Ages* (Princeton, N.J., 1967), deals with the first resident ambassadors, especially the Venetian ones.

bassadors' reports is widely believed to have remained high through the sixteenth century and later as well.

One might ask, why did a small state take the conduct of her international relations so seriously? For Venice by the latter sixteenth century was no longer a major European power. She was now dwarfed—and occasionally threatened —by the large territorial monarchies and empires elsewhere on the Eurasian continent. The answer to the question may lie precisely in this perilous position. The Venetians knew how limited were their means, yet they wanted to survive. The solution was to maintain a consistent neutrality (toward European powers, not Turkey) and to be so well informed through their ambassadors that they could make no fatal missteps.

To understand how the ambassadors observed events of their time, one should have in mind a picture of how these men carried out their missions. The typical Venetian envoy during the reign of King Philip had probably grown up in a family with an ambassadorial tradition, and while a youth he may have accompanied his father or an uncle on an embassy. Consequently he was well imbued with a knowledge of the duties, traditions, and skills of an ambassador even before his fellow nobles in Venice first elected him and sent him abroad as a representative. Once elected, he put his affairs in order, assembled the secretary, servants, horses, fine clothing, and expensive furnishings he would need, and set out for the capital in which he was to serve for a period of three years. The trip itself could be exhausting and dangerous. An assignment to France meant a horseback ride of about two weeks and at least one sixteenth-century ambassador died en route. To go to Madrid one sailed from Venice or Genoa to Barcelona and then crossed half the Iberian peninsula on lonely bandit-ridden roads. As for the sea journey to Constantinople, Dalmatian pirates infested the islands along part of the route, and we know that deteriorating seamanship was causing a rise in the number of Venetian shipwrecks in the latter sixteenth century. No wonder that Giovanni Michiel in 1577 spoke of himself as "used up in these duties, it being more than twenty-six years without interruption that I have been wearing out my boots. I can honestly say that traveling on your orders I have followed every valley, crossed every mountain, and passed over every river in Europe."[5]

When the ambassador and his secretary and servants arrived in the assigned capital, he usually took over an official residence vacated by his predecessor and then presented himself for an official audience with the king or sultan. In all probability he would talk to the monarch only infrequently in the rest of his three-year term, though this depended very much on the traditions of the court, the personality of the king, and the relations between Venice and the country in question. The Venetian ambassadors to Philip II of Spain found that they could see the king whenever they asked for an interview, but in Spain as elsewhere the ambassadors often did much of their official business with a minister or favorite. They found that a present of a painting by one of the famous Venetian masters helped to keep these relationships friendly.

Most of the ambassador's time was spent in collecting news and gossip which he could report in his frequent dispatches to the Senate and the Council of Ten. He obtained

5. *Fontes rerum austriacarum,* series II, vol. 30 (Vienna, 1870), p. 379.

3. Dalmatian Pirates Attacking Merchant Ship.
(*From Alberto Tenenti,* Venezia e i corsari, *1961.*)

some of this information by cultivating friendly courtiers and other ambassadors. A fifteenth-century Venetian ambassador commented that he found it useful to interrupt with irrelevant remarks someone who was revealing a choice piece of information, because the less he seemed to want to hear, the more people wanted to tell him.[6] An ambassador could also pick up some information by direct observation. When he wanted to discover if the Turks were ready for a naval war in the 1590s the Venetian ambassador in Constantinople simply walked by the unguarded shipyard, observed that there were only a few cannons and these were lying in disorder, and concluded that the Turks had no plans for immediate hostilities.[7]

But ambassadors and their secretaries were also capable of using paid informants, guile, theft, and force. In 1621 the ambassador in London hoped to get information which was in the possession of the agent of the Duke of Tuscany, a man named Antelminelli. He wrote to Venice that he was considering using violence (presumably torture) on Antelminelli. However, he wrote significantly, "in this island [England] it is not nearly so easy to use force as at home and elsewhere and possibly it would be better to intercept letters." By a fortunate chance his secretary learned that Antelminelli sent letters to Antwerp by means of the Merchant Strangers' Post. The secretary entered the room where outgoing letters lay on a table, pretended to be writing a letter of his own, filched Antelminelli's packet of letters, and took it to his chief. When the Venetians were then accused of the theft the ambassador pretended indignant rage and the matter was dropped.[8]

There were two ways in which ambassadors provided the home government with news and analysis. The more important was the dispatch, a letter sometimes of only a few lines

6. Mattingly, *Renaissance Diplomacy*, p. 114.
7. Federico Seneca, *Il doge Leonardo Donà la sua vita e la sua preparazione politica prima del dogado* (Padua, 1959), p. 307.
8. *Calendar of State Papers and Manuscripts, Relating to English Affairs, Existing in the Archives and Collections of Venice . . .*, various editors, 38 vols. (1864–1940), 17: 99, 111.

but often of many pages. Ambassadors wrote dispatches at very frequent intervals, even daily in periods of international tension, and in them they reported their conversations with kings and ministers, other news and gossip, and their own predictions and suggestions. If secrecy was needed to confound an enemy who might open the Venetian courier's pouch the ambassador's secretary put key passages in cipher.

The other way in which ambassadors reported to their fellow Venetians was in the famous *relazioni*, or reports, which they read aloud to the Senate soon after returning home from three years' service in foreign capitals. (About four-fifths of the documents in this book are abridged from reports, one-fifth from dispatches.) The purpose of the reports was to further the political education of the ruling class, especially the younger senators and other officials who were entitled to attend Senate meetings. Where the dis-

4. Senate Chamber in the Ducal Palace.

(*Foto Anderson. Courtesy of Art Reference Bureau.*)

patches had carried the fresh news on which statesmen in Venice had based their policymaking, the reports were more general discussions of the rulers, peoples, armies, finances, and foreign policies of the countries where they had served. Sometimes the ambassadors offered very unfavorable private views of men and events, reminding the senators to treat all they said as secret.

Some of the reports are very long—they often took as much as four or five hours in the reading[9]—and most of them are fairly polished works. Clearly a lot of work went into the collection of facts and figures, orderly discussion of the elements of a country's power, thoughtful characterization of kings and their intimates, and adornment with medical metaphors, old sayings, and even some humor. A marked stylistic trait is that whole sections of a report are often organized in a rhetorical framework. Typically an ambassador will describe three qualities which lend strength to a country, then show at length how these assets in time of stress can turn into three corresponding weaknesses. This fondness for rhetorical organization was probably inspired by an education which stressed the Greek and Roman classics, especially Cicero. While the reports are sometimes florid and tedious, they are more often candid, informative, and luminously revealing of the outlook of some marvelously cosmopolitan men, who knew sixteenth-century European civilization as few others did.

What the ambassadors have to say in these reports naturally reflects their loyalties and values. The ambassadors were among other things Roman Catholics and Venetians and aristocrats, and each of these three attachments is reflected in what they wrote. But it is not enough to let it go at that, because a man's loyalties and self-interests in the sixteenth century, as in all times, sometimes combined with and sometimes even contradicted each other. Consider their religious beliefs and their economic or class interests as Venetian aristocrats. The ambassadors were of course

---

9. A few were half the length of this book.

deeply committed to Catholicism. Sometimes their belief and religious practice may have been conventional and superficial, but many of them read devotional books, interpreted events as the will of God and—especially relevant for our purposes here—often viewed international affairs as a struggle between Catholicism and heresy or unbelief. This is not to say that they viewed all Protestants as tragically deluded, or despised every Turkish infidel, but they clearly hoped for the victory not merely of Christianity, but of Western Catholicism. Whether or not Venice was on good terms with King Philip of Spain, the ambassadors usually considered him the champion of the holy cause, and they hoped for peace between Spain and France so that all Catholics could join forces against the Turks.

However, the commitment to Catholicism was also in good part a feeling of loyalty and gratitude to the Church as an enormous mutual-benefit society from which they as Venetian nobles profited enormously. Probably there was not one who did not have at least an uncle, a brother or sister, a son or daughter in the Church. An interesting study by an Italian historian has shown that most mid-sixteenth-century Venetian bishops were nobles, that their positions were handsomely paid sinecures, and that these bishops handed their bishoprics on to their cousins and nephews in such a way as to keep a family hold on the lucrative posts for generations.[10] Two of the ambassadors whose reports appear here later became bishops and cardinals.

If the ambassadors were Catholics, they were also Venetians. Their patriotism was partly that love of the beauty of one's own native land which is an ingredient in all nationalisms. Their uniquely lovely island city was a natural object for such devotion, and they cherished it as the contemporary Shakespeare cherished his own "precious stone set in the silver sea." Beyond the purely physical attachment was a more idealistic and abstract one. When they spoke of Venice as "the state" and "the fatherland," these terms bore with

---

10. Giuseppe Alberigo, *I vescovi italiani al Concilio di Trento (1545–1547)* (Florence: Sansoni, 1959), pp. 47–80.

5. Gabriele Emo, Venetian
Nobleman, by Tintoretto.

*(Seattle Art Museum, Seattle, Wash.,
Samuel H. Kress Collection.)*

them an emotional freight made up of the sacrifices of effort, wealth, and life which countless generations of Venetians had made for their society. The Venetian nobility had led in making such sacrifices, and so the ambassadors' sense of loyalty and devotion was even keener than the loyalty of the ordinary citizen.

But just as Catholicism carried with it an attachment not only to high spiritual ideals but also to an aristocratic mutual-aid society, so the Venetian government evoked not merely lofty patriotism but also a class interest in the government which gave Venetian nobles wealth and status. It was enormously good fortune to belong to the ruling class of such a state, for the happy sharers of power enjoyed a semimonopoly of international trade, regulated this trade largely in their own interest, shared major government offices, and called each other *nobil uomo* (nobleman). Their outlook, naturally, was that their wealth and privileges were the rewards society paid them for assuming the responsibilities of rule. When he reported to the Senate after his return from Turkey, Leonardo Donà commented with wonder that the Turkish sultans always confiscated the fortunes of their wealthy subjects when they died and avoided the forming of a hereditary nobility.[11] To Donà this explained the insolence and ineptitude of Turkish officials (since they were all upstarts) and led him to voice doubt that any state that lacked a class with a financial "stake in the country" could ever survive a determined enemy's attack. For Donà, and most Venetian nobles, aristocracy and patriotism came close to being synonymous.

Religion, we have seen, overlapped or combined with class interest, and class interest with patriotism. It remains to be shown that religion and patriotism also merged. In fact, the Venetians probably found it rather hard to separate love of God from love of native land. Ancient legends held that a sign from Heaven had shown the early Venetians that they should flee to the islands to escape the pagan barbarians, and that Mark, their patron saint, had always shown a special interest in the republic. In the sixteenth century especially, when the Venetians several times had to fight the infidel Turks, their cause was considered also a divine one, and many Venetian paintings make it clear that the God of Battles was on their side. When Andrea Donà, older brother of the ambassador Leonardo, went to war in 1570 he wrote in his will that he hoped to die in battle so that he might "with my death wash away some of the many offenses I have committed" against God and (in the next phrase) "sacrifice my life for my country." He regarded the Turk as simultaneously the perfidious attacker of the Venetian state and an infidel so clearly the enemy of God that if Andrea died fighting him his sins would be remitted and he would make of the sea "an honorable and glorious sepulcher and monument."[12]

11. The writer will soon complete and publish a study of the con-
~ion of family wealth in early modern times which focuses on
 à family.
~l of Andrea Donà. Arch. di St. di Venezia, T.N. 1262, 3: 37.

"The age of Philip II." As mentioned above, this group of reports and dispatches was selected with the aim of portraying the world of the Venetian ambassadors as they saw it during the reign of a great Spanish king. But, a reader might ask, why use the reign of a king to fix the size of the portrait? Haven't we learned that it is not great men but surges of great social forces that shape events? The answer is that while the Venetian ambassadors were aware of those forces, they also knew that strong kings did a great deal to channel and direct them, and in their reports they devoted much of their time to analyzing the qualities and policies of those rulers. To use the sixteenth-century catch phrase for the attitude which puts the interests of the state ahead of morality and tradition, the ambassadors were concerned with the kings' "reasons of state."[13]

Now of all the latter-sixteenth-century rulers King Philip of Spain most impressed and most captured the imaginations of the Venetians. Philip ruled more people, worked harder on behalf of his government, and held his religious beliefs more deeply than any other contemporary ruler. Even though he scarcely moved from his palace, agonized over every decision, and lost as well as won great battles, it was this in many ways paradoxical ruler who, more than anyone else, shaped public events in the last half of the sixteenth century. And therefore it would have seemed very natural to the ambassadors to use his reign to set the time brackets for this book.

The ambassadors' task was to understand and influence (as far as possible) the empires and monarchies of Europe, and we may take it for granted that their opinions about the powers struggling for European hegemony in the latter sixteenth century were as expert as any. As well as one can synthesize their collective opinion from a number of stated

13. On the history of this phrase see Friedrich Meinecke, *Machiavellism: the Doctrine of Raison d'État and Its Place in Modern History* (New Haven, 1957), pp. 47–48. For examples of its use by Venetian ambassadors see Willy Andreas, *Staatskunst und Diplomatie der Venezianer im Spiegel ihrer Gesandtenberichte* (Leipzig, 1943), pp. 5, 68, 158–59.

judgments and a greater number of implied ones, they believed that the great powers of their time were Turkey (the Ottoman Empire), France, and Spain. In 1559, soon after Philip became king, one ambassador offered his view that "world affairs have had the effect of thrusting many formerly separate and distinct domains into the hands of just three rulers. . . . One of them is the king we have been discussing [Philip of Spain], and the others are the king of France and the sultan of Turkey; they are the important ones."[14]

True, another ambassador, thirty-four years later, used very similar phrasing to say that the greater part of the "powers and empires" had gone into the hands not of three kings, but of two, which were the sultan and the king of Spain. He thus excluded France from his list, and as a matter of fact, if one considers only the accumulation of lands and ignores the question of power, he probably should leave France out of consideration, because sixteenth-century France did not mushroom in size as did the Turkish and Spanish empires. But if one considers power France belongs on the list. As a matter of fact, this same ambassador mentions that before 1559 Spain and France had been "major forces which pulled the rest of Europe along behind them," that France was at the moment "weakened, fallen to the ground, more like a bloodless cadaver than a living body," but that she was nevertheless *"potentissimo"* and a grave threat to Spain if she could pull herself together.[15] The other ambassadors did not provide capsuled opinions about which powers dominated Europe, but it is clear from the way they discussed international relations that they too put Turkey, France, and Spain at the top.

Perhaps the best way for the modern reader to understand the relationships between the great powers in the last part

14. Eugenio Albèri, ed., *Le relazioni degli ambasciatori veneti al senato durante il secolo decimosesto*, 15 vols. (Florence: Società editrice fiorentina, 1855), series I, pt. 3 (report of Michele Suriano), 374.

Ibid., series I, pt. 5 (report of Tommaso Contarini), pp. 414–16,

of the sixteenth century is by comparison with the international cold war tensions of the late 1940s, 1950s, and early 1960s. The latter sixteenth century, like the mid-twentieth, had its uncertainly belligerent giants, its lesser powers nervously watching the sparring Goliaths, its fierce ideologies and ancient national rancors, its spy hunts, brink-of-war confrontations, violent clashes, and global fly swattings. In the sixteenth century, however, the great powers came to blows with each other more than has been true during the cold war—perhaps because there was no danger of a nuclear holocaust.

It is time to take a closer look at these powers which were struggling for what the ambassadors called "universal monarchy." It seems best to begin with Philip II's Spain.

Spain in the sixteenth century was enjoying her all too brief period of great political power, of intellectual vigor, even of moral force. From his father, the great Charles V, Philip II had inherited not only Spain but also the Netherlands; little Franche-Comté on France's eastern border; Milan, Naples, and Sicily; and vast areas of North, Central, and South America. (See map on the next page.) Although the highest of his many titles was king, Philip was really an emperor—ruling the largest empire the world has ever known. He did not inherit his father's lands in central Europe, because Charles had turned these over to his brother (Philip's uncle) and thus started a new royal dynasty. However, Philip added the Philippines to what he had inherited, and in 1580 he pressed and won his claim to Portugal and her wealthy colonies in South America (Brazil), Africa, India, and the spice-rich islands of south Asia. Here indeed was an empire on which the sun never set. His lands made Philip a very powerful ruler, but also provided him with overwhelming responsibilities.

Philip was probably as well equipped by nature and training as a mere man could have been for the superhuman tasks of holding together his vast empire and championing the beleaguered Roman Catholic world. To be sure, he was indecisive, suspicious, and overly concerned with details.

(On one occasion the Spanish ambassador in London, knowing the king's concern to have every kind of information, wrote at length about some insects he had seen crawling over his windowpanes. In the margin Philip solemnly wrote: "probably fleas.") But Philip's driving sense of duty to God and his people and his capacity for unending study and supervision of literally global problems were the essential qualities for his position, and they overbalanced his weaknesses. Not every historian would agree with that judgment; most of the Venetian ambassadors certainly did.

Historians of Philip's reign are fond of balancing his successes against his failures. There certainly were many

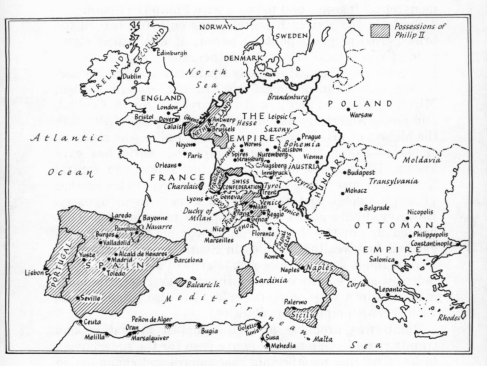

6. Philip II's European Possessions.

(From Sir Charles Petrie, Philip II of Spain, *1963, p. 196. Courtesy of Eyre & Spottiswoode, Publishers.)*

defeats and disappointments. Early in Philip's reign (1568) the nobles and burghers of his Netherlands possession began their revolt against Spain. The causes included Philip's attempts to increase taxes, reorganize the bishoprics, and wipe out heresy, and the Netherlanders' Calvinist beliefs (or more tolerant Catholicism), their national feeling, and (in the case of some nobles) personal ambitions. This revolt lasted a decade beyond the reign of Philip,[16] but long before his death it was obvious that Spain had lost the northern part of the possession (the modern Netherlands, or Holland). Because the Venetian ambassadors to Spain were stationed at Madrid, and not in the Netherlands, where the fighting took place, they have comparatively little to say about this struggle.

As if the loss of the northern Netherlands was not enough, Philip also suffered the defeat of his great fleet, or Armada, by the English in 1588. In France, his support of the Catholic forces in the French Wars of Religion had mixed results; his archenemy Henry of Bourbon became king and Catholic, changed the civil war to a national war against Spain, and forced the Spanish to make peace. Philip also had to cope with staggering financial problems, which four times made him declare humiliating bankruptcies. And he endured more than his share of personal family tragedy. Before he was sixty he had seen seventeen members of his family buried in the Escorial monastery-palace. One of these was his first son, the demented and physically deformed Don Carlos.

But not everything turned to ashes. Philip successfully crushed a revolt of the Moriscos (Moorish nominal converts to Christianity), although it should be added that their uprising had resulted from an inept effort to Christianize them. He joined his ships to those of Venice and the Pope in 1571 and, with his half brother Don Juan in command, virtually annihilated a Turkish fleet at the Battle of Lepanto. The winning of the wealthy Portuguese empire in

16. A peace treaty formally liberating the northern Netherlands (Holland) was not signed until 1648.

7. Ambassador Leonardo Donà with King Philip II, by Marco Vecellio. *(Collection of Count Lorenzo Donà dalle Rose, Venice.)*

1580 was another triumph for Philip, a victory won by skillful use of arms and diplomacy. Though successfully resisted by King Henry IV of France, Philip at least contributed to keeping that country Catholic. And finally, he put down a revolt in the province of Aragon (1591–92) in such a way as to preserve the federated pattern of the Spanish monarchy; the liberties of Aragon were respected, but future revolts were discouraged.

France in the latter sixteenth century was very different from the Spain of Philip II. One of the most obvious differences was that she was not an empire but rather what historians call a "territorial monarchy." This means, obviously, that she was ruled by a king, but a king who (unlike

Philip II) had roughly the same kind of authority in all the land he ruled. More important, a territorial monarchy usually comprised only a governable amount of land—one which it was feasible for the ruler to traverse from time to time, seeing his subjects, making laws for them, and if necessary defending them in battle. A territorial monarchy usually included people most of whom spoke one language, and who shared a number of historical traditions. Thus it resembled a modern nation-state except that its people felt loyalty not so much to the abstract idea of a state as to the person and family of their king. Sixteenth-century France is a classic example of a territorial monarchy. England was another, and in a way central Spain (Castile) was another territorial monarchy, if one considers it apart from all the other lands Philip ruled.

While Spain under Philip II was still enjoying her "golden century," France underwent one of the grimmest periods in her history. This depressing chapter begins in 1559, when Philip II and the French king, Henry II, finally concluded a long war begun by their predecessors. During a tournament which was held in France to celebrate the return of peace, Henry was accidentally wounded in a jousting match, and he died soon after. He left his widow, the fat, durable, cunning Catherine de Medici, with three young sons, and for thirty chaotic years these boys successively reigned. The sickly Francis died after a year as king; he was succeeded by his ten-year-old brother, Charles, who lived largely in his mother's shadow until his death in 1574; and the last of the brothers was Henry III, who was intelligent but unstable and eccentric. For most of these three decades Catherine guided her sons and gave the throne what little stability it had. She made many mistakes and played a leading role in planning an infamous massacre of Protestants, but perhaps one should not blame her for assuming responsibilities her sons could not handle, for being cunning rather than intelligent, and for often losing control over passionately religious or violently ambitious Frenchmen.

The religious turmoil began when Calvinism—the same

form of Protestant belief which would motivate many of
Philip II's enemies in the Netherlands—began to find many
converts among professional people, the lower clergy, and
the nobility. In 1560 and 1561 the Huguenots (as French
Calvinists were called) began to worship openly rather than
secretly. Soon groups of Huguenots and Catholics were
attacking and even massacring each other. But the religious
issue quickly became confused with a struggle for power
within the aristocracy. France at this time was dominated
less by the temporarily feeble monarchy than by three
powerful families: the Guises, who were very rich and
strongly Catholic; the Bourbons, who were closely related to
the royal family, but Protestants; and the Montmorencys,
who were religiously divided. These three families assumed
the leadership of the Catholics and Huguenots and fought
each other partly for religious reasons and partly out of a
desire to control and even take over the throne.

In 1562 the Duke of Guise permitted his retainers to
slaughter a group of Protestant worshipers at Vassy. Violence soon spread everywhere and from this time until 1598
eight different Wars of Religion alternated with periods of
fruitless negotiating. We cannot give the details here. Perhaps the most famous event of the wars took place in August
of 1572, when bands of armed Catholics all over France
carried out a massacre on Saint Bartholomew's eve. Some
three thousand Huguenots were killed in Paris alone. Philip
of Spain wrote to Catherine that the massacre "was indeed
of such value and prudence and of such service, glory and
honor to God and universal benefit to all Christendom that to
hear of it was for me the best and most cheerful news which
at present could come to me."[17] For a combination of
religious and dynastic reasons Philip helped the Catholic
League (led by the Guises) in the later Wars of Religion. In
1588 Henry III, who had been virtually replaced as king by
the Duke of Guise, had the leading Guises murdered; half a

17. Quoted in J. E. Neale, *The Age of Catherine de Medici* (New
York, 1962), p. 80.

year later he was himself stabbed to death by a Dominican friar. As a result the head of the Bourbon family, also named Henry, succeeded to the throne. Henry IV, an immensely likable man and a magnificent leader, realistically converted to Catholicism, brought the wars to an end, and arranged a religious peace within his ravaged country.

If France, a territorial monarchy, was far smaller than the great Spanish and Turkish empires, and was repeatedly devastated in this period by wars, why did the Venetian ambassadors consider her a great power? The answer is that they knew her potential strength. If French armies were being used against each other at this time, it would not always be so. French kings ruled about sixteen million subjects, more than there were in all of Philip II's European lands, and when Frenchmen, with their gallant military tradition, were once again united, all Europe would tremble. If the French treasury was often empty in the latter sixteenth century, French kings nevertheless had the authority to tax heavily. If French towns were sacked in the wars and farmers deserted their proverbially fertile fields, prosperity could return (as the ambassadors observed) even in the intervals between the Wars of Religion. Most important, if the sons of Henry II were weaklings, the institution of monarchy in France was still immensely strong.

Far to the east and south of France and Spain, in lands that sprawled over three continents, lay the third of the great powers of the age of King Philip. During the later medieval centuries the Ottoman Turks had conquered the Byzantine Empire, which was based at Constantinople and included Asia Minor, Bulgaria, and the Balkans. In the century before Philip became king of Spain they had won modern Romania, part of the Crimea (which they made a vassal state), Syria, Egypt, and the holy Arab cities of Mecca and Medina. Under one of their greatest sultans, Suleiman the Magnificent (1520–66), they had then turned west again and conquered much of Hungary and other lands north and east of the Danube. In North Africa Suleiman acquired Algeria, and in Asia he annexed what is now Iraq.

His ships dominated the eastern half of the Mediterranean. By the mid-sixteenth century the Ottoman Empire was so large, and such an extraordinary collection of religions and cultures, that to contemplate it makes the mind reel.

The government of Turkey blended institutions which the Ottomans had used in antiquity as Central Asian nomads with others they had borrowed from Arab Moslems, Persians, and Byzantine Greeks. Since the Venetian ambassadors describe them so well we need say here only that the sultan ruled through a bureaucracy of slaves,[18] that his revenues were so great that even while leading his armies on wars of conquest Suleiman had more money than he needed, and that a unique system of periodically levying children from the Christian subjects provided large numbers of the empire's soldiers and administrators.

After Suleiman died (early in the reign of Philip II of Spain), the Ottoman Empire began to show signs of deterioration. (This topic too is well analyzed by the ambassadors.) Many of the sultans displayed more vigor in the harem than on the battlefield, and the son of Suleiman the Magnificent was called Selim the Sot. The janissaries were just beginning to be insubordinate; later they would often depose sultans and choose their successors. And there were some signs of economic malaise. As a military power the Turks were still to be feared, but they were not invincible. In 1571 they captured the valuable island of Cyprus from the Venetians, but this led to the formation of a Christian league which annihilated a Turkish fleet in the great Battle of Lepanto off the Greek coast. The western powers did not recover Cyprus for Venice, and the Turks demonstrated considerable resilience by soon rebuilding their navy. But the Turks' enemies could find the same hope in Lepanto that Philip II's enemies later found in the defeat of the Armada. At the end of the century the Turks had so little success in a war with the Holy Roman Emperor Rudolf II that in

18. Half of the highest positions in the state were held by slaves, but obviously this was a peculiar kind of "slavery" with little social inferiority attached to it.

the peace negotiations they had to treat the Hapsburg emperor not as a contemptible lesser potentate but as an equal. If the Turk was not yet the "sick man of Europe" (the expression used by nineteenth-century European statesmen) he would never again be as vigorous as he had been half a century earlier under Suleiman the Magnificent.

While the Venetian ambassadors saw Turkey, France, and Spain as the great powers, they were not likely to forget that there were other countries quite capable of asserting themselves and perhaps only waiting for circumstances which would allow them to struggle for European hegemony. England, then thriving under the reign of Queen Elizabeth, had an exhilarating success in her defeat of the Spanish Armada. But she was a small country (perhaps four and a half million inhabitants, with Wales) and fairly content with the isolation that the English Channel forced on her. The Holy Roman Empire, which took in what is now Germany, Austria, western Czechoslovakia, and a good deal besides, should have played a bigger role than it did, but the emperors were harassed by religious dissension, pressure from the Turks, and an absolutely hopeless governmental constitution. As for the other European countries, they were too small, too bedeviled by internal conflicts, too rural, or too peripheral to count for much in European affairs.

How did the Venetian ambassadors view the conflict of Turkey, France, and Spain? Their attitudes again call the "cold war" forcibly to mind. The Venetian ambassadors were representatives of a small, conservative, fiercely pro-Western country. For them, the great enemy was a huge eastern land whose people held to an unspeakable ideology, obeyed ruthless tyrants, and were arrogant and uncivilized. To deal with this evil power they placed their hopes in a great Western power which shared their ideology. This power was devoted partly to its own selfish ends but partly also to defending truth and civilization, and its leader, for all his faults, was a determined leader of the "right" cause. Also in the West was another great country, one that had fought in the good cause for nearly a millennium, but where misguided "reformers" now twisted the ancient truths and opportunists joined them in dividing and ravaging the land. The sturdy institutions of government here had been nearly destroyed, blood had been spilled and wealth wasted, but the energies that were now being dissipated in fruitless internal conflict might yet be harnessed for the defense of truth.

Perhaps, however, the analogy with the cold war calls too much attention to the matter of ideology. The defense of

8. Pope (standing) and Venetian Doge and Philip II (kneeling) Thanking God for Victory in the Battle of Lepanto, by El Greco.

(*Detail from* Allegory of the Holy League, *National Gallery, London.*)

Christian civilization counted for a good deal with the Venetians, but they were also capable of a more dispassionate analysis of what each power brought to the struggle for hegemony. One might whimsically imagine them as sports reporters, viewing international relations as if it were a long-distance race. Just before the race starts the Holy Roman Empire withdraws because of bad muscle strains. Then the starter's pistol sounds and the race begins. Two men soon take the lead. One is Spain, a strong runner, determined to win because of personal pride and a feeling that much of the crowd is counting on him, but a trifle weary from too many recent contests. The other is Turkey, also a strong runner and a treacherous one, but somehow lacking his former concentration and will to win. Slightly behind is sturdy and gallant France, handicapped by a bad start and hampered because his faithless trainer yells abuse at him as he runs, but needing only an opportunity to put to use his explosive energy. Still farther back, but not so far as the runners believe, is England, a vigorous stripling who may not win this time but will certainly put the experience to good use in future races. The Venetian reporters stand on the sidelines, jeering at Turkey and cheering for France and Spain—but not neglecting their professional duty to note the qualities of each runner.

Venetian ambassadors provided their fellow nobles with information that was essential for a state's survival in the latter sixteenth century. What do they have to say to us, four centuries later?

On perhaps the least important level, the ambassadors' reports and dispatches provide certain kinds of information about specific events—information of use especially to professional historians. For instance, they tell us about the secret planning of the massacre of Saint Bartholomew's Eve, or the reasons that forced Philip II to lead armed men to the room of Don Carlos and place his demented son under arrest. True, the ambassadors often knew only what was common knowledge or rumor, but their diligence in finding out what was being said or done and the fact that they quickly reported it in their dispatches (before memory distorted it) make them good witnesses. There are cases where the ambassadors were the best or only witnesses to what happened, such as to the way Philip joyfully received the news of the victory at Lepanto, or to the way he greeted with "the very fleetest of ironic smiles" the news that Venice had made a separate peace with the Turks.

The ambassadors' reports, which are observations on a variety of countries by some very well traveled men, can also show the merits of a comparative approach to the study of European culture and provide materials for it. Suppose one is interested in ruling classes—in such questions as whether they were closed castes (like the Venetian nobility) or easily accessible, how they were controlled by kings, or what were the sources of their wealth. The ambassadors provide us with insights and observations for fascinating comparisons. They tell us of the Neapolitan nobles "in despair because they see themselves reduced to the status of their inferiors"; the Spanish grandees, who are remarkable only for their indolence and "Spanish composure"; the lesser nobility of France, gallant in war but financially troubled; and the Turkish viziers, drawn from the lowest ranks of Ottoman society, often grasping and incompetent, and (legally speaking) slaves who might at any moment have bowstrings looped around their necks from behind and drawn very tight.

But the ambassadors are interesting above all because they were such sharp-eyed witnesses of the great process of European state building and centralization. The story of Western civilization in recent centuries has been the story of rapid growth of certain kinds of control over the social and physical environment. Western man has learned how to move and communicate ever more swiftly over long distances. He has acquired some knowledge of how societies and physical organisms work, and with knowledge there slowly comes control. He has learned to form great unions of land, labor, machines, and other capital goods that give him the leverage with which to produce yet more capital and consumable wealth. He has learned not only to exert some control over the exit from life, with hospitals and medicines, but over entrance to it as well, as a birth-control mentality has slowly spread. But perhaps more obvious than any of these changes has been the growth of centralized and powerful states with the tax resources, the capable administrators, the monopoly of military power, and the determination to make all their citizens work and sacrifice for established state purposes. The struggle of the great powers for hegemony was the greatest force impelling rulers to develop armies, to crush rebellious aristocracies, to create loyal bureaucracies, and to collect taxes.

It was this particular aspect of the growth of control over the social and physical environment—the process of state building and centralization in the crucible of international conflict—which the Venetians observed most closely. The ambassadors realized that what counted in the international struggle was what the ruler did with his own holdings. Serving first in one country and then in another, constantly reporting what they saw, the Venetian ambassadors were among the greatest observers of this particular phase of the history of Western civilization. What they offer us, with their passionate interest and detailed knowledge well balanced by experience and excellent opportunities for comparisons, are valuable perspectives on the process of state building.

A few words are in order about the editing and translation of these reports and dispatches. All of the reports in this book and all the dispatches except those dealing with the Armada and the deaths of Philip II and Sultan Murad were translated by me. The exceptions are the work of Horatio Brown, a nineteenth-century English historian of Venice. All the reports (but not the dispatches) have been translated from the originals in Albèri's *Relazioni*.

Like even the best of reporters and commentators on recent events, the ambassadors sometimes had their facts wrong. If this were an edition intended only for scholars these mistakes would all be subjected to footnoting, tut-tutting, and correcting, but in fact this book is intended rather for the general reader. In it, therefore, such mistakes are called to the reader's attention in footnotes only when they are particularly important or when an alert reader might realize that a statement fails to jibe with something he is told elsewhere in the book.

Just as the ambassadors sometimes got their facts wrong, occasionally they did not write clearly, and occasionally they wrote in a style which to twentieth-century ears seems complicated or overblown. Their pronouns seem to refer to any of several antecedent persons or things, adjectives often appear in tautological duos (e.g., "strong and powerful king"), a habit of exaggeration sometimes results in too many *very*s and *many*s and *great*s as modifiers, sentences are really groups of sentences linked by semicolons, and paragraphs seem to be confusingly broken in the wrong places. A few of these matters result from just plain bad writing, others from errors which crept in when the reports were copied and recopied in longhand in the centuries before they were published in books, but the greatest number reflect what was considered good literary style in sixteenth-century Venice.

It would be foolish, obviously, for a translator to repro-duce all of these stylistic aberrancies in order to make his product "faithful." On the contrary, I did not hesitate to straighten out confusing references of pronouns, avoid tautologies and exaggeration, break up sentences, and even change paragraphing. In general I followed the practice of making the ambassadors express themselves as I imagined they would if they were addressing a twentieth-century senate (or writing to twentieth-century officials) in English. The result is a "free" translation, but should a translator ever aim at anything less?

I should like to thank the following friends and colleagues at the University of Pennsylvania for help they gave me in the preparation of this book: Elmiro Argento, John Bernheim, Frank E. B. Conaway, Werner L. Gundersheimer, Thomas Naff, Celia H. Newell, Otakar Odlozilik, Richard T. Rapp, and Martin Wolfe.

James C. Davis

University of Pennsylvania
January 1970

I.

The Catholic King of Spain — Victories and Defeats

1 "THE STRONGEST
AND SAFEST CHRISTIAN LAND"

Michele Suriano, 1559

"Spain" in the sixteenth century was both a European country and a far-flung empire. As a result of an almost unbelievable combination of dynastic marriages and untimely deaths, Charles V (who reigned from 1516 to 1556) had inherited the scattered parts of his empire, and he had added some territory to it by conquest. Then he had divided it (in effect) by turning over the central European part of it to his brother[1] and all the rest to his son Philip. The ambassador Suriano wrote this report three years after Philip II had shouldered his burden. Though here abridged, Suriano's *relazione* covers most of the standard topics of a typical Venetian report.

Your Serenity, venerable gentlemen, and Your Excellencies,[2] we all know from experience that to rule a state wisely and safely, nothing is more helpful and necessary than accurate information about the plans of the great kings and rulers and their means of carrying out these plans. With this information at hand one can remain at peace with those whose friendship he values and be so prepared that he has nothing to fear if trouble arises.

From a report by Michele Suriano, 1559, Albèri, I, 3: 333–78.

1. He did this by stages between 1519 and 1556.
2. Suriano is addressing the doge (Lorenzo Priuli), cabinet officials, and senators.

Every ruler eagerly seeks information through various channels, some with reports, others through conversations, still others with spies and various informers. But no source is better than ambassadors, especially when the ambassadors, because they serve great princes or have great ability, enjoy high standing in the courts. Ambassadors deal with important men and skillfully evaluate the words, customs, values, opinions, and methods of all of these men, including rulers. As a result they can understand past events more profoundly than those who are mere chroniclers and summarizers, and they are not limited to probing current events, as spies are. No, with a deep knowledge of both past and present, they can even guess at the future.

But since only an ambassador with great experience, skill, and judgment can analyze events in this way, I must ask you to forgive me if I undertake to report to Your Excellencies about such extremely important matters when I personally lack these qualities. I am not so foolish as to forget that I fall short of the skill needed to perform this task well.

However, Your Serene Highness is so respected by all kings and rulers in the world, and especially at the court from which I have just come, that I have been honored and favored to an extraordinary degree by the king and nobles. One person and another—even the king himself—have confided in me so much that with this information and what I was able to see for myself during my mission of twenty-eight months, it will not be so hard for me to carry out what I have promised Your Serenity. There will not be anything of my making in this account except the form and the order in which I propose to tell Your Serenity what I have learned and heard from other men. If my memory will not fail me and if Your Excellencies will grant me a quiet and receptive hearing, I hope that the report will be so concise and lucid that you will not find it boring or disagreeable.

The present Catholic King, who was born into the imperial family of Austria and inherited the wealth and destinies of the kings of Spain and the house of Burgundy, owns so many fiefs, kingdoms, and lands that no ruler in the world

has a larger realm,[3] greater stature, or more military power.
He has twelve [former] kingdoms in Spain, three in Italy
(Naples, Sicily, and Sardinia), Oran and control over the
kingdom of Tunisia in Africa, the Canary Islands beyond
the straits [of Gibraltar], and enough land in the Indies
[Latin America] to make up many kingdoms. In addition he
owns the County of Burgundy and the Low Countries, which
are the third part of the kingdom of France[4] and the duchy
of Milan, which may be considered another kingdom.

Spain lies between Africa and France. The Strait of
Gibraltar, not more than twelve *miglia*[5] wide, separates her
from Africa. The Pyrenees separate her from France from
sea to sea for a distance of two hundred *miglia;* on all other
fronts the country is surrounded by the sea with a coastline
of nineteen hundred *miglia.* This [measurement] includes
Portugal, which faces west on the Atlantic and is not near
the Strait. Portugal is like a narrow strip or belt, not wide,
but long, running from the border of Galicia to the sea near
Seville.

Larger than France, but not so fertile or populous,[6] Spain
produces wheat, wine, oil, salt, silk, wool, and other necessities of life. She has iron, lead, copper, silver, and gold
mines. Fine horses abound everywhere in Spain, but the best
are in Andalusia and Granada.

She is inhabited by a hard-working and intelligent people.
Those of the upper class have a certain haughtiness about
them, whereas the lower class are humble and have a pleasing way of speaking. I need say little about this because we
in Italy have come to know these qualities so well in recent

3. See the map on p. 18 of the Introduction.
4. He means that these lands roughly corresponded to Belgica in
the old Roman division of "all Gaul" into "three parts."
5. A Venetian *miglia* was slightly longer than a mile. In fact, the
Strait is from nine to twenty-four miles wide.
6. Other ambassadors had more to say about the Spanish landscape
and climate. Antonio Tiepolo, in 1572, described Spain as "a land so
dry that I saw men and horses suffering from the lack of so much as
a drop of water, and where I later nearly drowned in muddy torrents."
(Albèri, I, 5: 227–28.)

decades.[7] Our fathers knew little about Spain because in their time that country was so preoccupied with internal wars that she could not wage external ones. But after King Ferdinand with great courage and prowess had driven the Moors from his realm (and so gained the title of "Catholic King") he was not satisfied with having preserved and defended his own territories, but set out to win other countries and territories. First, to the great glory of his country, he discovered the Indies and the New World. But he did not

7. King Ferdinand of Spain (mentioned below, same paragraph) had conquered Naples, and Ferdinand's grandson, Charles V, had later won Milan. Until the eighteenth century, Spain exerted strong influence over much of Italy.

9. Spanish Peasants Outside Valladolid.

(*Detail from Braun and Hogenberg*, Civitates orbis terrarum, *1576, I, pl. 3. Rare Book Division, New York Public Library.*)

avoid resorting to arms: he won Africa, conquered Italy, attacked France and Germany, and fought the Turks on land and sea. All this he did without suffering any losses to speak of in his own territories.[8]

Although Spain can be considered the strongest and safest Christian land, even she cannot be sure that hostile neighbors will not make trouble. These neighbors are Portugal and France on the landward side and the Turks, the Arabs, and the Moors across the sea. The Portuguese would attack because of old enmity and because the haughty never get along with each other. The Moors and Turks are natural enemies and the French are hostile for well-known reasons. But Spain is safe from the Portuguese because of the friendship of the ruling families, who have long been closely related as a result of many intermarriages, and who forbid quarrels between their peoples. They are protected from the French by nature, science, and manpower. Nature has provided the harsh mountains which separate the kingdoms from each other; military science produced the many fortresses which guard the passes (at Perpignan and Salces opposite Narbonne on the Mediterranean, and Fuenterrabia on the Atlantic coast opposite Bayonne) and other suitable places. By manpower I mean the soldiers customarily assigned to guard Navarre and all of the kingdom.

Militarily, Spain is most vulnerable from the Mediterranean, where the nearness of her enemies in Africa makes a powerful assault possible. Even though there are always twelve galleys in readiness along the Spanish coast to protect those beaches, and (following the custom of former kings) three thousand infantry and an equal number of cavalry are deployed to protect the kingdom, all these would not suffice against strong enemies. This is why they feared the sherif of Morocco when he became so powerful, and for this reason they also fear the Turks, because they have a

8. The ambassador credits Ferdinand with much that was really done by his wife, Isabella, who ruled Castile (central Spain) and played a larger role than Ferdinand in the discovery of America, the expulsion of the Moors, and the African ventures.

foothold in Africa. It was because of Spain's vulnerability that Charles V conquered Tunisia, and also tried, with the full consent of all Spain, to win Algeria.[9] And for the same reason Oran and Bejaïa, two places in Africa opposite Spain, were fortified for many years at great expense. Since Bejaïa was lost they have tried all the harder to keep Oran, because that is now the only obstacle to the might of the infidels in that region. As a result there is no task the Spaniards consider more important, and no place where they would fight more willingly or use more force than in the conquest of the Barbary Coast, since control of those shores would protect them from their enemies and keep war far from their home. While they would fight this war eagerly, counting on an easy victory if they could concentrate all their forces on it, they are reluctant to fight in France and Italy, where the dangers would be great, the outcome unsure, and the benefits for the kingdom nil.

These are the only worries the Spaniards have about external enemies. Internally, there have sometimes been uprisings because of the rivalry between Aragon and Castile and the hatreds of the great noble families for each other. Sometimes the towns have revolted against the kings. This happened frequently during the reigns of King Ferdinand and the Emperor[10] Charles V; it is all well known and would take too long to narrate. At present, the whole kingdom is quiet and tranquil since the people are all united in obedience to a king who was born in Spain, is loved by all, and favors his Spanish subjects over the others. Also, there is no one else alive of royal blood who could take advantage of the old rancors and arouse the nation against the present government.

Spain is divided into two principal parts. One is Castile, to which are added the kingdoms of León, Galicia, Anda-

9. The Algerian expedition in 1541 was a disastrous failure.
10. Charles, grandson of Ferdinand and father of Philip II, was not only king of Spain but also head of the Holy Roman Empire (in central Europe) and was therefore known as "Emperor" rather than "King." The Comuneros revolt took place early in his reign; through the rest of his life there were no revolts.

lusia, Granada, Toledo, and Murcia, and in addition to these, Navarre. The other part is composed of Aragon, with Valencia and Catalonia.[11] To this part are attached Majorca and the other islands, and the kingdoms of Naples, Sicily, and Sardinia, just as the Indies and Africa are dependencies of Castile.

The Aragonese claim to be independent and to govern themselves as a republic of which the king is head. He may not succeed to the government unless they have elected him. They are so zealous to preserve their independence that they contest every little thing to prevent the king from having greater authority over them. They make difficulties even

11. The crown of Aragon was made up of three states: the kingdom of Aragon, the kingdom of Valencia, and the principality of Catalonia.

10. Sixteenth-Century Map of Spain.

(From Ortelius, Epitome, *1602, fol. 10. Rare Book Division, New York Public Library.)*

where they have no right to, so that Queen Isabella used to say that her husband, King Ferdinand, would have been pleased if the crown of Aragon had actually rebelled, since he would then have been able to reconquer it and impose his own laws.[12] The kingdom of Castile, on the other hand, is governed by councillors and ministers whom the king appoints, because he is the supreme arbiter of laws, finances, grants, justice, and matters of life and death. All the nobles, however, are so privileged that they have no other obligation than to serve the king in time of war, at his expense, and then only for the protection of Spain. When Charles wished to abolish their privileges, he was opposed by all the grandees, and the grand constable Velasco[13] was the greatest objector of all, even though he was a friend of His Majesty and enjoyed his favor more than any other. If this plan had not been quietly dropped there would have been a revolt in that kingdom. So the Aragonese maintain their liberty, and the nobles of Castile their privileges, openly challenging their kings if they try to abolish or modify their privileges and jurisdictions.

His Majesty's revenues are very limited, because he cannot add to them by imposing new taxes except with the consent of all his people. The ordinary revenues total no more than 1,500,000 [ducats] in gold. The taxes of Castile, his quarter of the tithes, and the other regular dues amount to 1,200,000 ducats. The grandmasterships of the three orders of Calatrava, Alcantara, and Santiago contribute another 200,000, the revenues of Navarre 40,000, and those of Aragon from 60,000 to 70,000. . . .

As irregular additional revenues he has, when the Cortes are held, 800,000 ducats from Castile and 700,000 from Aragon, spread over three years. Together these come to 500,000 ducats a year. They might be considered as regular income, since the Cortes meet every three years providing the king is present. These revenues are used for the expenses

12. Within the crown of Aragon there were revolts after Ferdinand's time in the kingdom of Valencia (1520), the kingdom of Aragon (1591), and the principality of Catalonia (1640).

13. Don Inigo Fernandez de Velasco.

of His Majesty's household. He also has a Crusade levy and tithes from the Church, amounting to 500,000 ducats per year. These are regular revenues if the popes grant them, but the present king has not had these funds because he has been at war with His Holiness almost continually.[14] It is true that he has had big loans from various bishops and priests who, in order to win His Majesty's favor or retain it, have lent him money when he needed it for his battles.

We can safely conclude that since Spain is very large, fertile, rich, and secure (because of her geographical position and the number and character of her people), she should not be considered inferior to any other kingdom in Christendom.

Spain owns those dominions in Africa and the Indies which her kings won and have kept. . . . Leaving aside the Indies of Portugal, which have nothing to do with this report, I shall speak only of the Indies of the king of Spain, which consist of two vast mainland provinces and many nearby islands. One is called New Spain and was discovered during the reign of King Ferdinand; its capital city is Mexico or Themistitan [Tenochtitlán]. The other is Peru, which was discovered in our own times.[15] Its capital city is Cuzco.

In New Spain they mine gold and silver, and they produce such things as hides, cotton, sugar, and little insects, like flies, from which they get red cochineal dye; but from Peru they get only metals. A fifth of everything produced belongs to the king, but since the gold and silver is brought directly to Spain, he also receives a tenth of all that is sent to the mint for refining and coining. In this way he ends up with a quarter of the total amount, which does not exceed 400,000 or 500,000 ducats, although it is counted not only in millions but in millions of pesos.[16] But it is not likely to continue

14. In the latter 1550s, the papacy under Paul IV was at war with Spain.
15. New Spain, or Mexico, was conquered in 1519–21; Peru in 1531–35.
16. The sense of the words *"sebbene si conta non solamente a milioni, ma a milioni di pesi"* is not clear.

this way much longer, because less gold and silver is found
on the surface than in past years, and if they wish to dig
deeper into the bowels of the earth that will take more
trouble, more work, and more money. The Spaniards refuse
to do the work, and the natives cannot be forced to do it
because the emperor freed them from all labor services if
they were converted to Christianity. Therefore they have to
use Negro slaves, who are brought there from the north and
west coasts of Africa. The price they have to pay for them
has been rising steadily. These slaves are feeble to begin
with, and they suffer both from the change of air and from
their masters' foolishness in working them hard and feeding
them little. So they sicken, and most of them die.

It was very easy to conquer these lands, because the
natives have no courage, no military discipline, and no
weapons (since they lack iron). Besides this, as they have no
aims in life and no energy, they care nothing about money
and do not mind being ruled by others. But while this land is
free from problems that other states generally have, much
more danger arises from the Spaniards themselves, because
almost all the men who go out there are either failures who
are desperate, or criminal fugitives fleeing justice. There is

11. Brazil (a Spanish possession from 1580 to 1640).

(Detail from Ramusio, Delle navigationi, *1556–83, III, 427. Libraries of the
University of Pennsylvania, Philadelphia.)*

much to fear from such men, as past rebellions have shown. The government has provided for this danger in two ways. The first is that anyone who wants to go to the Indies must leave his wife and children behind as hostages. The other requirement is that he may not stay longer than three years at a time, and this rule applies even to the governors of these lands. . . .

The African territories are partly beyond the straits [of Gibraltar] and partly on this side of them. Those outside the straits are the Canary Islands, about which nothing much need be said because they neither produce significant revenues for the king nor cost him much money. Private citizens profit from wine, meat, sugar, fodder, and other products of the islands. Inside the straits lie Oran and Goletta, important fortresses with harbors big enough to shelter the fleet— the best on all that coast. And even though they are so far apart that one could not relieve the other, nevertheless they are so well placed that they protect both Spain and Italy by preventing the Moors and Turks from winning control of these waters. They also enable Christians to carry on profitable, honest trading in that area. . . .

There is nothing new that I could tell this illustrious Senate about the lands which His Catholic Majesty has in Italy—Milan, Naples, Sicily, Sardinia, and part of Tuscany —so I shall only touch on them briefly, limiting myself to three principal points: military offense and defense, the morale of the subjects, and income and expenditure.

Milan is a state which is fatal not only to whoever controls her, but to anyone who seeks to control her, to Italy, and to all Christendom. I say this because she is the origin of so many wars, which consume the wealth of kingdoms, the blood of their subjects, and energies which should be spent on worthier efforts for the general welfare. At first glance this state seems even more dangerous to whomever controls it than to others, because she is not strong enough to threaten others and she needs a good deal of outside help for her own defense. But experience shows that whoever rules Milan has always been able to disturb the peace of her

neighbors. Leaving aside what the dukes of former times
did—especially Lodovico il Moro, the most restless of them
all—we remember very well the damage she did in recent
times to our republic, the affair in Genoa, and the occupation
of Piacenza. . . .

The kingdom of Naples yields revenues of a million in
gold and has expenses of a million and a half. They make up
the difference with grants, assessments, subsidies, new taxes
and increases of old ones, confiscations, and other unusual
methods. You can't imagine a method of extracting money
from subjects which has not been used in this kingdom. As a
result a majority of Neapolitans are bankrupt and desperate, and many of them take to the streets because they have
no other way to make a living. This situation breeds more
thieves and outlaws than there are in all the rest of Italy.
The causes of the revenue shortage are well known: the
sources of the kingdom's income have mostly been sold or
mortgaged, and expenses, instead of diminishing, increase
because of the added interest payments, and because of
unexpected events which require unexpected expenditures.
An example is the French attack on the kingdom in 1557.

As for the morale of the Neapolitans, I can only repeat
what they themselves always say: every government sickens
them and every state displeases them. As things now stand
Spain has ruled these lands for such a long stretch of years,
and is so powerful, that she has extinguished all the passions
of the kingdom (except their affection for Your Serenity's
government, which is deeper than ever). However, if the
present king [Philip II of Spain] should run into trouble in
Italy or anywhere else he could not rely on the loyalty of
these subjects. This is all the more true because of the
present discontent of the nobles and people. The latter are
disaffected because of the heavy taxes and the former because of the slight attention their rulers pay them, and
everybody is discontented because of the many defects in the
government. Three of these are outstanding. One is that His
Majesty rules by force, and being afraid of the temper of his
subjects, he always wants to have a large body of Spaniards

12. Spanish Soldiers on Guard Duty, by Franz Hogenberg.

(Detail from view of Philip II's court. Prints Division, New York Public Library.)

stationed there. While the people of newly acquired territories will put up with foreign troops, in a kingdom long under one dynasty, and held by inheritance, foreign troops are more of a burden on the populace than a necessary safeguard for the kingdom.

The second difficulty is that the benefits and honors of the kingdom, which should be distributed among the native subjects, are generally given to the Spaniards and to "janissaries," as they call those of mixed blood, the children of the native subjects and Spaniards.[17] Therefore, the Neapolitans cannot hope to hold any offices in their own country or at the court of their king, and yet such things count with these people more than with any other on earth.

The third defect lies in the sphere of justice, which in this kingdom is meted out without taking into account the differences between nobles and commoners. Governments should

17. Janissaries were the sultan of Turkey's elite soldier guard, recruited among Christians and converted to the Moslem religion. See below, pp. 131–136.

inflict punishments in geometric proportions, that is, according to the rank of the person. To do it otherwise is unjust, since the shame of disgrace matters very little to a plebeian, but very much to a nobleman. But in Naples the judges measure out rewards and punishments, favors and deprivations to nobles and commoners in the same amounts. They don't take into consideration the differences that nature and fortune have made between one class and the other—differences that one cannot change unless he changes human nature and the customs of the whole world, or imitates the Turks, who treat all people equally as slaves. As a result, the nobles are in despair because they see themselves reduced to the status of their inferiors, and the common people, seeing themselves treated like nobles, become insolent and presumptuous.

All these considerations, and others which I omit for the sake of brevity, unsettle these people so much as to raise the danger that they might be ready, if an opportunity came, to change rulers, hoping to change their fortunes. They might try this even though they have already learned many times that this evil [of bad government] is like the fever of a sick man. Even though he moves from bed to bed and from room to room, he carries his illness with him everywhere. That is enough about the Neapolitans.

The Sicilians would have no reason to want a change of government if they were not divided into factions. Don Ferrante Gonzaga and other viceroys have tried to make peace among them but have never been able to do enough, because an ancient hatred is like a poisonous disease spread throughout the whole body. If medicines or plasters soothe one affected part, the disease breaks out in another where it was least expected. Hatreds among the populace, especially those between nobles and commoners, have always caused great harm in cities, towns, and kingdoms. Because of this danger the emperor was advised to build a fortress in Palermo to keep the city under control. Since this enormous city is full of barons, nobles, and heads of the government, whatever happens there, good or bad, is imitated throughout the rest of the island. As for attacks from the outside, all they have to fear are naval attacks, and the fortresses and militia guard against these. . . .[18]

I have discussed Spain, her territories, and Italy enough for my purposes. Now I shall turn to the County of Burgundy and the Low Countries, which form the third principal part of the lands of His Catholic Majesty.

The County of Burgundy borders on France, Switzerland, and another part of the Holy Roman Empire.[19] The Netherlands, which comprise Flanders, Artois, Hainaut, Luxembourg, Brabant, Holland, Zeeland, Gelderland, and Friesland, are all in one body and contiguous to each other. On

18. Other remarks about Sicily, Sardinia, and Tuscany have been omitted. (Ed.)

19. The Free County of Burgundy (Franche-Comté) and Switzerland were, themselves, parts of the Empire.

13. Netherlands Villagers, by Pieter Breughel the Elder.

(*Detail from* The Numbering at Bethlehem. *Musées Royaux des Beaux-Arts, Brussels.*)

the north their border is the English sea [the North Sea];
on the east, Germany, and on the south and west, the
kingdom of France. To protect themselves against France
they have twenty-three fortresses—at least, they call them
fortresses—but many which I have seen do not deserve this
name.

In respect to length of borders, size of population, wealth,
accessibility by sea and rivers, beauty and magnificence of
lands, this country has no rival in any kingdom of Europe.[20]
There is no country in the world that is at the same time
richer and more [agriculturally] unproductive. It is the
most unproductive region partly because of nature and the
climate, which is cold and wet, and partly because of the
indifference of the inhabitants. They are more interested in
business and other pursuits than in farming, and they let
the countryside go to pasture and woods, as the English do
with their lands. This is the richest country because of the
heavy trading that goes on with England, France, Spain,
Germany, Italy, and the whole world. It supplies all these
countries with many things, and is in turn supplied by them
with many other products, some of which are sold on the
home market, while the rest are exported to other places.
Among the products they ship throughout the world are
tapestries, woolens, and linens. Their tapestries show what
can be achieved in that art by fine workers, because, just as
master mosaicists working with tiny stones create various
pictures of things, so these artisans, working with the tiniest
silk and wool threads, not only decorate their work with
various colors but also create the illusion of light and
shadow, and make the figures stand out in relief just as the
greatest painters do.

Commerce and industry continually bring riches to these
lands from other parts of the world. As a result, the emperor
was able to raise 24 millions in gold there within a few

20. The ambassador is discussing the Netherlands, of course, and
not the County of Burgundy. He is certainly wrong with regard to
the length of borders and population, though the Low Countries may
have had the highest population *density*.

years, and the present king raised a large part of the costs of the recent war. Even if they had provided only what they promised for the duration of the war, which was 90 infantry companies, 8,000 cavalry, all the necessary armaments, and warships to guard those seas, this would have been fully as much help as one might have looked for from much larger lands. They also pay the costs of building and manning many fortresses in peace and war, the living expenses of

14. Netherlands Tax Collector.

(Detail apparently based on frontispiece in Damhouder, Pratique iudiciaire, *1572. Historical Pictures Service, Chicago.)*

governors, officials, and generals, and the expenses of the
court and His Majesty's household.[21] The Low Countries
pay all these expenses as beyond-the-ordinary services, since
the king does not have a single ducat of income of his own
from all these lands. This is because the predecessors of
Duke Charles[22] gave the rights to the ordinary tax revenues
to some of their subjects, and then the special taxes, which
had become ordinary and gradually rose to the sum of
400,000 ducats, were all used with the people's consent for
the wars which have been fought almost continuously in
that area. To have more money from time to time, therefore,
it has been necessary to pile taxes upon taxes and duties
upon duties. (As a result, the cost of living is higher than
anywhere else on earth. What costs two in Italy costs three
in Germany, and four or five in Flanders.) In this manner
the king raises more than 800,000 ducats annually in these
states in peacetime, and in wartime more than a million and
a half. . . .

These are the treasure chambers of the Spanish kings, the
mines, the Indies, which so long sustained the emperor in his
wars in France, Italy, and Germany, and saved his kingdoms, honor, and prestige. They are also the surest, easiest
route for attacks on France; many times armies have
started here and rapidly penetrated to the heart of the
French kingdom. But there are two things to fear in these
territories. One is the disaffection of the subjects, who are
worked up because of the heavy taxes and also because
Spaniards now run the whole government, which used to be
in their own hands. The other problem is the French, who
are strong and near and lose no chance in peacetime or war
to harm their enemy. To protect himself from his subjects
the emperor made it a policy always to station a large
Spanish force there, and he built the fortress in Ghent and
planned to have more of them in other places. And to guard

21. Philip lived in the Netherlands in the latter 1550s, but not
thereafter.
22. Charles the Bold, duke of Burgundy, Philip's great-great-
grandfather.

himself from the French he planned to use English arms, which have always proved so deadly to France. So he and King Henry VIII made a treaty in which each pledged to supply the other with a certain number of men if he was attacked. But then Henry died, and Edward after him, and Mary succeeded to the throne. The emperor, always a drafter of large-scale plans, decided he could win that kingdom by marrying his son to the queen.[23] The result was not what he had hoped for, however, because King Philip experienced so many difficulties and problems that I remember hearing from a very important person that His Majesty [Philip] became sorrier every day that he had ever carried out that plan. He had gained no kingdom, no power, no influence, nor even a crown, but only a title which was more appearance than reality.[24]

Since I have mentioned England, I think I should briefly discuss the kingdom. I will touch on only a few details, which are relevant to my subject, and so maintain the brevity that I am aiming at in my report. Of all the northern kingdoms, England is the richest and most powerful. Even though the crown has only a small regular income of no more than 500,000 ducats, the king can easily raise whatever he needs for peace or for war. Special tax collectors are authorized to demand large amounts from some, small ones from others, as they see fit. Whatever taxes they levy they collect within two months without meeting any outcry or opposition; it was that way last year even when they were raising a million and a half in gold. England's strength lies in her numerous soldiers and in the might of her fleet. Her sea power gives her an advantage over all her neighbors because her site is convenient for attacks on others but easily defended. But because of both the character of her people and some errors of judgment, this country has suffered, not benefited from her military power. She lost

23. Philip married Queen Mary (his second wife) in 1554. She died childless four years later.
24. The marriage arrangements expressly forbade Philip's having any part in ruling England.

Calais [in 1555] by not facing up to the danger soon enough, and her many internal struggles have weakened the kingdom. Another problem has been that the English always want to try something new, are hostile to foreigners and not too civil to each other, and try to carry out every idea that comes into their heads, as though it were as easy to carry out a project as it is to conceive of it.

For this reason[25] more uprisings have taken place in that one kingdom than in all the rest of the world. The latest was that of Thomas Stafford, a nephew of the cardinal, who thought he could overthrow the government with a mere sixty men whom he had taken to France. He paid dearly for his rashness. This also made them change their religious faith. This is the greatest change that can take place in a kingdom, because it offends Our Lord, and it also leads to changes in morals, laws, and civil obedience, and ultimately in the government itself. We know how such things have happened in Asia, in Africa, in Greece, and in much of Europe. It is this which has caused so many downfalls of great men and elevations of lowly ones, so many imprisonments, so many exiles, and so many deaths. It seems incredible, and yet it is true, that in that kingdom in the past twenty years three queens, four dukes, forty earls, and more than thirty thousand others have met violent deaths.

If their own rulers are so insecure it is obvious that an outsider could never control such people. Despite all this King Philip tried every means that his father suggested or that he and his own advisers could think of to gain influence with these people. To win their liking he was friendly to everybody, went among them unguarded, claimed he wanted nothing from them, spent money lavishly, courted the nobles, reduced the queen's council from a group of twenty-two to one of only six of his most trusted advisers, and avoided using force for any purpose.

But he observed how they became increasingly suspicious of him, and he knew that if he had no children he would be

25. A typical example of careless Venetian syntax. (The ambassador has just suggested several reasons.)

15. Young Woman Presumed to Be Queen Elizabeth, British painter, unknown, sixteenth century.

(Queen Elizabeth [?]. Metropolitan Museum of Art, New York, gift of J. Pierpont Morgan, 1911.)

excluded from the government as soon as his wife died. He also realized that the people favored Lady Elizabeth, who is now queen. So he hit on the plan of marrying her to the duke of Savoy, a man he could count on as his client. In this way he would not lose with shame what he could not keep with honor and he would be able at least to keep England friendly, even if not subject to him. But his plans ran afoul of two obstacles. One was that Elizabeth would not marry without the permission of the English Parliament, which was a requirement her father had laid down, and Parliament seemed opposed to allowing her to marry a foreigner. The other obstacle was that her sister, Queen Mary, would not allow Elizabeth to marry with the expectation of inheriting the crown. This problem looked even more serious than the other, because the queen loathed Elizabeth, and would not even admit they were sisters.[26] Since she was a hot-tempered

26. They were half sisters, but Mary believed that her father's marriage to Anne Boleyn was illegal and Elizabeth was therefore illegitimate.

and stubborn woman the king gave the task of persuading
her to his confessor, a very clever man who was in good
standing with the queen. The confessor did his work so skillfully that he won her over. For the moment she seemed
pleased with the plan, and she promised to discuss it with
the king the next evening. But she did not do this, and when
the confessor returned the next day he found she had
changed her mind completely. . . .

With the project thus stymied, nothing further was done
until the queen fell ill. This provided a pretext for the king
to send the count of Feria to England to bring the matter up
again, with orders that whether he won the queen's agreement or not, he should make the princess [Elizabeth] appreciate the fact that she would owe her crown to the king's
support. Both the count and the confessor told me that in
important matters like these it does not pay to spare a
woman's feelings. But in this way Philip lost one woman
and failed to win over the other one. Queen Mary, partly
because of her ingrained scorn [for Elizabeth] and partly
because she saw herself forced to consent to a measure she
disapproved of, died of a broken heart, whereupon Elizabeth
inherited the throne through her own good luck. Since she
has the same proud spirit as her father, she wants to stand
completely alone, even if she remains on friendly terms with
all comers. For several reasons she has not yet changed her
religion, but she does prefer the sect in which she was born
and raised. Because of this preference and also considering
the kind of people she has brought into the government, it is
believed that she will return to the religion she practiced
during the reign of King Edward.[27]

As for her marriage, the English are convinced she will
not choose a foreigner. Rumor has it she is negotiating with
His Catholic Majesty, but the truth is that the king is not
interested, partly because he has no desire to get involved
again in that kingdom, and partly for other secret reasons.
At the time when I left the court His Majesty had only one

27. And so she did, a few months later.

hope of keeping England friendly. This hope stems from the fact that Queen Elizabeth must always be on guard against the French, who claim a right to her kingdom because of the queen of Scotland.[28] This queen is a descendant of King Henry VIII's sister, and is the first in the legitimate line of succession to the throne, if one reckons that Elizabeth is ineligible to be queen because she was born while her father's legal wife was still alive. But Your Serenity will receive clearer and fresher news about these and other events which happened after I left the court from the distinguished [ambassador] Tiepolo. Since he is on the spot, he can write authoritatively about what is actually being done, while I can only guess. I shall conclude by observing briefly that if the Catholic king wants to hold on to his lands in Flanders he must keep open the sea route from Spain. To do this he must make every effort to remain at peace with England and keep it from falling into the hands of some other ruler who might go to war against him.

Most Serene Ruler, I have discussed as briefly as possible—perhaps more briefly than the importance of the topic called for—the state of each of the lands of His Most Serene Spanish Majesty, and I pointed out that we must keep in mind that he has large armies and big revenues, the products of his many lands and great wealth. There is no part of the world, on land or sea, in India, Latin America, Africa, or Europe, where that king does not have a major possession.

Now I must turn to two other things, which are so essential for both offensive and defensive war that unless he has them a ruler can neither carry on a war nor live safely at peace. One is money, and the other is an armed force.

In peacetime His Majesty has an annual income from all his possessions of five million in gold: one and one-half from Spain, a half million from the Indies [Latin America], one million from Naples, one million from Milan and Sicily, and

28. Mary Stuart, queen of Scotland and wife of Francis, oldest son of the French king Henry II. Henry died in the year this report was given, and Francis and Mary became briefly king and queen of France (1559–60).

another million from Flanders and the Low Countries. On
the other hand, his expenses amount to over six million. He
makes up the difference with special taxes which he imposes
at will. You might think he would have great trouble finding
the money for military operations, since he uses all the
revenues from his kingdoms for ordinary needs. But you
may remember that when his father, the emperor, held the
same responsibilities he was able to wage many wars and
carry on other projects in Italy and elsewhere on sea and on
land. And this present king in recent years has found the
means to maintain so many armies in Flanders, Piedmont,
Lombardy, and Sicily, and so many soldiers guarding Africa
against the Turks, that someone estimated the total cost at
more than ten million in gold. This example shows that even
when their expenses exceed their incomes, powerful rulers
can usually find large sums of money in emergencies. This is
especially true of the king of Spain, and not so much because of his mines in Spain and the Indies, which the Spaniards, who are very boastful, are always talking about. More
important than those are his many lands and vassals, almost
all of them rich. They supply him with many grants of
money, not because they are forced to but because the subjects see that both the state and they as individuals stand to
gain. I believe the mines are not as important as the Spaniards believe, because we can see on the one hand that the
kings of France and the sultan of Turkey are very rich
without mines, and on the other hand that the present
emperor,[29] who has as many mines in his lands as there are
in all the rest of Europe, is always in financial straits. . . .

I have discussed the way the king raises his revenues,
which are the sinews of war and the ornaments of peace.
Now I shall turn to his armed forces, which fall under two
headings, sea and land. Part of the sea forces are his own
and part are mercenary. I call the twelve galleys of Spain,
the four from Naples, and the four from Sicily "his own"
because the timber, guns, slaves, and oarsmen are all sup-

29. Ferdinand I, Holy Roman Emperor, brother of the late Charles
V and uncle of Philip II of Spain.

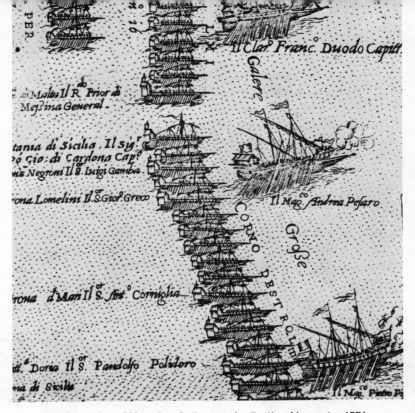

16. Spanish and Venetian Galleys at the Battle of Lepanto, 1571.

(Detail from Camocio, Isole, famose porti, *1573, pl. 65. From an original in the Free Library of Philadelphia.)*

plied by His Majesty. The fleet of Prince Doria is a mercenary one and consists of twenty galleys: six belong to Sir Antonio Doria, six to Cicala, two to the ruler of Monaco, two to the marquis of Terranuova, and six, which used to belong to Pappacoda, to Sir Stefano da Mare. His Majesty spends 3,500 ducats a year on each of his own ships and 6,000 for each of the hired ones. He spends less on his own (and his captains make larger profits from them) because they are not kept ready for action more than eight months a year, while the others are on duty the whole year round and the captains have to keep spending money to feed the [galley] slaves and replace them when necessary. Since they cannot go slaving on the Barbary Coast, as they used to (because the Turks defend it so heavily), they have great trouble in finding oarsmen, and their ships are often undermanned and cannot leave port for naval actions. Therefore, although the king has sixty galleys, he can use only forty-five or fifty. But these are the best managed, the best armed, and the best commanded in the world. . . .

On land His Majesty has as many forces and is just as powerful as at sea, because he raises a great many men and arms of every kind from all his lands, and he gets superb breeds of horses from Spain, the Low Countries, and the Kingdom [of Naples]. In one respect he has the advantage over all other rulers: since he governs so many peoples and countries he can use subjects of his own for all the different needs of war. Spanish infantrymen, because they are cautious, bear hardships patiently, and are easily disciplined,

17. Measuring a Cannon.

(*From Luys Collado*, Practica manuale dell'artiglieria, *1606, p. 46. Libraries of the University of Pennsylvania, Philadelphia.*)

are better than any other soldiers when it comes to ambushing, defending passes, retreating, and undergoing a siege. Because the Italians are more spirited, they are good for gun loading, skirmishes, assaults, and fighting with light arms. The Walloons are best suited for artillery warfare and fighting in the open country, and the same is true of the Germans, of whom His Majesty can have as many as he wishes when he has the money. Of all these, the Spaniards, like firstborn sons, are the best loved and the best treated; they are the ones who get the rewards and the glory and who are trusted with the defense of the kingdoms and provinces; and—in order to maintain their loyalty—they are always paid and honored more than the others. About thirteen thousand Spanish troops are stationed outside Spain in such places as Africa, Flanders, Lombardy, Tuscany, Sicily, and the kingdom of Naples. They could send even more than that number out from Spain, but not enough to make up an entire army.

As for cavalry, their men of arms are the best in the world. They have not only held their own against the French, who have a great name in this kind of fighting, but on two occasions they easily scattered and routed them. The reasons for their success lie in their battle order, armor, and fine horses. The French battle order is a wide front with weak flanks, because everyone wants to be right at the front. The Flemings,[30] on the other hand, use more ranks and thus build a unit that is more solid and firm. The difference in armor is that the Flemings are completely covered, while the French show their courage by not protecting their shins or knees, from which one pushes when thrusting or warding off a blow. As for their horses, the Flemings have a great advantage here because they have their own bloodstock and they can choose the best; the French do not have any bloodstock and must use whatever they can get. There would be nothing new or important to say about the other [Spanish] cavalry if the *ferrajoli*, or German cavalry, did not have

---

30. The Flemings, of course, were Spanish subjects.

such a great reputation. Actually these men do more harm to
their friends than to their enemies because they are so
insolent and undisciplined. If there are few of them, they
are no use at all, and if there are many, they disrupt the
whole army and devastate the countryside. In addition to all
this, they are so expensive that many believe they will soon
lose their repute, and no ruler will use them.

It is not hard to calculate how many troops and what
force the king of Spain can organize when need arises, when
we remember that several times in recent years he has
simultaneously maintained four armies totaling over
100,000 men in different places. The Italians were the
smallest group because they have a reputation for disobedience, bad discipline, and doubtful loyalty. (Several times
they have changed sides because they were badly treated.)
Everybody despises the Italians for these reasons, but they
know what passion and force this people would show if they
were united and led by brave and experienced leaders. As a
result they aim to humiliate this land and deprive it of the
glory it won in wars with every other country, and put the
whole region under their power. . . .

That is all I can tell you about the armed forces of the
king of Spain. However, we must remember that while a
ruler, when considered alone, may appear very powerful if
he has vast lands, ample revenues, and many troops, we
know his relative strength only when we compare him to
other kings and rulers. It will be useful, therefore, to consider in what respects His Catholic Majesty is stronger,
weaker, or equal to other rulers. And since world affairs
have had the effect of thrusting many formerly separate and
distinct domains into the hands of just three rulers, I shall
concentrate on these three. One of them is the king we have
been discussing, and the others are the king of France and
the sultan of Turkey; they are the important ones.

The king of Spain has the same strength, when compared
with the sultan, that his father, the emperor Charles V, had.
He has the same lands that his father ruled,[31] the same

---

31. He did not have his father's central European lands.

influence in Italy (as we know), the same naval power, and the same help from Germany. (Perhaps more of the latter, because Germans pitch in more readily when they can count on being paid than they do when they are merely obeying a command.[32]) This much is sure, that if the emperor Charles was strong enough to stand up to the Turk and even attack him, this king can do the same, and he could be just as valuable an ally as his powerful father. While the emperor was never able to assemble as many soldiers at one time as the sultan could, he still had enough men under arms in Hungary and at Tunis to frighten his enemies. The same can be said of the navy; it has never been so large as the Turkish one, but the ships are always better constructed, the sailors more skillful, the admirals more distinguished, and the marines braver and more seasoned in battle. The fleet would also be larger, if they would carry out the program I discussed earlier.

As for arms, ammunition, cannon, and all types of matériel for land and sea warfare, His Majesty is the equal of the Turk in respect to the amount and quality of this equipment and the skill of those who use it. With respect to food and pasture for his regular troops, and for entire armies and fleets in time of war, the king will never have any problems as long as he rules Sicily and Apulia. . . .[33]

You might compare the forces of the Spanish and French kings in this way. The king of Spain has many lands, but they are all separate from each other, while the king of France has only one kingdom, and that is in one piece and obedient. The Spanish king's subjects are wealthier—many of them in Spain, Flanders, and Italy have incomes of thirty, forty and even fifty thousand ducats a year—but Frenchmen are swifter to provide money to their king. Perhaps the king of Spain could find more ways of raising money than the French king, because his realms are rich in

32. The ambassador is explaining why Germans gave less help to Charles V, who was not only king of Spain but also Holy Roman Emperor and therefore their ruler, than to his son Philip, who was not their emperor.

33. A fertile area of southern Italy.

minerals and include many great trading centers (notably
Antwerp and Genoa),[34] and he owns Flanders, which is
very rich, and India [Latin America], which is overflowing
with gold. And yet the king of France, even if he has no
mines and no India, knows better how to use the money he
raises in his kingdom and spends only two-thirds as much on
his wars as the king of Spain. In naval forces Spain is
stronger, and this is why France has made use of the Turkish fleet. On land there is not much difference between them.
The Gascons are not far behind the Spanish in respect to
skill and energy; the Germans who are used by the king of
Spain are equaled by the Swiss and the other Germans in the
pay of France; and Fleming and Walloon cavalry and infantrymen are no better than the French from the [north-
ern] borders. The king of France used to have a great lead
as far as generals were concerned, with no less than twelve
men who were experienced in commanding armies, while the
king of Spain had only two. But a stroke of luck helped the
Spanish king to even the balance. [Unwisely] believing that
King Philip and his counselors were still new and inexperienced, the French lost, almost in one blow, three fortresses
and seven of their leading generals.[35]

So the armed forces of these two kings are very evenly
matched. They are, to be sure, capable of damaging each
other in their wars, but neither will ever be stronger than
the other unless he has an ally. You may remember how
Emperor Charles V, that great, successful, powerful commander, was humiliated after his many victories by a king
of France who at that time was young, inept, and inexperienced.[36] Not too long after that, this same French king,
whose own successes in battle had by now made him prosperous and arrogant, fell into danger[37] because of the good
luck of a young Spanish king [Philip] who was a newcomer

34. Nominally independent but virtually a Spanish protectorate.
35. In the Battle of Saint Quentin, fought August 10, 1557.
36. A reference to Charles's loss of the bishopric of Metz to Henry
II in 1552.
37. After losing the Battle of Saint Quentin, referred to above.

in his own state and lacked generals, ministers, counselors, and (as Sir Ruy Gómez told me) experience, soldiers, and money. So much for the comparison of the forces of the kings of Spain and France.

Your Serenity,[38] however, is superior in naval power and fortresses to both these countries, and everyone holds that it lies in your power, if you should join either of them, to defeat the other with ease. The new emperor is poor in men, money and spirit, beleaguered by powerful enemies, and scorned by the Germans, from whom he should be getting most of his support. Neither in his own right nor with the help of his relatives[39] can he be compared in splendor and power with the king of Spain. No other ruler in the world has so big a realm as that king, nor so much money, so many subjects, or such a potential for offensive or defensive wars. What else can we say then about the strength and might of the king of Spain? Consider these points: A duke of Milan and a king of Naples were able on one occasion to torment Italy and throw the whole world into confusion.[40] A king of Spain[41] freed himself from bondage to the Moors by his own efforts, drove powerful enemies from his own lands, and won kingdoms in Italy and Africa and formerly unknown lands in the Indies [Spanish America]. A duke of Burgundy,[42] sometimes with English help and sometimes alone, repeatedly attacked the Swiss, upset France, and frightened Germany. Fifty years ago a person who could round up a million gold ducats could start a major war, and a ruler with twenty or thirty thousand troops in his army could plan sweeping campaigns of any kind. Remembering all these things, we must surely place at the top of the list a ruler who

38. The ambassador addresses the doge, but is actually speaking figuratively of the state of Venice. His estimate of Venetian power is optimistic.

39. The words *"nè per industria de' suoi"* seem to refer to other members of the Hapsburg family.

40. The reference is to the events which led, in 1494, to a French invasion of Italy and decades of subsequent Italian wars.

41. Ferdinand (1474–1516). Here again the ambassador credits Ferdinand with much that was really done by Isabella.

42. Charles the Bold, duke of Burgundy (1467–77).

has put together all of those duchies and kingdoms, who has collected so much money in these few years, and who keeps more than twenty thousand infantrymen under arms in his lands in time of peace and has maintained one hundred thousand and a powerful fleet in time of war.

We should remember, however, that if armed force is not handled with good judgment it is worse than weak and useless, it is usually downright harmful to the man who has it. Used with prudence and good sense, on the other hand, it can have splendid results, giving his friends hope and a sense of security, and throwing his frightened enemies into confusion. So the remaining task is to discuss whether these great powers are used wisely and with the benefit of good advice. I hope you will listen carefully and reflect on this subject. If we know what to think about the nature of the king and his counselors we will find it easier to decide how to stay at peace with His Majesty, or how to avoid the worst if war should break out.

18. King Philip II in Council, by Franz Hogenberg.
(Detail from View of Philip II's court. Prints Division, New York Public Library.)

The Catholic King was born in Spain in May, 1527. He spent his early years and most of the more recent ones in that country. In accordance with the customs of the kingdom and the desires of his mother, who was Portuguese, he was always treated with the awe and deference owed to the son of the greatest Christian emperor of all times and the future heir of so many lands and such power. The result of this upbringing was that when His Majesty left Spain for the first time and passed through Italy and Germany on his way to the Netherlands, he made everyone feel that he was harsh and unbending, so that the Italians found him unlikable, the Flemings, disagreeable, and the Germans, odious. First the Cardinal of Trent, then Queen Maria,[43] and lastly his father, with more effect, warned him that it was unwise for someone who had to rule dissimilar lands, and people with varying traditions, to be so aloof and harsh. As a result he changed, and from the time he passed through Spain in the other direction on his way to England, he has always shown a gentleness and warmth unsurpassed by any other ruler. He still has the reserve and royal gravity which are his by nature and upbringing, but far from making him less likable, they only make the courtesy with which he treats everyone stand out the more. His bodily grace, his manly behavior, his words and deeds, which are at the same time kingly and gentle—all these add to his attractiveness. He is small, but he is so well formed, with every limb perfectly proportioned to every other, and he dresses so neatly and tastefully, that you have never seen anything so perfect.

His Majesty's health is very delicate, and so he regulates his life carefully. He usually eats very nourishing food, and avoids fish, fruit, and other things that give rise to evil humors. He sleeps a lot and takes little exercise, and his amusements are all tranquil ones. He has sometimes been known to take an interest in physical exercise, but this was clearly against his nature, which is inclined more toward restful calm than sport or work.

43. Philip's first wife, a Portuguese princess and his first cousin.

19. Emperor Charles V in 1546, by Augustin Hirschvogel.

(National Gallery of Art, Washington, D.C., Rosenwald Collection.)

At his age most kings have a youthful ambition to win new lands, but His Majesty has been aiming not to wage war so that he can add to his kingdoms but to wage peace so that he can keep the lands he has. At the beginning of his reign he made peace with the king of France even though the emperor was opposed[44] and the bishop of Arras[45] publicly deplored it; he corrected abuses by the governors in his kingdoms, forgave debts, speeded up the processes of justice, which used to drag on under the emperor, was generous to everybody, and allowed no one to leave his presence unsatisfied. The emperor's prudence and experience at first bolstered his son's authority. When Charles left for Spain,[46] however, his son found his new responsibilities almost too heavy for him and in a short time he was in several difficulties.[47] These would have destroyed him, if he had not been helped out both by Fortune and the imprudence of his enemies.

If he wanted to imitate the emperor, or for that matter the old Catholic King [Ferdinand], his enormous resources combined with some good luck would make him feared throughout the world. He looks like his father, speaks like him, and has the same piety and the same habit of always professing his friendship and goodwill. But he differs from him in many of the respects which make rulers truly great. His father loved the battleground and had mastered the arts of war, but his son dislikes warfare and knows little about it. The emperor undertook great campaigns of conquest, but the king avoids them. Charles planned great projects and eventually carried them through with enormous profit to himself, but Philip cares less about his own grandeur than he does about blocking the progress of others. . . .[48]

44. Charles V abdicated the Spanish throne in favor of Philip, his son, in 1556, two years before his death.

45. Subsequently Cardinal Granvelle, formerly Charles V's chancellor.

46. The father and son had been in the Netherlands because of the war with France.

47. A reference, apparently, to military events after the Battle of Saint Quentin.

48. The ambassador proceeds to discuss Philip's counselors.

2 "MOST SPANIARDS ARE EITHER VERY RICH OR VERY POOR"

Gianfrancesco Morosini, 1581

More than most of his colleagues, Morosini liked to depict the social structures of the countries in which he served. Here he discusses the distribution of wealth in Spain, the magnificence and political impotence of the grandees, and regional differences in the king's control of his subjects. (In the section on Turkey below, he vividly analyzes the very different organization of that semi-Oriental land.) Late in life Morosini entered the Church and was made a papal nuncio and cardinal.

Most of the men in this country are small in stature and dark in complexion, haughty if they belong to the upper classes or prudently humble if they are common people, and unsuited for any kind of work. As farmers they are the most lackadaisical in the world, and as artisans they are so lazy and slow that work that would be done anywhere else in one month in Spain requires four. They are such stupid craftsmen that in all their provinces you can hardly find a building or anything else of interest except for antiquities done in Roman times or works built by the Moorish kings. Most of the Spanish live in houses so ineptly built of inferior materials that it is remarkable if one lasts as long as the man who built it. The cities are badly run and dirty; they

From a report by Gianfrancesco Morosini, 1581, Albèri, I, 5: 286–94.

throw all their refuse into the public streets instead of having the conveniences in their houses which are used in Italy and other parts of the world. They give no thought to food supplies; as a result the common people often have to fight each other to get bread, not so much because there is a shortage of grain as because there is no official whose job it is to make sure that there is bread. . . .

On the other hand, in bearing arms and making war they have worked miracles. They put up well with discomforts, are very comradely with each other, and are particularly clever at battlefield strategems (they make a specialty of this). In battle they are bold, eager, and united, as they have shown not only in their own country, where they won fame for the prowess they showed in driving out the Moors, but also outside of Spain. I have in mind the conquest of the Indies and the new world, their attacks on France, Germany, and Italy, and their warfare on land and sea with the Turks, in none of which they have ever suffered any real damage to their homeland. More recently there were the

20. Peasants and Gentry Outside Granada.

(*Detail from Braun and Hogenberg,* Civitates orbis terrarum, *1576, I, pl. 4. Rare Book Division, New York Public Library.*)

events in Flanders when a mere three thousand Spaniards, garrisoned in the citadel of Antwerp, had the courage to assault and sack the city. Antwerp had a large population and more than fourteen thousand friendly soldiers with fairly experienced officers, but all of these were not enough to prevent the sack. The Antwerp soldiers considered themselves lucky to escape, after killing only a dozen of the Spanish.[1] The Spaniards reached the point where they were a threat to all countries, and even to their own king, who dreaded their return to Spain because he thought that when

1. The sack of Antwerp, or "Spanish Fury" (1557), cost the lives of about seven thousand persons. The Spanish dead probably numbered nearer two hundred than the twelve of which Morosini speaks.

21. The "Spanish Fury," Antwerp, 1576, by Franz Hogenberg.
(Detail. Prints Division, New York Public Library.)

they had been paid off these capable soldiers might stir his whole kingdom into rebellion.

Spain might be quick to rebel if there were a leader courageous enough to direct a revolt. All of the people are discontented with their king and his current ministers. The nobles are dissatisfied because they are virtually ignored, and everyone else because they pay such unbearably heavy taxes; no other people in the world carry such a tax burden as the Castilians. True, the Aragonese and Castilians have ended their quarrels and there have been no more of those rebellions of the cities against the kings which happened in the reign of the emperor Charles V, and earlier during the reign of King Ferdinand. But when the king dies—or if he should get into serious problems—these and even more unpleasant humors might recur in the body politic. There would be a special danger if the rebels used religion as a battle standard, since religious faith lends itself very well to subverting and destroying monarchies. Spain would be particularly susceptible because there are so many there who are Moors at heart, many others who secretly remain Jews, and even some heretics. They are all very cautious because they fear the Inquisition, a high tribunal so powerful and harsh that everyone is terrified of it. Without the Inquisition Spain would be more lost than Germany and England, even though the Spanish look at first glance like the most devout Catholics in the world.

Most Spaniards are either very rich or very poor, and there would seem to be a cause-and-effect relationship between the wealth of some and the poverty of the rest. It is as if four men had to divide this [Senate] chamber among them. If one man took three-quarters there would be very little to divide among the other three. The Spanish clergy is very rich; the church in Toledo alone has revenues of 400,000 ducats a year, and all the other fifty-seven bishoprics are also very wealthy. The incomes of the churches have been estimated at four million in gold per year. Then there are twenty-two dukes, forty-seven counts, and thirty-six marquises in those lands, and their incomes total nearly three million in gold a year. The richest of all is said to be the duke of Medina Sidonia,[2] the governor-elect of Milan, whose income exceeds 150,000 ducats a year.

One group among these nobles are called the "grandees" of the kingdom. The only things that set them apart are that they remain covered in the presence of the king, whereas everyone else must remove his hat, and when His Majesty is in church they sit on a bench, called the grandees' bench, while everyone else stands. These grandees are all addressed as *"Vuestra Señoría"* even though they are dukes. (The sole exception is the duke of Alva, whom many call "Your Excellency.") All the nobles *except* the grandees—including the counts and marquises—are addressed as *"Vuestra Merced."* But then the rest of the men and women right down to the peasants and the scoundrels who beg in the streets and churches are called *"Señor"* and *"Señora."*[3]

The grandees then are those to whom previous kings or the present one conceded the right of remaining covered in their presence. Many of the other nobles constantly implore the king to grant them this honor, which the mere fact of being dukes, counts, or marquises, and very rich, does not entitle them to have. The honor is conferred on them only if the king so desires, and he grants it to those he likes best. He does not confer it only on Spaniards; recently he indicated that he plans to give this honor to Sir Giovanni Andrea Doria,[4] who had never received it. Doria plans to go to court to be given the dignity. The king makes as little use as possible of the grandees; on the contrary, he does all he can to keep them from becoming important. If one of them manages his affairs well or has a stroke of luck and becomes very rich, the king finds a way to make him spend his money and thus weaken him. As a result, even though they have

2. In 1588 he commanded the defeated Spanish Armada.
3. What strikes the ambassador as paradoxical is that the highest social group (the grandees) and the lowest are both addressed in approximately the same way.
4. Genoese naval commander in Spanish service, grand-nephew of the more famous admiral of the same name.

large incomes, as I said, none of them has money to spend. Quite the opposite; they are deep in debt.

Because the king does not use them in his service, very few of the grandees know anything about running a government, nor do they know anything else. They consider it beneath them to leave their estates unless to take major government positions; on the other hand, they are not suited for life on their own estates. They do not read; they do not discuss anything of value; they simply live in ignorance. The only noteworthy thing about them is a certain loftiness and dignity which in Italy we call "Spanish composure"[5] and which makes all foreigners hate them. They let it be understood that not only is there no other people which bears comparison with them, but that everyone should be grateful to be ruled by them. And they do not forget to use this haughtiness even among themselves. Before addressing a person as *"Señor," "Vuestra Merced,"* "you" (plural), "you" (singular), or *"el,"* they give the matter a great deal of thought, because they believe that any distinction they confer on someone else reduces their own importance.

Because they remain on their own lands they have seen and they know nothing about the world. Their lack of schooling makes them ignorant and their lack of contacts

5. The ambassador uses the Spanish word *sosiego.*

22. Spanish Noblemen, by El Greco.
(Detail from Burial of Count Orgaz. *Church of Santo Tomé, Toledo.)*

with others makes them arrogant. This arrogance is very common among the young people, especially those who are surrounded by great wealth. Revered and deferred to by their own domestic servants, they soon come to believe that everyone should behave that way toward them, and that no one is so important as they. The result is that they look down on others—indeed, they often despise them—and only late or never do they realize their error, when they have been damaged and shamed.

The Spanish grandees consider attending to business matters just as ridiculous as book reading; both pursuits are detestable, or at least completely at odds with the life of a knight. And yet they do not take much pleasure in horsemanship. Instead they pass the time idly, even depravedly. The reasons for this are that they have been poorly brought up and they believe that exercise in Spain is "unhealthy," and also that the king lives in great seclusion and has no interest in watching tournaments.

The grandees and other nobles are subject to the laws of the kingdom just as much as the poorest, wretchedest commoner. Not even the richest and proudest of them would dare to refuse to go to prison if a constable (called an *alguacil*), armed only with a billy club, came to arrest him. While I was in Spain the duke of Alva provided an example of this obedience. The duke is closely related to many of the grandees and nobles of Castile, is respected, dignified, and more than eighty years old. He has served the emperor Charles V and the present king more than fifty years continually and received honors that those rulers never conferred on anyone else. And yet a single *alguacil* with a warrant from the king took him to prison. If he had refused to go, and turned not toward Uceda, where he was imprisoned, but toward his own easily defended district of Alva, he would have frightened the king and agitated the country so much that those who know the kingdom well think the king would have had to leave him alone.

Spain is divided into two major sections. One is Castile, which in 1034 was changed from a county into a kingdom, with the kingdoms of León, Galicia, Granada, Toledo, Murcia, Andalusia, and Seville added to it. The Indies and the king's lands in Africa are also linked to Castile. The other section is Aragon, with Valencia and Catalonia (to which Majorca and those other islands are attached) and the kingdoms of Naples, Sicily, and Sardinia. The kingdom of Navarre is not grouped with these, nor is Portugal,[6] because the former is not completely under Castile and the system of government for Portugal had not yet been decided when I left. The king was planning to join it to Castile, but I will discuss it separately.

The people of Aragon claim to be independent, as in effect they are, since they govern themselves almost as if Aragon were a republic. The king is the head of the state, but he does not inherit the position, they elect him to it. He appoints no official there except a viceroy, who has no part in governing the land or administering justice. These tasks are the responsibilities of officials elected in that kingdom. The viceroy has charge only of the armed forces, and the safety and defense of the region. His Majesty collects no revenues from this region unless he goes there to conduct a meeting of the Cortes, in which case they grant him 600,000 ducats. They keep the rest of the taxes and duties and spend them for the benefit of their own land. They guard their liberties very jealously and bitterly contest each point so that the king and his ministers cannot enlarge their control over them. As a result they frequently and unnecessarily hinder measures which are not their business.

The kingdom of Castile, however, is governed very differently, because there the king has supreme authority. It is he who chooses all the judges, officials, ministers, and councillors, assigns the bishoprics (as he does throughout all of Spain), grants all the benefices and sinecures of the kingdom, and draws up whatever laws he chooses. He abolishes old laws and imposes new ones entirely as he sees fit, although with the apparent consent of the Cortes of Castile,

6. Portugal was added to Philip II's lands in 1580 and remained under Spanish rule until 1640.

who assemble whenever he gives so much as a hint and then
do just about what he wants. He has total control over the
revenues, completely controls the courts (that is, pardons,
executions, and fines), and generally does whatever he
pleases. The one exception is the imposing of new taxes and
customs duties, which he cannot change without the consent
of the Cortes, which represent all of Castile. But this requirement serves more as a salve to his conscience and a way
of facilitating the collection of the money than anything
else. Even in tax matters he has such power and is so
revered and respected that if he wants something, not one of
the deputies in the Cortes would dare to oppose him openly.
What makes them all the more docile is their knowledge that
when the Cortes are over, the king invariably rewards with
presents those who openly supported him. He does this to
help his projects along; it keeps everyone from speaking out
against him and he always has his way.

The nobles and other aristocrats are all tax exempt; they
pay the king no head or property tax at all. Their only
obligation is to serve in his army at their own expense, and
even then only when it is a question of defending Spain from
attack. They are very firm and determined about guarding
their tax immunity, just as the Aragonese defend all of their
liberties. Once when the government tried to impose a very
light tax on them they raised such an uproar that the matter
was dropped.

The nobles and grandees of Castile have so little legal
authority in their own jurisdictions that most of them have
courts only of the first instance; and few of their courts may
hear appeals. All appeals eventually go to the chancelleries
and the royal council. Their own vassals can have them
summoned to these higher courts on the slightest of grounds,
and they are often treated worse there than the lowliest
subjects. This happens both because such is the king's wish
and because the judges usually come from the lower classes.
The reason for this is that judges have to be university
graduates; since the nobles consider it beneath them to
study anything, the power of the courts goes by default into

23. Spanish Gentleman.

(From Deserps, Recueil de la diversité des habits, *1562. Prints Division, New York Public Library.)*

the hands of plebeians. Professional learning is the only route by which men from the lower classes can rise to important posts. This explains why not only the law courts but almost all of the bishoprics are also in the hands of commoners, who are enemies of the nobility. This in turn is another of the grudges the upper classes have against the present regime. At one time most of the bishoprics were given as a matter of course to younger sons of the grandees, as a way of compensating them for not being the heirs. Despite all I have said, however, the king still has ample means to gratify the nobles, since he has many knighthoods in the military orders to distribute, all of which may be conferred only on nobles. Some of these have incomes of up to twelve thousand ducats.

The king rules the people of Castile with an iron hand, as experience has proved is necessary. They are an obstreperous people by nature, and if he treated them otherwise they would be violent and ungovernable. If someone resists the authorities even slightly, by word rather than deed, they punish him as harshly as another government would only

24. Toledo, Ancient City of Castile.

(Detail from Braun and Hogenberg, Civitates orbis terrarum, *1576, I, pl. 3. Rare Book Division, New York Public Library.)*

for very serious and important crimes. The law officers behave so outrageously that no other country would tolerate them. Frequently they will arrest prominent people without reason, showing no respect for them, and put them in prison. If these people then complain to higher officials about the damage and injustice done to them, these officials are so determined to support the authority of their subordinates that they merely release the injured parties. And even then they have to pay the expenses of their arrest and imprisonment! Because of this there is no shame attached to going to jail in Spain, so at least one does not have insults added to his injuries. . . .

3 PHILIP II: "PHLEGMATIC,"
"ASSIDUOUS," "KINDLY AND NATURAL"

Paolo Tiepolo, 1563

The preceding selections presented the general, almost pe-
rennial aspects of early modern Spanish government and
society. The remaining selections, arranged chronologi-
cally, show how Venetian ambassadors analyzed Spain's
use of her power during the reign of King Philip, or
viewed events which revealed the extent and limitations of
that power. Here, in vivid word portraits reminiscent of
their compatriot Titian's paintings in oils of the same
man, Tiepolo and Soranzo depict the views, the daily rou-
tine of government, and the very human amusements of
an immensely powerful ruler.

PAOLO TIEPOLO, 1563

The king was born of the Empress Isabella, daughter of
the king of Portugal, on May 21, 1527. He is slight of stature
and round-faced, with very pale blue eyes, somewhat prominent lips, and pink skin, but his overall appearance is very
attractive. His temperament is very phlegmatic[1] and his

From reports by Paolo Tiepolo, 1563, and Giovanni Soranzo, 1565,
Albèri, I, 5: 61–72, and 113–14; and a dispatch by Girolamo Lippo-
mano, 1587, *Calendar of State Papers . . . Venice . . .*, 8: 266
(April 14, 1587). The translation of Lippomano is by Horatio F.
Brown.

1. That is, dominated by phlegm, that one of the four humors which
in early physiology was believed to cause sluggishness.

25. King Philip II, by Titian.
(*Cincinnati Art Museum.*)

condition weak and delicate; he often takes to his bed, sometimes with chest pains and shortness of breath and sometimes, others say, with more serious illnesses. I have heard
doctors say that it is unlikely he will live for long. Like other
Spaniards he sleeps a great deal; not only does he take a
long siesta after dinner, but he does not get out of bed in the
morning in any season of the year until two and a half hours
before noon. As soon as he rises he hears mass, and then he
has little time for anything else before dinner. Sometimes he
dines with his court and sometimes privately—in fact, usually alone, since he rarely eats with his wife, child, and sister, and others are not considered worthy to be at his table.
His meals are very simple, with no more than fifteen different dishes. He eats very little and only safe, substantial
foods—hardly any kind of fruit and no fish at all. He dresses
very tastefully, and everything that he does is courteous and
gracious. He preserves his kingly dignity, but with all comers he is very natural and cordial—especially by Spanish
standards.

He appears to be extremely religious, since he goes to
church very often and takes communion four times a year.

When he assigns bishoprics and benefices what concerns him most about the candidates is their Christian learning and morality. He accepted the Council[2] against the wishes and advice of the Spanish bishops, who enjoyed a very comfortable position and had no desire to endanger it. He maintains nearly perpetual hostilities with the infidels, persecutes heretics more than any other ruler, and claims to be the readiest and loyalest defender of the pope and the apostolic see. In everything he does he seeks to appear as a true Catholic king, guided by his conscience. But what religious zeal inspires always seems to coincide with his own purposes. . . .

His amusements include conversations with those he knows best, the chatter of buffoons, occasional hunting, tournaments, and lance throwing, but more than anything else, women, in whom he takes a great deal of pleasure, and with whom he is often secluded. Above all else he likes to loaf in peace, forgetting the business of government, which he hates and avoids as much as he can. Quite often, as I have informed Your Serenity in my letters, he will surprise everyone by leaving the court with only five or six others, sometimes before daybreak, and going to some solitary place where he spends his time resting in utter tranquillity and refusing to listen to anything that would bother him or demand thought.

From this anyone can see that his natural inclination is to avoid difficulties; he showed this trait during the fighting in the Netherlands when he got angry and frustrated over the way things were going. Anyone who ponders this king's way of life—how he enjoys staying in Spain and how unwillingly he wrestles with problems—is sure to conclude that when he can the king will stay at peace with everyone and keep far from the noise of battle. If he does start a fight with anyone, it will be with the infidels [Turks], because he could attack them without having to go in person; his soldiers would run all the dangers.

One can never be sure, however, about the inner natures and impulses of other men. With the passage of time their

2. But it was only in 1564 that Philip allowed publication of the reforming decrees of the Council of Trent.

personalities change, they develop new habits, and they
come to hate what they once delighted in. A long period of
sluggish inaction will often weary a man as much as many
troubles and a lot of work would do. Then, too, it sometimes
happens that a bad minister of state, especially one who
thinks he might profit monetarily or otherwise from
changes, will drag his ruler into war against his will. And
sometimes luck and circumstances will produce tricky situa-
tions that a ruler just cannot avoid. . . .

The queen[3] is little more than seventeen years old, and she
has a lively personality but is not very pretty. So far she has
shown no symptoms of pregnancy, but the truth is that she
is still very young. The indications of maturity as a woman
only appeared about ten months ago, as her own doctor told
me. In public the king treats her as if he loves and respects
her very much, but actually he does little to make her happy.
He frequently stays away from her for long periods, and
when he is at court he purposely visits her late at night; if
he finds her sleeping he goes away, as if he does not want to
awaken her, satisfied with having made this gesture. So the
queen, in order not to miss having his company, many times
has stayed up most of the night. She knows that the king has
many affairs with other ladies, but she has learned from her
mother[4] to put up with this, and she patiently endures it
without a murmur of complaint. . . .

GIOVANNI SORANZO, 1565

In his public dealings His Majesty is very kindly and
natural. While walking from his chambers to the church
where he hears mass he receives all the petitions which are
handed to him, and if someone wants to speak to him he
stops courteously to listen. He does the same as he leaves the
church to go to the dining hall, or to his chambers, walking
very slowly so that everyone will have time to reach him. As
he receives the petitions he smiles cheerfully, and if he

3. Elizabeth, sister of the king of France, Charles IX. She was
Philip's third wife and died five years after Tiepolo gave this report.
4. Her mother, Catherine de Medici, for years tolerated the attachment of her husband, Henry II of France, to Diane de Poitiers.

answers anyone he does it in very polite and general terms. That happens rarely, because he usually glances at the petitions without making any answer. However, while he listens to all who want to speak to him and receives all the petitions, he acts on very few of these, or, in fact, none. As soon as he has entered the church, or his chambers, he hands all the letters to a servant, who then distributes them to different officials according to their contents. To get any satisfaction the supplicant must then go to the official who has received his petition. The process is a long one, because the official must take the petition to a council, which decides what response to make, and if they decide favorably, their answer must then be taken to the king, who, if he approves, signs it with his own hand. If the council rejects the petition, they answer *"no hay lugar,"* which means nothing further will be done about it, and then the petitioner has no recourse. This whole complicated process requires a great deal of the petitioner's time and money. Most of them exhaust their energies and their wallets, give up, and go home disgusted and despairing. I have seen many such cases.

When the ambassadors desire an audience they send a request to the king, who promptly grants it and states the time at which they should appear. I never had to ask twice for an interview; one was always courteously arranged. His Majesty listens to what one says with great friendliness and then answers in very general and polite terms, and that is usually the end of the interview. But if the subject is very important and the ambassador needs a definite answer, the king will usually suggest that he speak to the duke of Alva, or if he is not in court, Ruy Gómez, and the ambassador must then go to them to discuss the problem and have an answer. . . .

GIROLAMO LIPPOMANO

[Dispatch from Madrid, April 14, 1587] His Majesty, praised be God, is in good health, and attends assiduously to affairs, though he gladly avoids seeing many people, and is averse to public audiences. I am informed by one who is always in his private apartments that he is never idle, for besides his wish to read for himself all the correspondence which passes between his ambassadors and governors in all parts of his great domains, and besides the prayers which he says, he writes every day with his own hand more than a quinternion of paper between minutes, opinions, and orders, which are transmitted to his councillors, judges, secretaries, and ministers in this way; and it is hardly to be believed how much time he spends in signing letters, licenses, patents, and others affairs of grace and justice, which on certain days amount to two thousand; and he always insists on being informed, at least in substance, of the content of these papers, and frequently he rejects them if he thinks them unjust. I must add that notwithstanding this mass of work he does not omit to attend to the minutest details, such as his household accounts for the expenses of the Escorial, Madrid, Aranjuez, and Pardo palaces.

26. Philip's Comments (left) on a Letter from His Inquisitor General.
(British Art Museum, London, Egerton MSS., 1834, fol. 1.)

4 "THE UNHAPPY AND UNFORTUNATE PRINCE OF SPAIN"

Giovanni Soranzo, 1565

Philip's first three marriages produced only one male heir, the pathetic Don Carlos. The significance of this demented young man's story[1] lies not in the details of his imprisonment and death but in its relation to the government of an empire. Spanish history had demonstrated the necessity of a strong monarchy. As far as historians can tell from the Spanish, Venetian, and other documents, Philip decided that Carlos could not possibly rule Spain, and hiding emotions which he must have felt, he bleakly arrested and imprisoned his son, who died six months later.

GIOVANNI SORANZO, 1565

His Royal Highness Don Carlos [the king's] only son, was born on July 9, 1545, and is now nineteen years old.[2] He is ugly and unpleasant to look at, with a face not so much pale as it is wasted. His temperament is melancholic,[3] and

---

From a report by Giovanni Soranzo, 1565, and dispatches by Sigismondo Cavalli, 1568, Albèri, I, 5: 119–21, and Louis P. Gachard, *Don Carlos et Philippe II*, 2 vols. (Brussels, 1863), vol. 2, app. B, pp. 668–70, 699–701.

1. Don Carlos's life provided material for a Schiller play and a Verdi opera, in which King Philip plays a more villainous role than he does in these dispatches.

2. Soranzo wrote his report late in 1564 and delivered it early in 1565, before Don Carlos's twentieth birthday.

3. That is, dominated by black bile, the bodily humor believed to cause irascibility or gloomy depression.

27. Don Carlos, by
Sanchez Coello.
(*Museo del Prado, Madrid.*)

he is quick-tempered and very difficult to control. His eating
habits are so irregular and undisciplined and his appetite so
voracious that he has a fever much of the time. But His
Highness is accustomed to the fever, and takes it very
lightly; the moment he is free of it he resumes his excesses.
He listens to and respects no one. If I may say so, he has
very little regard even for the king, who simply pretends to
be unaware of many things he does. When he is angry, His
Highness goes immediately to bed with a fever, which he
gets because he is so enraged. Up until this point in his life
he has learned very little. He has never taken any interest in
books, horsemanship, or any of the other worthwhile things
that one would expect a man who is going to inherit so many
lands and kingdoms to know about. By nature he is very
cruel, and there are many stories told about this which I
cannot repeat in this place.[4] In conversation he is downright

4. The ambassador Paolo Tiepolo in 1563 told the Senate that Don
Carlos as a little boy had "not merely bitten but bitten off the nipples
of three of his wet nurses, who almost died as a result," and that as a

uncouth. He bears a grudge against many people, especially the gentlemen assigned to his service. He takes sudden dislikes to them, and if it weren't for the king he would always be changing them. There are very few who know how to get along with him and win his favor.

His health is very bad. I have been assured it is true that by order of His Majesty they brought pretty girls to him to see what he would do, and that he showed not the slightest interest in them or desire for them. For several reasons, then, the king is very disturbed about his son, and cannot make up his mind to have him marry. This is the private reason why he keeps stalling about completing the betrothal with the emperor's daughter.[5]

His Majesty has assigned as Don Carlos's chief majordomo Sir Ruy Gómez,[6] who intensely dislikes the job of coping with that totally unreasonable young man. For Don Carlos is full of strange whims. He has tailors make him vast quantities of clothing, and buys jewels without letting anyone appraise them for him. Sometimes he will have his portrait engraved on a diamond or ruby and then when he has worn the ring for a week he doesn't want to see it again. He gives no presents and far from showing affection for anyone else, he always plays the proud lord. He makes a show of scorning most things that the king takes pleasure in, and nobody has discovered anything he does like.

In short, there is a great deal I could tell you about this prince which is better left unmentioned. Suffice it to say that if Our Lord does not give him better judgment and more intelligence he will turn out very badly. As far as that goes, if he does not learn to eat more wisely, and stop behaving wildly, and cool his hot temper, he will not live long; his health has already suffered.

The king took Don Carlos on one occasion to a meeting of

---

youth of seventeen or so he had men stabbed and flogged and tried to have one individual castrated. (Albèri, I, 5: 73.)

5. Anne, daughter of the Holy Roman Emperor Maximilian II and Philip's sister. Five years later Philip himself married Anne, his niece.

6. Ruy Gómez de Silva, prince of Eboli (1516–73), a very influential courtier in the early years of Philip's reign.

the Council of State, led him in and had him seated, and left him there, but clearly neither government nor anything else interests him at all. All the king's officials at the court are afraid of Don Carlos because when they refuse to do what he wants he curses them and goes to bed with a fever. They know they must not obey him without the king's permission, so they are at a loss what to do, and as far as possible they avoid his presence. . . .

SIGISMONDO CAVALLI

[Dispatch from Madrid, January 22, 1568] Most Serene Prince, I hope you will forgive me if I go into details in this letter to an extent I have tried to avoid when discussing other subjects. It seemed to me that the importance of the topic was such that Your Serenity should be told every particular.

For quite some time now, the prince of Spain has been very angry with the king, his father, and his father has been very displeased with him. Several times the king has punished his son, or severely rebuked him for insolent behavior unsuitable to a prince. Every once in a while Don Carlos insulted important gentlemen at the court, and all night he went around armed with light arquebuses committing various outrages. He spent money wildly, and when he needed more he would force different men to lend it to him; among others he made Nicolò Grimaldo, a Genoese, lend him forty thousand escudi. Despite many stern warnings from his father, the prince continued on this course. Frequently he would try in different ways to wheedle money from his father, only to find that the king refused his requests, and was highly irritated by them. And so, as the prince realized he was in his father's bad graces, he began to cultivate Don Juan of Austria.[7]

No one can be sure just what happened but as of this writing it is believed that the prince confided in Don Juan

7. Don Juan was an illegitimate son of Charles V, hence Philip II's half brother. In 1571 he commanded the fleet which defeated the Turks in the Battle of Lepanto.

28. Don Juan, Philip's Half-Brother.

(*From Stirling-Maxwell*, Don John of Austria, *1883, I, 452. Libraries of the University of Pennsylvania, Philadelphia.*)

that he planned to shoot his father to death with an arquebus, and that he urged Don Juan to join him in this plot. He tried to convince Don Juan that the king would never do anything for him, that he would certainly make him live in poverty (seeing how he treated his own son), and that if Don Juan would help him in the murder he would reward him with Milan or the kingdom of Naples. It is not known how Don Juan answered him, but a few days later he pretended to be summoned by the king to discuss naval matters, came to the place where the king was staying, and remained there ten days. When the prince learned that his father was making a great display of goodwill toward Don Juan he began to suspect that he had been betrayed. He wrote to Don Juan that he wanted very much to talk to him without the king's knowledge, and urged him to meet with him at a designated rendezvous. His plan was to murder him if he would not go along with the plot, but Don Juan, perhaps realizing this, did not show up.

The prince remained determined to carry out this plan.

The next day, having returned here to Madrid with the king, he sent a messenger to ask Don Juan to come to his chambers, and he prepared a light arquebus with which to murder him when he appeared. One of the gentlemen in his suite, however, suspected something was afoot and took the powder from the firing pan. As a result, when Don Juan came in the prince found the gun unloaded; he then drew his sword to give Don Juan a thrust, but by God's grace he failed to wound him.

When word of this came to the king he said nothing for the moment. In the middle of the night, however, when the prince was already in bed, King Philip took four important gentlemen of the court and set out for the prince's rooms. When the prince was told that the king was coming he leaped from bed and asked his father if he planned to kill him. The king answered no, but he was certainly going to punish him and treat him as if he were insane, to which the prince responded that he was not insane, but that he was indeed miserable. The king made no answer, but with his own hands he took away his son's sword and dagger, which he later carried to his own quarters. As he left he told the prince that he could no longer leave his rooms, and he immediately posted guards and had the windows nailed down. The prince is not allowed to have any kind of arms; when he eats they do not even give him a knife. And so he remains, confined and closely guarded.

The next day the king summoned all his counselors and told them what he had done during the night. He told them he had had no other choice, that it was his duty to God and necessary for the safety of the kingdom, and that he would explain the circumstances later. He sent word to all the Castilian grandees and the officials of the Cortes of Castile to convene here. . . . My friend also tells me that the prince had never intended to take his father's life, but that he had wanted to go with Don Juan of Austria and the fleet to Italy, incite revolution in His Majesty's holdings there and make himself their ruler, and then go to the Netherlands and win them as well. He planned to go to the emperor, on whose help he was counting very much, and he had also written about his plans to several of the German princes. When His Highness told Don Juan about all these plans of his, he took twenty-four hours to decide what to do, but once he had made up his mind he went to the king and told him everything, as I explained above.

The reasons for Don Carlos's imprisonment are being kept very secret, and Your Serenity should not be surprised if I cannot vouch absolutely for the truth of any of them. . . .

SIGISMONDO CAVALLI

[Dispatch, July 24, 1568] Most Serene Prince . . . I must now report the death of the unhappy and unfortunate prince of Spain. These are the pathetic events of his death.

As soon as His Highness was imprisoned and saw that he would be confined for a long time, he decided to kill himself. He said that a prince who was injured and shamed as he had been could no longer live. Since he had no weapon or no other quick way of committing suicide, he decided to starve himself to death. For several days, as I remember reporting to Your Serenity, he ate almost nothing, but finally he got so hungry that he began to eat again. It appeared that his fasting had actually benefited him; his body is full of gross humors caused by his wild living, but his abstinence from food had made them dwindle and disappear. Seeing this, he tried another course. He had heard someone say that if a man eats a diamond it will kill him, so he swallowed one which he wore on a ring. But since it was hard, rather than a powder, in two days it emerged from his body without having hurt him anywhere.

So, having failed in that, he made up his mind to die of overeating. This method was easier and more natural for him, and it succeeded. Six days ago something happened which started the final decline. Among the dishes they served him was a pie filled with large partridges, and after he had eaten some of the other things he turned to this pie and ate not only the fowl but also the *pasta* around it. Since this *pasta* had been seasoned with many different spices, it made him so thirsty that all day he drank quantities of water cooled with snow. (This was his usual beverage; he did not drink wine.) The great volume of water and indigestible food led to a terrible stomachache that night, and this was followed by vomiting and continual diarrhea. Because he was so unhappy His Highness refused to take any medicines or eat any food for quite some time, and the result was that when he finally accepted what they gave him, his stomach could not hold it down. He became terribly weak, and within a few days the poor boy came to the end of his days. May Our Lord give him more peace and happiness in the next world than he ever knew in this one.

[In cipher] *During this final illness, His Majesty has appeared very harsh, not to say cruel. Not only did he stay away from the prince, but he forbade the queen, the princess, and all others to visit him, except for his doctors and regular attendants. Nor would he let them console the prince, or cheer him, or encourage him to recover. This makes me believe the king held something extremely important against him. However, His Majesty has already gone into mourning and looks very sorrowful. He will order the court to dress in black, and he will hold all the ceremonies which are customary in these events. . . .*

SIGISMONDO CAVALLI

[Dispatch, July 31, 1568] Most Serene Prince, because I had no way to send a letter directly to Italy, I sent one by way of France on the twenty-fourth with the news of the death of the prince of Spain. I will enclose a copy with this letter. That evening he was buried amid much funereal pomp and ceremony, with everyone in tears. At the interment were the princes of Bohemia, the cardinal, the usual ambassadors, and the rest of the court, dressed in mourning. The grandees of Spain were the pallbearers. The next morning a solemn requiem mass was celebrated. There will be no other ceremonies until they have prepared for the funeral, which will be lavish and magnificent. Four days before he died the poor prince spoke in the wisest and most Christian manner one could ask, as if our Lord God had given him in abundance at the time of his death the wisdom that he lacked during his life. He bequeathed his mother's dowry of 200,000 escudos to his creditors and begged that his father should relieve his conscience by paying the rest of what he owed. He commended his servants to the king and begged His Majesty to reward them, saying that they had served him well even though he had often treated them badly. He left several gold cups to religious institutions and his favorite courtiers, and he gave his crystal drinking goblet to Ruy Gómez, to show that he did not die hating him, even though he used to blame all his woes on Ruy Gómez's advice [to the king]. He said that he was content to think that with his death he would free his father of all the pain and worry he had suffered, or would have suffered, on his account. . . .

Philip's third wife, Elizabeth, died soon after Don Carlos. (She was survived by two daughters.) Two years later Philip married his fourth and last wife, his niece Anne of Austria. Anne bore him four sons and one daughter, but of them all, only one, who was to succeed his father as Philip III, lived to be more than eight years old.

5 "THE SPANISH ALWAYS CLAIM TO BE THE MOST CATHOLIC"

Leonardo Donà, 1573

Was it their religious fervor, coupled with patriotism, which made the Spaniards such vigorous colonizers and warriors in the sixteenth century? Why did Spanish kings treat their converted Moorish subjects with such apparent cruelty? Was the Spanish Inquisition an instrument for political despotism as well as religious purity? Were religious heresies—or indifference—already beginning in the latter sixteenth century to weaken the Spanish sense of purpose? Donà's remarks on Spanish religiosity are colored by his own deep Catholicism. Years later, nevertheless, he acquired fame as the doge of Venice who led his city-state in defiance of the Church's temporal authority.

. . . I will end my report on the kingdoms of Spain by giving Your Excellencies an account of the state of religion there. Besides being the chief concern of every Christian, religion is so involved with questions of state that governments tend to rise and fall according to whether religious faith is preserved or upset. The Spanish always claim to be the most Catholic of Christians, and whenever they speak of the Church they make a point of saying, "as the Holy Roman Catholic Church believes and commands. . . ." There is no doubt that in all those externals by which Christians

---

From a report by Leonardo Donà, 1573, Albèri, I, 6: 410–12.

show their reverence for God and their observance of Christian duties the Spanish try to surpass all other peoples. Granted, the externals of behavior are not certain proofs about the will and the soul, but there's no doubt that it is a rare thing for someone evil at heart to be good on the surface. Following that line of argument, if the surface is very good it is logical that the interior may be very good, just as if the surface were very bad we might suppose that the interior similarly would be very bad.

But even though everyone in Spain appears to be staunchly Catholic and Christian, and theology flourishes in the cathedral chapters, the monasteries, and the universities on a level unsurpassed elsewhere, there are nevertheless so many baptized Jews and Moors,[1] so many "new Christians" that we can be sure there is a good deal of contamination. Some say there are many Spaniards who in questions of faith *male sentiant* but keep silent for fear of the Inquisition. One proof of this is the discovery in Valladolid in 1559 of a group of heretics which included many nobles and gentry who had been infected with Protestant worship and beliefs by a former chaplain of Charles V named Cazzala. Many believe that if this poisonous weed had not been quickly and violently uprooted it would have spread and sickened all of Spain. If we could only see inside events, we might discover that this event played a major role in deciding the present king to make peace with France and return to Spain, where he has remained ever since. I have heard that in Aragon and Catalonia the Inquisition has for a long time suspected many people of heresy, and that in Valencia the Inquisition very recently discovered some landholders who confessed they had profited by allowing baptized Moors in their villages to live almost openly as Muslims.

Once an idea takes root in a Spaniard's mind it is very hard to remove it. If some misfortune allowed religious dis-

1. The Spanish Moors had been forced to accept Christianity or leave the peninsula. Those who remained were considered a religious problem, as only nominal Christians, and a political one, as potential rebels and possible allies of their coreligionists the Turks.

29. A Spanish Inquisitor, by El Greco.

(Cardinal Don Fernando Niño de Guevara. *Metropolitan Museum of Art, New York. Bequest of Mrs. H. O. Havemeyer, 1929. The H. O. Havemeyer Collection.*)

sension to spread, some claim that present circumstances would make stamping it out a very dangerous process. The peasants might prove especially susceptible to this disease, because the tithe on all income which is paid to the churches is a particularly heavy burden for them, and in addition to that there are agreements with local priests according to which each year they have to turn over a sizable part of the first crops that are harvested.

Among those who are sentenced by the Inquisition each year there is almost always someone who is punished for having believed that ordinary fornication is not a sin which *occidat animam* [kills the soul—i.e., a mortal sin]. Since this vice itself *late patet* [is widespread] in Spain, and those in charge don't repress it as they should, it has given rise to the heresy I just mentioned, and if not carefully attended to, that could very easily lead to other heresies. [Marginal note by Donà: *This is a topic which could harmfully influence a reader; perhaps I should leave it out.*] But these dangers, and the disturbances that could rise from them, are taken care of by the powerful and vigilant Inquisition, which is indispensable in Spain, and by the present king's unwavering determination to uphold the Catholic religion. His personal example and his fixed purpose of upholding our religion have the result of nipping all troubles in the bud. What also helps to eliminate heresies, in the opinion of some observers, is the self-interest of the great body of noblemen who customarily hold church benefices. In order not to lose these benefices—so it is said—the nobles zealously merge their human interests with those of God.

6 "VICTORY! VICTORY!"
AND "THE LESSER OF TWO EVILS"

Leonardo Donà, 1571

On October 7, 1571, an allied Spanish-Venetian-papal fleet annihilated virtually the entire Turkish naval force in a spectacular battle in the Greek bay of Lepanto. European Catholics saw the battle as a great Christian crusading victory over infidels, and Cervantes later wrote of it in *Don Quixote* as "the noblest occasion that past or present ages have seen or future ones may hope to see." Lepanto was not decisive. The Turks soon rebuilt their fleet, Spain was forced to divert much of her attention to the Netherlands revolt, and Venice in 1573 deserted the Holy League and made a separate peace with the sultan. Despite all of this, the victory at Lepanto foretold the approaching demise of Turkey as a great naval power. In these dispatches Donà describes Philip's jubilation at the news of victory, and his politeness and suppressed irony when later told that Venice had left the alliance.

MADRID, NOVEMBER 2, 1571

The news of the glorious victory which the loving hand of God has given to all Christendom, and especially abundantly

Dispatches by Leonardo Donà, 1571 and 1573, *Corrispondenza da Madrid di Leonardo Donà (1570–1573)*, ed. Mario Brunetti and Eligio Vitale, 2 vols. (Venice-Rome, 1963), 1: 372–75; 2: 680. By kind permission of Dr. Vitale.

30. The Battle of Lepanto, 1571.

(Detail from Camocio, Isole, famose porti, *1573, pl. 64. From an original in the Free Library of Philadelphia.)*

to Your Serenity, and which you were pleased to advise me of by special courier, arrived here at two o'clock in the afternoon on the last day of October.

As I read the news the first sentences overcame me with joy and delight, and at the same time it made me more aware than ever that God's mercy toward us surpasses not only what we deserve but even what we hope for. Not knowing how nor being able to give him my small thanks in any other way, I lay down with my face and lips to the ground in all humility, and I praised and blessed and glorified his indescribably divine compassion. Then I took Your Serenity's packet and after not reading but hastily devouring your letters I went immediately, without sending any advance word, to His Majesty's palace and learned that he was in his chapel at an All Saints vesper service. I sent a message with his major-domo, the count of Chinchón, that I wanted urgently to tell him something that would delight him, and His Majesty was pleased to welcome me within the curtains of his baldachin and hear what I had to say. I approached him at that very moment when the chapel resounded with *"magnificat anima mea Dominum et exultavit spiritus meus in Deo salutari meo,"* and crying "Victory! Victory!" and praising God, I told His Majesty briefly what Your Serenity had written me. I added that I had come there to join him in reciting the *Te Deum laudamus* in the presence of the Blessed Host on the altar, that to do this I would go to my place in the chapel, and that later I would like to see His Majesty in his reception room and tell him all the news in a more leisurely way and carry out some other commissions Your Serenity had given me. The king, however, obviously elated with the news and showing great respect for Your Serenity, insisted that I remain with him behind the curtains, and after the incensing of the chapel, he had me read at length all Your Serenity had written to me. When I told him I also had with me a packet of letters from his own ambassador[1] he wanted to see it then and there, and after he

---

1. That is, Philip's ambassador in Venice.

had opened it we read all the letters together. He was very happy and praised God for showing us such favor and wanted me to thank Your Serenity warmly for sending this wonderful news.

Then he told me that he wanted not only the two of us to recite the *Te Deum* but that all in the chapel should solemnly join in singing it. And so, when vespers were over, all of the court knelt down and with immeasurable joy and in the most perfect harmony that I have ever enjoyed we gave our thanks to the all-powerful King of Kings and Lord God of Hosts. After this I accompanied the king to his rooms talking all the while of this great victory, and I stayed with him until after nightfall. . . .

That night the king had it proclaimed in all the streets that everyone must attend a solemn All Saints procession which was to be held the next morning to thank God for infinite grace. This was carried out with great ceremony; all the ambassadors of the various kings took part, and His Eminence the cardinal legate said the mass. During the long procession His Majesty was pleased to do me great honor by having me walk by his side for some distance, discussing various aspects of this remarkable event with great satisfaction. Considering how much joy this news has brought to the king and all his court, I would say that Your Serenity has never spent your money on couriers with better results than this time. Another result has been to reflect great honor and respect on your embassy here. . . .

I will conclude by saying that I join with Your Serenity in rejoicing over what has happened, and I only want very humbly to remind myself, first, and then all the distinguished and venerable gentlemen of your councils that our Lord God has granted us this victory *ut sine timore de manu inimicorum liberati, serviamus illi in sanctitate et justitia coram ipso omnibus diebus nostris.*[2]

2. Bible (Revised Standard Version), Luke 1: 74–75: "that we, delivered from the hand of our enemies, we should serve him without fear, in holiness and justice before him all our days."

MADRID, APRIL 17, 1573

. . . After telling him how much trust Your Serenity and people everywhere place in his goodness and wisdom we[3] asked him, on behalf of our republic [of Venice], to understand that Your Serenity was forced to take this action to avoid worse troubles, and as the lesser of two evils. We also said that in making this decision and carrying it out Your Serenity had believed that for the reasons we had mentioned it was in His Majesty's interest as well as ours. And we added that we knew of His Majesty's remarkably sound judgment, and were sure that when he had considered the circumstances Your Serenity's decision would not look so selfish as it might appear at first glance.

The king listened to us very attentively. The more he realized that we were explaining our position in a suitably friendly and respectful manner, the more His Majesty gave us his attention and directed his gaze right at us. His face gave no hint of what he was thinking, except that at the moment when he heard that the conditions of the peace treaty had been accepted his mouth moved ever so slightly in the very fleetest of ironic smiles, almost as if His Majesty wanted to say, without interrupting us, "In short, you've done it, just as everyone told me you would!" Then the king, without losing his composure at all and behaving to us just as he always does, followed his custom by answering us in few words: "Ambassadors, you have never troubled me unnecessarily, and you did the right thing to seek an audience with me. However, this news comes to me as a complete surprise, and what has been done is very important, so it would not be wise for me to give you my reactions without some thought. I will consider the matter and see that an answer is given to you."

3. Donà and his successor-to-be as ambassador, Lorenzo Priuli, together had an audience with the king to break the news that Venice had deserted her alliance with him and made a separate peace with the Ottoman Turks.

In subsequent weeks it became clear that high Spanish officials understood why Venice had been forced to seek a separate peace with the Turks, but were highly annoyed that she had negotiated the treaty without the knowledge of her allies. The king himself proved to be friendlier and more sympathetic than his ministers.

7 "THE ARMADA HAS GIVEN BATTLE"

Girolamo Lippomano, 1586

The first two decades of Philip's reign were very difficult, although there were some successes among the tribulations. The king suppressed a revolt of the Moriscos in Granada and countered Turkish naval pressure with the victory at Lepanto. But Philip did not succeed during these years in coping with his greatest problem, the revolt in the Netherlands, and he was hampered by a lack of revenues. In the 1580s and 1590s, however, dramatic increases in the supplies of silver reaching the king from the New World allowed him to carry out much bolder ventures than he had undertaken in the past. A more venturesome, imperialistic Philip now added Portugal to his empire (1580), recovered the southern (but not the northern) Netherlands (1578–85), launched the Armada against England (1588), and intervened (1589–98) in the French Wars of Religion. Of these ventures, perhaps the most famous is the Armada. By sending a fleet and army against England, Philip hoped to halt English persecution of Catholics, punish Elizabeth for several impudences, and stop English piracy in the Spanish New World possessions, but most of all to block the English from allying with the rebellious Netherlanders.

Dispatches by Girolamo Lippomano, 1586–88, *Calendar of State Papers . . . Venice . . .*, 8: 182–406. Translation by Horatio F. Brown.

JULY 20, 1586

[In cipher] *His Majesty hears with great displeasure the account of the damage which the queen of England is doing in Flanders and in the Indies,[1] besides the understanding which she maintains with Portugal through the medium of Don Antonio,[2] and her negotiations at Constantinople. But what has enraged him more than all else, and has caused him to show a resentment such as he has never before displayed in all his life, is the account of the masquerades and comedies which the queen of England orders to be acted at his expense. His Majesty has received a summary of one of these which was recently represented, in which all sorts of evil is spoken of the pope, the Catholic religion, and the*

1. In August 1585, Elizabeth allied herself with the Dutch rebels and she soon sent troops to the Netherlands. Meanwhile Sir Francis Drake raided the Spanish West Indies.
2. Pretender to the crown of Portugal.

31. Queen Elizabeth, by Crispin van de Passe.

(National Gallery of Art, Washington, D.C., Rosenwald Collection.)

*king, who is accused of spending all his time in the Escorial
with the monks of Saint Jerome, attending only to his buildings, and a hundred other insolences which I refrain from
sending to Your Serenity. All this, taken in conjunction with
the continual exhortations of the pope and his promises of
help from church revenues, has once more stirred the king,
who is naturally inclined to peace, to make vigorous preparations for war; such is the general interpretation of these
many levies of troops in Italy, and the galleys and gal-
leasses, and the Spanish reserves from the Neapolitan garrisons. Public rumor says that the king will go to Portugal in
November, and points to the activity displayed in laying by
money, of which two million in gold are already set apart
for the express purpose of this campaign. They say the king
has resolved to sell three thousand titles of that status of
nobility called* hidalgo *to anyone who wishes to buy them for
two thousand crowns apiece. There have been fresh appointments to the Council of War. . . .*

A<small>UGUST</small> 6, 1586

*[In cipher] . . . His Majesty desired the Council to con-
sider the whole question and to report what action they
advised him to take, with a view to achieving a single but
complete revenge for all the injuries which the queen inflicts
daily on this crown. The king shows a lively desire to shake
this disgrace from his shoulders, and among many other
insults he cannot conceal his indignation at the infamous
comedies which the queen causes to be enacted. For although
His Majesty professes never to show his emotions, still I am
assured that when an account of these plays was given to
him by an Englishman, he rose from his chair with every
sign of wrath and indignation. The members of the Council
have held long deliberations on this subject, and although
they take pains to keep their proceedings very secret, yet I
have found means to come by many of their memoranda
and speeches on the subject at hand. As these are very
voluminous I do not send them to Your Serenity, I merely*

enclose a short summary drawn up by the Marquis of Santa Cruz and sent from Lisbon; it contains a statement of all the provisions which will be required for the attack on England. I gather that all seven councillors are of opinion that next spring the king should undertake this war. In favor of this resolution they urge that His Majesty cannot do less than punish the queen, if he desires to preserve his reputation and his possessions, for she is the foe of all good people, aye, and of God himself; that her subjects are in part Catholics, and they are waiting anxiously for this day; that in part they are deeply attached to the queen of Scotland, while all are ill-affected toward their sovereign, who tyrannizes over them; that the English race is little accustomed to arms, having the use of the bow only, and they cannot put together more than seven or eight thousand trained infantry, without any cavalry, without any arquebusiers, without generals of experience; that there are no forts of any importance in the kingdom; that it will be impossible to prevent a landing if the right moment of the tide be chosen. In this way the war in Flanders may be finished at a blow, these seas and the Indies swept clear of corsairs, and all that poor people of England brought back again to the Catholic faith. Thus the king would acquire a new crown on earth to add to his others and a still greater one in heaven. God will fight for the king, for that woman in the wickedness of her heart and the folly of her intellect has reached such a pitch of insolence as to attack the pope and the king in public comedies, though His Majesty, when king of England, caused her to be freed from her prison[3] and saved her life.

JANUARY 12, 1587

. . . Although the king has been living in retirement during Christmas and attending to his devotions, yet he has not omitted to make various provisions for the Armada. It is indeed a miracle to see how he governs this great machine

---

3. When consort of Queen Mary of England, Philip persuaded her in 1555 to release Elizabeth from confinement.

without any council of state, and almost, one might say, without any ministers; but his long experience, and his singular prudence, joined to his great power, easily point out to him alone sound and excellent lines of action more easily than they could occur to many, however wise they might be. . . .

FEBRUARY 13, 1588

[In cipher] . . . *His Majesty shows no signs of changing his first resolution; indeed, one of his most intimate courtiers had occasion to say that he would never have expected to see such prudence, judgment, knowledge, and intelligence as His Majesty displays in this business. He urges forward the preparations so that the Armada may take the sea as soon as possible, for he believes that by rapid action it is still possible to remedy the mischief caused by previous delays, or, perhaps, he hopes that the sailing of the fleet will greatly facilitate the conclusion of an honorable treaty.* . . .

APRIL 30, 1588

Day by day we are expecting news that the Armada has sailed. It has drawn down the river to Belém at the mouth of the port, three miles from Lisbon. The blessing of the standard was performed with great pomp and many salvos of artillery. . . .

Here in all the churches they make constant prayers; and the king himself is on his knees two or three hours every day before the sacrament. Everyone hopes that the greater the difficulties, humanly speaking, the greater will be the favor of God.

JUNE 4, 1588

The Armada set sail from Lisbon at length on the twenty-ninth of last month, a Sunday. The weather was most excellent. They are now waiting the news of its arrival at Corunna, in Galicia, to embark more troops, and then to sail.

I have from time to time reported the great preparations which have been made; but we here must expect news of its progress from other quarters now, unless the peace is effected in Flanders.

JULY 12, 1588

[In cipher] . . . *The wiser wonder what can induce the king to insist, quite against his natural temper, that the Armada shall give battle to the English, who are known to be awaiting the attack with eager courage, and so they surmise that, over and above the belief that God will be on his side, two motives urge the king to this course; first, that he has some secret understandings which will fail if there is any delay; secondly, that these expenses of a million of gold a month cannot be supported for long, and so he has resolved to try his fortune, believing that if the enemy win a battle it will have been so bloody that they will immediately be compelled to make peace, whereas if they lose a battle they lose all at one blow.*

AUGUST 20, 1588

. . . Don Bernardino de Mendoza[4] announces from France, in letters of the second of August, that the Armada has given battle to the English, sunk some of their ships, won a victory, and passed on to join the duke of Parma;[5] but the report is so confused, and that ambassador is so accustomed to deceive himself, that they are waiting confirmation of the news; no public rejoicings have taken place, nor have the ambassadors congratulated the king. His Majesty exclaimed that he trusted God would favor his cause to the full, for he was moved by no desire to increase his possessions, but only to increase the faith and the Catholic religion; and even if he conquered England he would not in many years recover the expenses of the Armada for a single day. . . .

4. The Spanish ambassador.
5. The Spanish commander in the Netherlands.

His Majesty will give audience to no one until he has more certain news of the Armada.

AUGUST 27, 1588

[From the Senate, in Venice, to the ambassador in Spain] From many quarters we hear of the success of the Armada and we rejoice. We order you to offer our congratulations to His Majesty.

SEPTEMBER 6, 1588

[In cipher] *The bad news received in dispatches from the duke of Parma, and dated the tenth of August, though kept strictly secret, yet pain the king and the court all the more that they were unexpected, and moreover quite contrary to*

32. Battle of the Armada, 1588.

(*Detail from* The Armada, Design for Tapestry, *by an unknown artist. Courtesy of the Trustees of the National Maritime Museum, Greenwich, England.*)

the news sent by Don Bernardino de Mendoza, the ambas-
sador in France, who by three different couriers confirmed
the statement that the duke of Medina Sidonia had sunk
many of the enemy, and was on the point of effecting a
junction with the duke of Parma. The dispatches from the
duke of Parma detail the misfortune which befell the Ar-
mada on the eighth of August, and how it has been driven
toward Scotland and Norway. But what distresses them
most is the news that Drake is following up the Armada,
harassing it continually and picking up all the vessels that
become separated from it. . . .

It is a blessing that the bad news did not reach Spain
while the king was suffering from fever, for though His
Majesty professes to allow no occurrence to disturb his
equanimity, yet this war moves him in such a way as to
prove clearly that on other occasions he was only acting, and
that now he is unable to do so, perhaps because this war is
entirely conducted by himself alone; and that it should not
succeed brings to light all his anxiety. He lives very retired
and gives audience to no one. He has lately remade his will,
and spends hours together with his confessor; though many
say that this is owing to the question of appointments of
benefices.

SEPTEMBER 17, 1588

As the misfortunes which have befallen the Armada up to
the tenth of last month have caused great anxiety to the king
and his ministers, who keep the news secret, so the reports
from Rouen and Don Bernardino de Mendoza, the Catholic
ambassador in France, have done much to console His Majesty, for they announce that the English fleet, in its en-
deavor to prevent the Armada from entering a certain port
in Scotland, has been severely damaged, with the loss or
capture of many ships. They are anxiously awaiting more
positive news of this event from the duke of Parma and
from the duke of Medina Sidonia, who is, according to Don
Bernardino, now lying in an open roadstead in Scotland,

recovering his ships and men, and waiting to see whether his condition will compel him to return to Spain, or whether he can follow up his victory by joining the duke of Parma, not allowing time for the enemy to recruit himself and to call in foreign aid. The ambassador affirms that the queen and the whole country are in a panic, for only thirty ships have come home, and those very roughly handled; also that in various parts of the English army mutinies have broken out; and much more which, if true, Your Serenity will already have heard from elsewhere. We only know what is published here, and all letters and dispatches pass into the hands of the king and Don Juan de Idiáquez only. All I can say is that after the last news His Majesty was in excellent spirits, and so were his ministers. . . .

SEPTEMBER 29, 1588

On the twenty-third of this month Don Balthasar de Zúñiga arrived at the Escorial; he had been dispatched by the duke of Medina Sidonia on the twentieth of August, while the Armada was off the Orkneys, in sixty degrees of latitude. He made a report of all that had taken place since the fleet left Calais, and of the bad state in which it was at present. The fleet will return to Spain, as Your Serenity will gather from the enclosed letter written by a friend of mine on board the fleet. All this has made still clearer the falsity of the news which Don Bernardino de Mendoza has been publishing to the world; and for his conduct in this matter he is in but little favor with His Majesty. Yesterday we had news that the whole Armada had reached Biscay, but today a courier from San Sebastian announces that only Captain Oquendo, with ten ships, had sailed into that port, on the twenty-fourth of this month, having been separated from the rest of the Armada by a great storm. God grant that it may come home safely after all these misfortunes; and its return at all would be taken as good news by the ministers, who at one time expected much worse.

His Majesty feels these misfortunes profoundly, but

shows that he is more than ever determined to follow out his enterprise with all the forces at his disposal. He is resolved that by March next a most powerful fleet shall be put to sea. Orders will be sent out to raise men in Italy and also in Spain. All ships of every build will be seized, all the grain throughout Spain will be made into biscuits, and every other sort of provision will be got ready. Six ships with provisions have sailed from Lisbon for Corunna, and another six in their company, and this will be a most useful reinforcement when the Armada comes into that port. His Majesty has given orders to build in Lisbon twenty galleys fit to sail in English waters; they are to be shorter and higher than the usual model, and already the wood is prepared.

OCTOBER 1, 1588

. . . As no one is paid, as the king gives no audience and does not dispatch business, the cry of his people goes up to heaven; and Father Marian Azaro, who speaks very frankly, said to the king the other day that although his prayers and processions were very good things, yet it was certain that God gave ear to other voices before his; when the king asked "What voices?" Father Marian replied, "Those of the poor oppressed who stay about the court in pain, without being paid and without having their business attended to. . . ."

OCTOBER 12, 1588

I have received Your Serenity's instructions to congratulate His Majesty on the success of the Armada. I, however, have not mentioned the subject, and, as Your Excellencies will know by this time, there is occasion to condole rather than to congratulate, and this office had better be deferred to the happier issue of next year's enterprise.

OCTOBER 22, 1588

[In cipher] . . . *The king has fully made up his mind that the late disasters are to be attributed not to the ability of the enemy nor to the unfavorable weather, but rather to the want of courage shown by his officers. He declares that if they had lost, as they have, fighting instead of flying—for one must call it flying when they showed no heart for the fight—he would have considered all his expenses and labor as well invested. Above all he feels the stain on the Spanish name, and declares that with a prudent and valorous commander they can still recover the honor they have lost. In short, His Majesty outwardly displays a fixed resolve to try his fortune once again next year; though it is quite possible that he may have a different design in his head, perhaps because he recognizes the actual impossibility of carrying out the enterprise. . . .*[6]

6. Spain and England continued their naval war in a desultory way until 1604.

8 "THE KING IS DEAD"

Francesco Soranzo, 1598

In 1563 the ambassador Paolo Tiepolo reported (see page 82) that doctors claimed it was not likely Philip would live very long. Periodically thereafter Venetian ambassadors told the Senate of the king's illnesses—gout, gravel, pains in the flank, colic, catarrh, tertian and "double tertian" fevers, and phthisis—and allowed him few more years of life. That he lived to the age of seventy-one seems miraculous in view of the burdens he bore and the purgings and bleedings he endured. When the end finally came, the ambassador Francesco Soranzo sent to Venice the somber, eloquent, often-quoted dispatch which begins, "The king is dead."

AUGUST 31, 1598

Since the date of my last dispatch it has always been thought that the king could not last more than three or four days, and yet he has dragged on, aided by the prayers put up for him and by his constitutional strength. That he can hold out against so many ills is considered a miracle. The fever is continuous, and the doctors declare it is phthisical. The paroxysms are violent and have reduced his strength, and continue to do so every attack; his vital forces sometimes

Dispatches by Francesco Soranzo, 1598, *Calendar of State Papers . . . Venice . . .*, vol. 9. Translation by Horatio F. Brown.

33. The Escorial (completed 1584).

(Braun and Hogenberg, Civitates orbis terrarum, *1576, VI, pl. 4. Rare Book Division, New York Public Library.)*

run so low that his death is expected from moment to moment. But in the intervals between the paroxysms His Majesty, thanks to rest, sleep, and food, recovers sufficiently to resist the new attack. So the days pass in a great fear that he cannot recover; and the news of last night reports him worse.

All this time His Majesty has displayed incredible patience in his acute sufferings caused by the gout and the numerous sores all over him. His courage has never deserted him; he has made himself most familiar, not only with the thought of death, but with the details and the discussion thereof, and with all that should be done after he is gone. He has arranged every detail of his funeral, and has ordered the purchase of a large quantity of black cloth to drape the church of the Escorial. He has caused them to bring into his room and to his bedside a shirt of lead in which he is to be wrapped after he has breathed his last, and a leaden coffin for his corpse when his hour is come. He examined both and caused himself to be measured, and gave orders for the necessary alterations. At the moment when the nuncio was about to consecrate the archbishop of Toledo, His Majesty sent for him and begged him as the pope's minister to impart his blessing at this extreme moment of his life.

Three days ago he summoned the prince and the infanta to his presence and gave them his blessing in words full of affection. He exhorted them to govern their subjects with love, to administer justice impartially, and to support and defend religion and the Catholic faith with all their might. He gave the prince two sealed packets, with instructions to open them only after His Majesty's death; and he charged him to read, to study, and to observe the contents, as they would prove of the highest value to him, a fact to which His Majesty himself could testify.

The prince through tenderness shed a few tears, whereupon the king, to avoid the contagion, turned his face away and dismissed the prince.

SEPTEMBER 5, 1598

Two days ago they wished to change the king's bed; in doing so he had such a sinking fit that for some time they thought him dead. He recovered, however, but remained so weak that at night they administered extreme unction for the first time. Though very feeble, the king was in full possession of his senses, and asked for the cross which his father, the emperor, held when he was dying. But what was more surprising was that he sent for the prince and told him to remain during the ceremony, and contemplate this example of mundane misery: exhorting him never to forget, when he had entered on his kingdom, that he too must come to a like pass and must die. The prince burst into tears, but the king continued to speak calmly in most Christian spirit.

His Majesty continues in this state, neither better nor worse, though it seems that he experienced some relief from

34. Prince Philip, the Future King Philip III, by Peter Perret.

(Galleria des Estampes de la Biblioteca Nacional, Madrid.)

the bursting of a gathering in his leg yesterday. Everyone says he can last only a few days. He has begged those about him not to conceal his death. All affairs are at a standstill, and Don Cristóbol de Moura plucked up courage to ask if it was the king's pleasure that the prince should dispatch business. His Majesty shook his head.

SEPTEMBER 13, 1598

The king is dead. His Majesty expired at the Escorial this morning at daybreak, after having received all the sacraments of the Church with every sign of devoutness, piety, and religion.

Although change is usually popular, yet nobles and people, rich and poor, universally show great grief.

His Majesty lived seventy-one years, three months, and twenty-four days; he reigned forty-two years, ten months, and sixteen days. He was a prince who fought with gold

35. Philip II, Near the End of His Life,
by Pantoja de la Cruz.

*(Photograph provided and authorized by
El Patrimonio Nacional.)*

rather than with steel, by his brain rather than by his arms. He has acquired more by sitting still, by negotiation, by diplomacy, than his father did by armies and by war. He was one of the richest princes the world has ever seen, yet he has left the revenues of the kingdom and of the crown burdened with about a million of debts. He owes to his good fortune rather than to the terror of his name the important kingdom of Portugal, with all its territories and treasure; on the other hand, he has lost Flanders. In Africa he has gained Peñón, but lost Goletta.[1] Profoundly religious, he loved peace and quiet. He displayed great calmness, and professed himself unmoved in good or bad fortune alike. He had vast schemes in his head: witness his simultaneous attack on England and on France, while assisting his son-in-law to acquire Saluzzo, while attempting to expel the French from Italy, while facing the revolution in Flanders.[2]

On great occasions, in the conduct of wars, in feeding the civil war in France, in the magnificence of his buildings, he never counted the cost; he was no close reckoner, but lavished his gold without a thought; but in small matters, in the government of his household, he was more parsimonious than became his station. He sought aggrandizement for his kingdom by ceding Siena to the grand duke, Piacenza to the duke of Parma, Flanders and Burgundy to his daughter.[3] He held his desires in absolute control and showed an immutable and unalterable temper. He has feigned injuries, and feigned not to feel injuries, but he never lost the opportunity to avenge them. He hated vanity, and therefore never allowed his life to be written. No one ever saw him in a rage, being always patient, phlegmatic, temperate, melancholy. In short, he has left a glorious memory of his royal name, which may serve as an example, not only unto his posterity and his successors, but unto strangers as well. . . .

1. The fortress before Tunis.
2. Events of the mid-1590's.
3. Philip ceded to his daughter and his son-in-law Albert the sovereignty of the Netherlands (in effect, the southern part) but when they died without issue the land reverted to Spain.

II.

The Great Lords of the Turks—in Dissolution

9 "TURKEY IS A REPUBLIC OF SLAVES"

Gianfrancesco Morosini, 1585

To the east of Philip's Spain, to the east of Venice lay the
Turkish colossus. The Venetian ambassadors probably
knew this empire better than any other westerners, as
they had not only observed it firsthand for years as Venetian representatives, but traveled its waters as merchants,
fought its navy as galley commanders, and coped with its
foreign policies as statesmen. In this report as in the one
he wrote on Spain (see pages 70–80) Morosini zestfully
explains the structure of a complicated society. Though
pungent details of his report suggest the beginnings of
Turkish decline, the emphasis is on the semipermanent
features of the Ottoman Empire.

Of all the subjects this excellent Council can discuss, none
is so important or deserves so much attention as the great
sultan of Turkey, his empire, his people, his forces, his
wealth, his form of government, and finally, what should be
hoped for or feared from that quarter. Since this Most Serene government shares such a long stretch of border lands[1]
with that potentate, and since he is the only power from
whom we need fear any serious hostilities, no senator should
ever tire of hearing every detail about this topic. He should
be as well-informed as possible, and he should know, if need

From a report by Gianfrancesco Morosini, 1585, Albèri, III, 3: 253–
322.

1. Chiefly on the Dalmatian coast of modern Yugoslavia.

36. The Sultan and His Guard.

(Detail from Braun and Hogenberg, Civitates orbis terrarum, *1576, I, pl. 51. Rare Book Division, New York Public Library.)*

arises, how to keep peace with this ruler as long as possible, or else overcome him in a war, if it should please God to afflict us in that way.

The present Turkish sultan, Murad III, is the thirteenth[2] in the Ottoman dynasty, which, it is generally thought, had its origins among people who inhabited the borders of Scythia on the Caspian Sea. They lived in abandoned villages, eating only fruit and game. About 800 A.D., this tribe came down from Scythia into Asia Minor and conquered many villages in that area, where the cursed religion of Mohammed was already established. Since they had no religion, and this one seemed to conform to their own customs, they embraced it. Because they were very numerous they terrified all the inhabitants of these villages and overcame a number of cities without having any king or recognized chieftain. They were organized as military squadrons or commando units until 1300 A.D., when one of their number,

2. Murad was the twelfth unless one counts Suleiman, son of Bayazid, who was sultan of part of the empire from 1403 to 1411.

named Ottoman, a man of low birth, began to build a reputation as a strong and spirited leader. Shrewd and clever, he
took advantage of the rivalries among his people, attracted
many of them to him, and led them in war and conquest,
making himself master of various towns and provinces of
both the Turks and their neighbors.[3] In this manner, he
became powerful and founded the kingdom and empire
which his descendants have ruled to the present day, marvelously handing it down from father to son. I say marvelously because it is their custom, in order to stay safely in
power, that when one of them succeeds his father, he immediately puts to death all his brothers. In view of this
custom it seems extraordinary that in such a long time this
family line has never died out, even though it is always
carried on in each generation by one man alone.

They succeed to the throne without any kind of ceremony
of election or coronation. According to Turkish law of succession, which resembles most countries' laws in this respect, the oldest son should succeed to the throne as soon as
the father dies. But in fact, whichever of the sons can first
enter the royal compound in Constantinople is called the
sultan and is obeyed by the people and by the army. Since he
has control of his father's treasure he can easily gain the
favor of the janissaries and with their help control the rest
of the army and the civilians.

Because this government is based on force, the brother
who overcomes the others is considered the lord of all. The
same obedience goes to a son who can succeed in overthrow-
ing his father, a thing which bothers the Turks not at all. As
a result, when his sons are old enough to bear arms, the
sultan generally does not allow them near him, but sends
them off to some administrative district where they must
live under continual suspicion until their father's death.
And just as the fathers do not trust their own sons, the sons
do not trust their fathers and are always afraid of being put

3. This account of the early history of the Ottomans is based on
legends. For a more accurate view, see appropriate headings in the
Encyclopaedia of Islam.

to death. This is the sad consequence of unbridled ambition and hunger for power—a miserable state of affairs where there is no love between father and sons, and much less between sons and father.

This lord has thirty-seven kingdoms covering enormous territory. His dominion extends to the three principal parts of the world, Africa, Asia, and Europe; and since these lands are joined and contiguous with each other, he can travel for a distance of eight thousand miles on a circuit through his empire and hardly need to set foot in another prince's territories.

In Africa the sultan has a common border with the kingdom of Fez and with the Moors. And also, I might add, with the king of Spain, because of the strongholds which His

37. Ottoman Empire, with Constantinople Near Upper Left Corner.

(*Ortelius*, Epitome, 1602, fol. 10. Rare Book Division, New York Public Library.)

Catholic Majesty has in Africa, and because of the narrow straits which separate Spain from Africa.

In Asia he shares common borders with the Persians for a very long distance, and with the Georgians, Tatars, Circassians, Mingrelians, Arabs, Prester John [Ethiopians], Moors, and Nubians; and in Europe with the emperor, the king of Poland, Archduke Charles, and Your Serenity.

The principal cities of the Turks are Constantinople, Adrianople, and Bursa,[4] the three royal residence places of the sultans. Buda[5] is also impressive, as are the Asian cities —Cairo, Damascus, Aleppo, Bagdad and others—but none of these have the things which usually lend beauty to cities. Even Constantinople, the most important of them all, which is posted in the most beautiful and enchanting situation that can be imagined, still lacks those amenities that a great city should have, such as beautiful streets, great squares, and handsome palaces. Although Constantinople has many mosques, royal palaces, inns, and public baths, the rest of the the city is mazy and filthy; even these [public buildings], with their leaded domes studded with gilded bronze ornaments, only beautify the long-distance panorama of the city. They dazzle the eyes of those approaching the city for the first time, and raise high expectations, but as I said above, as soon as these people enter the city they are greatly disappointed.

The security of this country does not depend on the numbers or the quality of fortresses, because the Turks do not try to fortify their borders extensively, much less the interior of their empire. In the past they were even less careful about fortifications than they are now. In the recent Persian wars they did fortify various places they had seized from the Persians so that they could hold them and discourage their enemies from ever trying to retake them.

No, the security of the Turkish lands depends first on the

4. Constantinople, formerly Byzantium, was renamed Istanbul by the Turks, but the Venetians used the older name. Adrianople and Bursa are respectively west of Constantinople in the Balkans and south in Anatolia.

5. Modern Budapest, won by Suleiman in 1541.

38. Constantinople, with Sultan's Seraglio in Foreground.

(Detail from Braun and Hogenberg, Civitates orbis terrarum, 1576, I, pl. 151. Rare Book Division, New York Public Library.)

abundance it has of all the necessities of life. Not only is there enough for the daily needs of her people, but great quantities of foods and other goods are exported. From Constantinople go wool, leather, furs, and cambric; from

Greece, cotton and spun thread; from Syria, silk, ginger, spices, cotton, dyes, spun thread, pistachios, muslin, and carpets; from Alexandria, spices, ginger, vegetables, dates, *bordi*,[6] textiles, carpets, sugar and other things; and from the Morea, wheat and other grains. There could be even more if there were additional people to cultivate the fields. They also have mines of every kind of metal, though these are not very important.

The security of the empire depends more than anything else on the large numbers of land and sea forces which the Turks keep continually under arms. These are what make them feared throughout the world.

The sultan always has about 280,000 well-paid men in his service. Of them about 80,000 are paid every three months out of his personal treasury. These include roughly 16,000 janissaries, who form the Grand Signor's advance guard; six legions, or about 12,000 cavalry called "spahi," who serve as his rear guard; and about 1,500 other defenders, including the *muteferrika* [mounted royal guard], *ussineri,* and *cavusi.*[7] There are also armorers, artillerymen, *adjemi-oghlani* [cadet janissaries], grooms, servants, pages, doctors, and others; all together they bring the total to the figure I gave. They are not paid by the month, as in Christian countries; remuneration here is calculated at so much per day.

The other 200,000 cavalry are called timariots[8] because they are not paid with money like the others, but are assigned landholdings [called timars]. Each of them is required to maintain one armed horseman for every 5,000 aspers of income produced by his timar, and present them for inspection whenever the governor of his province so orders. These timars are made up of lands—we would say *campi*—throughout the Turkish empire. When these people take over a kingdom or other dominion they are not satisfied merely to

6. Ribbons and edgings of silk and golden threads.
7. The *cavusi* were sometimes guards, sometimes ushers, marshals, or messengers.
8. Or spahis (feudal cavalry).

have jurisdiction and manorial dues; they want the entire
revenues from all the lands in the country. They distribute
these lands to their soldiers for their pay and maintenance
and call them timars.

The timariots are in no way inferior as fighting men to
the soldiers paid every three months with cash, because the
timars are inherited like the fiefs distributed by Christian
rulers. Fief-holders [in Christian lands] don't count for
much militarily, because it often happens that the owner of a
fief is not a soldier and knows nothing about warfare; moreover, fiefs are often inherited by women or minor children.
But with the Turks, those who hold timars are sure to be
soldiers, since these lands are not assigned to anyone else.
As soon as a timariot dies, his timar is immediately given to

39. Fortress on the Dardanelles.

(*Detail from Camocio,* Isole, famose porti, *1573, pl. 13. From an original in the
Free Library of Philadelphia.*)

another soldier, so that this militia is always composed of professional fighting men. As a matter of fact, their number is always increasing, because as the Turkish empire expands they divide up land in the newly conquered countries just as they did with the other ones. In this way they maintain armies larger than another ruler could have if he paid them ten and a half million gold ducats a year.

What about the fighting qualities of these widely feared Turkish soldiers? I can tell you the opinion I formed at Scutari, where I observed the armies of Ferrad Pasha and Osman Pasha (Ferrad's army was there for more than a month, and Osman's for a matter of weeks). I went over to Scutari several times to confer with the two pashas and also, unofficially, to look at the encampment, and I walked through the whole army and carefully observed every detail about the caliber of their men, their weapons, and the way they organize a bivouac site and fortify it. I think I can confidently offer this conclusion: they rely more on large numbers and obedience than they do on organization and courage.

Although witnesses who saw them in earlier times claim they are not as good as they used to be, it appears that the janissaries are still the best of the Turkish soldiers. They are well-made men, and they can handle their weapons—the arquebus, club, and scimitar—quite well. These men are accustomed to hardships, but they are only used in battle in times of dire necessity. They always insist on guarding the person of the Grand Signor, or the general commanding the army, and they avoid joining in the attack even when they are needed.

As for the cavalry, some are lightly armed with fairly weak lances, huge shields, and scimitars; they look more like mummers than warriors. Others carry nothing at all to protect their bodies, although they do have lances and swords, and they rely chiefly on bows and arrows, with which they can do a lot of harm.

If I compare these men with Christian soldiers, such as those I saw in the wars in France or in the Christian King's conquest of Portugal,[9] I would say they are much better than Christian soldiers in respect to obedience and discipline. However, in courage and enthusiasm, and in physical appearance and weapons, they are distinctly inferior. In my humble opinion, 10,000 Christians could face 30,000 Turks with complete confidence. But it would be harder to govern 2,000 Christians than 100,000 Turks—much harder if the Christians were Italians!

The naval forces which the Great Turk uses to defend his empire are vast and second to none in the world. He has an enormous number of galleys in his dockyard and he can turn out more whenever he wants, because he has plenty of wood, iron parts, skilled workmen, pitch, tallow, and all the other things needed. True, at present they do not have at hand all the armaments they would need to outfit the as yet uncompleted galleys, much less those the Grand Signor has ordered made, and they are short of cotton sailcloth and other things. But his resources are so great that if he wanted to he could quickly assemble what he needs; he has already begun to attend to this.

The Turkish fleet has only thirty or forty galleys armed with Christian slaves, while all the others are as bad as the galleys that we man here with peasants. They may even be worse. The Turks themselves admit that most of their galleys are not as good as Christian ones. While I am on this subject I want to say how much I deplore the foolishness of Christian rulers. It never occurs to them that they could take away from the Turks the very heart of their naval force if they would discreetly ransom as many Christian slaves as possible, because these slaves are the shipwrights, the caulkers, the mates, the boatswains, and the captains, not to mention the oarsmen, who make their galleys as good as they are. Freeing them would not only be very easy, it would be to the glory of God, it would be a blessing to those poor devils, and it would make all of Christendom safer. . . .

The whole empire is inhabited by three groups of people:

9. Morosini had served as ambassador to Austria, Savoy, France, and Spain.

40. Jewish Merchant in Constantinople.

(From Nicolay, Navigationi, 1576, fol. 266. Collections of The Library Company of Philadelphia.)

Turks, Moors,[10] and Christians. In Asia and Africa the Moors are more numerous than the Turks, while in Europe the largest number are Christians, almost all of whom practice the Greek rite. There are also many Jews, since that[11] is really their homeland, even though they live in it like strangers rather than natives.

Control of the empire, however, is in the hands of the Turks, and so I will only discuss them. The others are a great deal more numerous, but they are all laborers or farmers, and more oppressed by the Turks than the Jews were under Pharaoh.

There are two types of Turks. One is composed of people native-born of Turkish parents, while the other is made up of renegades who are sons of Christians. The latter group were

10. By "Moors" the ambassador means all non-Turkish Muslims.
11. Presumably Morosini is referring to the Ottoman province of Syria, which included Palestine.

taken by force in the raids their fleets and pirates make on Christian lands, or else harshly levied in their villages from the sultan's non-Muslim subjects and taxpayers. They are taken while still boys, and either persuaded or forced to be circumcised and made Muslims. It is the custom of the Porte [Turkish government] to send men throughout the country every fourth or fifth year to levy one-tenth of the boys, just as if they were so many sheep, and after they have made Turks of these boys they train each one according to his abilities and what fate has in store for him.

Not only is most of the Turkish army made up of these renegades, but at one time they used to win all the chief positions in the government, up to the first vizierate, and the highest commands in the armed forces, because ancient custom forbids that the sons of Turks should hold these jobs. But the present Grand Signor ignores this custom and chooses whatever men he wants and believes can serve him best, without regard for their status.

After they have been taken away as young boys the renegades are sent to different places to be trained according to the jobs they will be given. The handsomest, most wide-awake ones are placed in the seraglio [palace] of the Grand Signor, or in one of two others used only for this purpose, and there they are all prepared for the same end, which is to rise to the highest government offices. The Turks care not at all whether these boys are the children of noblemen or of fishermen and shepherds. All of this explains why their major officials are all good-looking and impressive, even when their manners are uncouth.

The other boys, who are not so handsome but are strong and healthy, are made *adjemi-oghlani,* which means they are in a kind of seminary for the janissary corps. In order to accustom them to hard work and physical suffering they are made to tend the sultan's gardens, look after horses, sail on ships, transport lumber, building stone, and other goods, or work in the mills. They make them drudge day and night, and they give them no beds to sleep on and very little food. When these boys begin to shave they make them janissaries.

41. Janissary Under Arms.

(From Nicolay, Navigationi, *1576, fol. 152. Collections of The Library Company of Philadelphia.)*

The first group, the ones destined for higher positions, presently number about six thousand. They are trained under discipline which is stricter than that of our monasteries, they never leave the seraglios, nor even their own rooms, and they speak to each other only when it is urgently necessary. Eunuchs, most of them Negroes, have charge of them, and for any little offense they beat them cruelly with sticks, rarely hitting them less than a hundred times, and often as much as a thousand. After punishments the boys have to come to them and kiss their clothing and thank them for the cudgelings they have received. You can see, then, that moral degradation and humiliation are part of the training system.

The first thing they are made to learn is the Turks' false religion, which they know so well as to put us to shame. They pray together without fail at four prescribed times every day. They also learn to read and write in Turkish, but except for that they have no instruction in things pertaining to gentlemen and soldiers—no horsemanship, no training with arms. Far from that, they do such tasks as sweeping the place where they live, and cooking.

Four of these young men are assigned when they are at least eighteen or twenty to serve continually with the sultan. Each of these is almost sure to end in such an important position as aga of the janissaries, admiral, beglerbeg in Greece and Anatolia, and finally pasha in the Porte. These four have the task of dressing and undressing the Grand Signor, and guarding him at night while he sleeps. When he rides on horseback through the city or in battle or while hunting, one of them carries his arms, another his rain clothes, the third a pitcher full of an iced drink, and the fourth something else.

Every three years the Grand Signor allows those of the young men[12] who have reached an age where they can serve in battle to leave the seraglios if they wish. He gives them either the position of cesimir,[13] with forty aspers per day, or that of spahi, with twenty-five or thirty, according to how well they are thought of at the time they leave.

Perhaps I have discussed these young men a little longer than I should have, but Your Serenity and Your Illustrious Lordships will understand why the matter is important. It is these young renegades who will provide the future army officers of all grades, the governors of the provinces, and even the pashas themselves. They are usually the sons of the commonest peasants and other people and they have been taught nothing of any significance about the world, trained in no military matters except the use of bows and arrows, and treated vilely and cruelly. It is amazing that any of them turn out well, and yet it is these who end up governing that enormous empire.

The sphere of the native-born Turks includes such things as the management of the mosques, presiding over civil and criminal law courts, and running the chancery. They pro-

---

12. That is, the whole group of boys selected for special training, not merely those who served as the sultan's servants.

13. In Albèri's edition the word *cesimir* is followed by [?], presumably because the correct reading of the manuscript is unsure.

42. Mufti.

(*From C. Vecellio*, Costumes anciens, *1859, II, 365. Libraries of the University of Pennsylvania, Philadelphia.*)

vide the cadis and the cadi-askers, the sultan's advisers, and the grand mufti, who is the head of their false religion. The cadis [judges] are like our *podestà*,[14] and render justice to everyone, and the cadi-askers[15] hear appeals from the courts of the cadis.

The renegades are all slaves, and are proud to boast, "We are slaves of the Grand Signor!" As is well known, Turkey is a republic of slaves, where it is they who are in command. The other Turks, even though they are not technically slaves like the renegades, might just as well be considered such, and they hold it an honor to be referred to that way. This is especially true of the ones who serve the sultan in the positions just mentioned.

The Turks are a sordid and depraved lot, and very lazy.

14. Venetian governors of subject cities. They were judges as well as administrators.

15. Judges of the army, judicial officials second in rank only to the sheikh ul Islam, or grand mufti.

They spend most of their time sitting still and doing nothing. The favorite entertainment of all Turks—from the important men right down to the lowest of them—is to congregate in shops or on the streets and drink a black liquid called *kahvè* as boiling hot as they can stand it. They say it helps a man to stay awake.[16] Some eat opium so as to feel happy, while others take *teriaka*,[17] Galen's tonic,[18] and such things. The ones who drink wine don't leave the table until they are drunk. The Turks never walk for pleasure; they laugh at Christians they see out for a stroll, and say they are crazy to walk if they don't have to.

Very few Turks, especially in the areas I have seen, do any physical labor. They don't work the land, they don't take any exercise, they don't take pleasure in developing skills, they play no ball games or soccer, they don't ride horses, and they don't play at bowls. In fact, their only amusement is archery. However, sometimes the Grand Signor and some of his pages and a mute or buffoon will ride around on horses the way they do in Spain when they throw lances.

In appearance they are very pious adherents of their false religion. (I say "in appearance" because their piety masks a profound wickedness.) They are very regular in observing the hours of prayer and they always have the name of God on their lips, but never blaspheme. Every wealthy Turk builds a mosque, making it as splendid as he can, and provides a rich endowment for its upkeep. As a result, the mosques are kept so clean and orderly that they put us Christians to shame. They are built not only by the Grand Signor, the sultans [his sons?], and the pashas, but also by people of lower status. In addition to mosques they also build asylums more imposing than their own houses, and in many of these they will give food for three days to anyone who asks for it—not only Turks, but also Christians and Jews. For the good of their souls they also put up stone bridges to help wayfarers over streams, and they pave roads

16. Coffee became popular in Europe a few decades after this report was delivered.

17. Opium flavored with spices.

18. Perhaps a narcotic made from mandrake?

43. A Turk in His Home.

and build caravansaries to lodge pilgrims and travelers,
since there are no inns in the lands of the Turks.

The whole of the Turk's religion consists in praying four
times a day and fasting one month a year. Before their
prayers they wash their hands and arms up to the elbows,
and also their feet. Very few fail to pray at the prescribed
times, either in mosques or houses, or on the public streets
and squares. No one is afraid he will be considered sancti-
monious for carrying out his devotions in public; quite the
contrary, they deem it a great honor to be considered zealous
about their religion. They are also required to fast for one
entire month, during which they eat nothing at all during
the hours of daylight. After nightfall they may eat and
drink until daybreak, as many times as they want and
whatever they want, as long as it is not pork or wine.
(Consuming these things is considered sinful and is forbidden them at all times.)

Those who observe these requirements are called good

Muslims. If I were to tell you about the filthy and depraved lives these same good Muslims lead, I would sully the chaste ears of my distinguished listeners. But the Turks do know how to hide their vices better than Christians; they choose their words carefully so as at least to appear morally upright.

Although there is a great deal more I could say about the Turks, I want to let what I have just told you suffice, and I will say just a few words about the other peoples in the empire. I mentioned earlier that there was a larger number of Moors than Turks in Africa and Asia, just as there are more Christians in [the Turkish lands in] Europe. Both the Moors and the Christians are so oppressed, downtrodden, and discouraged, and their land so wrecked and wasted by the Turks, that the population is declining from day to day and things are going from bad to worse. The Turks carry away the little property their subjects have and even their sons, and continually persecute them with beatings, so that their lives are utterly miserable. We can well imagine—in fact, we can be certain—that the Turks cannot rely much on these people, who would seize any opportunity that came along to overthrow the government and escape from such misery. The tyranny of the Turks over their subjects is the reason why the country does not produce as much as it could, because human nature is such that men will work hard only for their own gain. When these people toil and suffer long hours to improve their miserable lot, only to have what little they produce snatched from their hands, naturally they decide it is better to settle for the bare minimum they need to sustain life than to wear themselves out for others.

I have tried very hard to learn the facts about the ordinary revenues the sultan receives each year from the whole empire. I have it on good authority that after deducting the incomes from the timars, which go to the soldiers, the Grand Signor annually receives eight million in gold. I could not, however, get the facts about his nonordinary income. He receives gifts from his officials and other people, and of course he can seize whatever he wants from his subjects whenever he pleases, but these sources do not provide a regular, fixed sum. The amount of the additional income depends instead on chance. When someone dies the Grand Signor, who is the real owner of everything, takes whatever he wants from the estate, and considers it a favor if he leaves anything to the widow and children. He can easily find pretexts to make it appear that justice requires him to confiscate the goods. He often takes property from the wealthy, a thing he can easily do because no one would dare to speak out against him. The mere whim of the Grand Signor is justification enough to do anything in the world. The sultan will never lack money when he needs it because he can always turn to wealthy private subjects and get from them, as gifts or by force, whatever amount he wants.

Many people think the Grand Signor's incomes are actually much greater than his expenses, and a widespread belief holds that he has accumulated a huge surplus in his treasury. I have not heard anyone say this on reliable authority, however, and anyone who considers the matter carefully will be skeptical. Think of the many large expenditures they have regularly in that Porte, including those which not everybody witnesses but which are very familiar to anyone who has been active in any government. Obviously the sultan can save very little of his revenues. . . . He spends 5.5 million in gold each year on his soldiers, and then he has all the expenses of a shipyard, in which he maintains a great fleet. Your Serenity, who knows how much he spends on his own shipyard, where things are better managed, will realize how much the Turks must spend on a yard where everything is run by slaves and thieves. They say that a galley costs the Turks only 1,000 ducats, but I can vouch for the fact that for a little pleasure boat built for the sultan's use they spent 100,000 ducats. It is not that they really spend that much, but everyone in the arsenal, from the admiral down to the lowest official, steals so much. They take the Grand Signor's lumber and ironware and use it to build commercial ships

44. Galleys Guarding Constantinople.

(Detail from Braun and Hogenberg, Civitates orbis terrarum, *1576, I, pl. 51. Rare Book Division, New York Public Library.)*

and boats of their own, and frequently even the houses they live in.

Then, too, anyone who knows on what a grand scale the sultan lives will realize that his household expenses must be huge. Each day he must feed more than 19,000 men, women, and children in the seraglios and provide their clothing and other living needs, and he does the same for all the pashas, sultanas, and many others. Every day when the divan [council] is in session he feeds the pashas and all the lesser officials, who are very numerous. He gives the ambassadors from other countries hay, fodder, firewood, and money, and he gives the ambassadors from Persia and the Holy Roman Empire not only those things but also chickens, mutton, rice, sugar, spices, candles, and other goods sufficient for their daily needs and for making gifts as well. Every year he gives ordinary clothes and fine ones too to foreigners (the custom of the Porte is to give only clothes as presents), and on every little occasion he also gives them to many other people. Clearly this is very expensive. . . . He gives clothes to the sultanas inside and outside the seraglios, and to many women and boys in the seraglios, and this costs a great deal because all the clothes he gives, from those of the janissaries on up, are made of silk and gold thread. Then there are the costs of the stables, where they keep many horses, mules, and camels, and expenditures for hunting and other kinds of recreation; anyone can see these must consume a great deal of money. To all these major expenses, which other rulers do not have, we must add those which are normal and inevitable for the conservation of a vast empire and the court of such a great ruler.

However, it would be a mistake to think this ruler would ever hesitate to go to war because of a lack of funds. He doesn't need so much extra revenue as other kings require to mobilize his army and navy. And furthermore, if he wants to seize the money of private individuals, he has only to give the word. Other kings have to be careful not to stir up resentment among their subjects, but the Turks are all the sultan's slaves, and he can do what he wants with them.

The armed might of this empire, and everything else about it, are under the sole command of the Grand Signor. It is not simply that he is the absolute master of everyone and everything, but he uses his great power in such a way that I can safely say that no one ever dreamed of such a tyranny, much less brought it into being. He not only puts his subjects to death at will, but he holds them in such awe that they accept their fate instantly and without the slightest resistance. He takes what he wants: their possessions, their children, and even, you might say, their bodies. He is of course obeyed when he gives a command, but even the mention of his name makes men tremble. He directs every aspect of their religion, appointing and dismissing priests, and making human and divine laws as he pleases. He hires and fires whomever he wants as officials, and has only to hint his wishes in order to be obeyed. He makes men and women marry each other whenever he wants to, and obliges men to divorce their wives at his order. In short, there was never a king or lord who was a more absolute master of his people than the sultan. True, the people he rules are all mere sheep

45. Turkish Woman.

(From C. Vecellio, Costumes anciens, 1859, II, 392. Libraries of the University of Pennsylvania, Philadelphia.)

and peasants; a tyranny like his would never work if there were a nobility around him, or even his own family and relations. (To ensure his power each sultan always has his kinsmen beheaded.)

The present Turkish emperor, Sultan Murad, was born on August 27, 1546. His father was Sultan Selim and his mother was a Venetian, as she herself used to say. She had been captured at Corfu,[19] she said, where her father was serving as governor, but she never could say what her family name was.[20] Sultan Murad had the pleasure of beginning to rule his great empire when he was only twenty-eight, an age

19. A Greek island in the Ionian Sea, formerly a Venetian possession.

20. Modern historians of the Ottoman Empire follow Joseph von Hammer (*Geschichte des osmanischen Reiches*, 10 vols., 1827–35) in saying that Murad's wife, not his mother, was a Venetian woman. But see Albèri, III, 3: 235 n. Some ambassadors said she was of the Venetian noble family Baffo.

when men particularly enjoy giving orders. He also escaped those worries and dangers that usually nag at Ottoman princes when they reach maturity, because as soon as he arrived on the throne he put to death his five brothers, the oldest of whom was just nine. He was not considered cruel for doing this, since the mufti had decided he must do it for the safety of the government. For that matter, if the Grand Signor alone believed the security of the empire required it, he could have a third of his people put to death.

The sultan is very small but well formed—perhaps a bit fat. He has large, pale eyes, an aquiline nose, good skin color, and a big, blond beard. He looks good when seated on horseback, wearing his turban, because then his smallness is not so obvious, but when he is seen standing on his own feet he looks almost dwarfish. His facial expression does not suggest an evil character. His health is rather delicate, and his life is not likely to be long.

He used to enjoy reading books on different subjects, and they say he still does this sometimes, but the questions he asks of his men of learning show clearly that he knows very little. In my opinion the sultan spends his time very unsuitably. He is almost always secluded in his seraglios in the company of eunuchs, pages, dwarfs, mutes, and slave girls (it would be bad enough if they were ordinary women). There is no worthwhile person for him to talk with, since except for a few of the women everyone in the seraglios is less than thirty years old and belongs to one of the types I mentioned.

In the morning he gets up quite late, leaves the women's quarters, where he sleeps every night without exception, changes his clothes, and then breakfasts. If it is a council day he gives an audience to the aga of the janissaries, the cadi-askers, and finally the pashas. If someone has just been made a beglerbeg [governor of a province], sanjakbeg [governor of a district], or something of the sort, he approaches and kisses the sultan's hand without saying a word or having anything said to him. At the same time any newly arrived ambassador or other representative from another ruler comes to him for the same purpose. Even if the ambassador explains his mission he receives no answer at all. The Grand Signor only deals with ambassadors by means of notes, just as the king of Spain did during my time there.[21]

He used to be self-restrained with the ladies, but now he has gone to the other extreme. For many years he was satisfied with a single woman whom he loved very much, and while he never made her a *kebir*, which means a freed woman, and gave her a dowry, nevertheless everyone considered her his wife and sultana. This woman was born of very common people in Albania,[22] but she has a very vital personality. Even without the aid of beauty her personality was enough to hold the Great Turk's affections for many years. Although surrounded by lovely women presented to him as gifts by various people, he ignored his mother and sisters when they urged him to consort with other women so as to have sons,[23] since this woman was no longer fertile. He loved her so much that they could not change his mind.

Finally, however, he was attracted by a slave girl given him by his sister, who was the wife of Mohammed Pasha. He had no intention of sleeping with her, and simply enjoyed looking at her and having her sing and play an instrument for him, but that was enough to rouse his wife's anger and jealousy. In order to hold on to her husband, she got some other women to help her use charms and spells to keep him tied to her with love and make him impotent with other women. But the poor woman's plans completely backfired. As I wrote to Your Serenity at the time, the Grand Signor learned from his mother about his wife's doings and lost all his respect for her. He had already been tempted by the slave girl but had resisted his inclinations because of his fondness for his wife. Now he gave himself over to enjoying this girl and found himself so delighted with this pastime that he decided to see if it would be the same with other

21. Morosini had been ambassador to Spain from 1579 to 1581.
22. Albania was then part of the Ottoman Empire. Modern historians, as indicated above, say this concubine, and not Murad's mother, was a Venetian.
23. In the course of his life he eventually fathered 102 children.

46. Sultan's Favorite.

(*From C. Vecellio,* Costumes anciens, *1859, II, 378. Libraries of the University of Pennsylvania, Philadelphia.*)

women. He tried out many other beautiful young girls, whom everyone brought to him, and in this way began the life he now leads. This is very different from his old ways; he is not satisfied now with one or two but has relations with more than twenty women. Every night he sleeps with two, and often with three. Since their religious laws require a man who has been with one woman to wash before going to another, he often bathes two or three times a night. This is a real danger to his life because his health is weak, and he suffers from epilepsy; he could easily drop dead without warning. While I was there it was believed at one time that he had died, and there was almost a sack of Constantinople and Pera.[24]

He is considered a pusillanimous man, but prouder than

24. Mobs often sacked palaces and houses of the wealthy when a sultan died. Pera was a suburb of Constantinople (Istanbul), where the European embassies were situated.

the devil. He does not seem very clever, even though you might say he governs his whole empire by himself, since he has no permanent councillor with whom he regularly discusses affairs, nor any intelligent and trustworthy man who can give him advice. The way he frequently countermands his own orders shows his lack of firmness of mind, and everyone says this results from his allowing first the women and then the eunuchs to twist him around. The reason they can do this is that while the pasha can reach him only by writing notes, which cannot counter objections to his proposals, the women and the eunuchs are always around him and can usually put in the last word. If the pasha then sends another note replying to what they suggest, the sultan is once again in doubt. I don't mean to say that he is not a very stubborn man, but he becomes stubborn only when he has finally made up his mind. Before he does that he is afraid of being tricked and he suspects the pasha of being bribed to advise him against what are his best interests. That is why he is indecisive, and constantly changes his mind about what to do. After he has once decided he cannot be moved.

He trusts no one, and is wise not to, because he knows that all the people who serve him can easily be bribed. He has no one but himself to blame for this. By giving offices to those who pay him most and oftenest, he teaches everyone else to take money in order to be able to make him gifts, since otherwise they would never advance at all.

Although Sultan Murad governs his empire by himself with complete authority and under no restraint from any kind of council, he still has to use officials to carry out his commands. No human being could run the whole organization by himself. The chief officials are his pashas, who are also called the viziers of the Porte. At present there are eight of these men, but there is no fixed number. The sultan appoints new ones and dismisses old ones whenever he wishes. (His predecessors in former times were much slower to change viziers than he is.)

Only the first vizier deals with all the other viziers. Usually that post is given to the one who became a vizier first.

When he goes, the next one in line succeeds him, and so on, and the custom is not to interrupt this order and promote one of them ahead of the men who were made viziers before him. When the sultan wants to appoint someone as first vizier who was made a vizer after some others, he simply dismisses the others until the man he wants is first.

In former times they never took his office away from a first vizier without also taking his life. But while I was *bailo*[25] two were dismissed and one was sent to the war zone, so that I had to negotiate Your Serenity's affairs with four different first viziers. You can easily imagine what problems this created. As soon as I had come to know one pasha, and had made friends of his staff, he would be dismissed, and I would have to start over again with another. This cost Your Serenity money, and gave me a lot of trouble.

That is all I think it is worthwhile to tell Your Serenity about the Great Turk, his family, his lands, the nature of his subjects, his armed forces, his incomes and expenditures, his way of governing, his personal qualities, and finally his viziers. . . .

Now, Serene Prince and distinguished gentlemen, I must turn to the relations of the Grand Signor with the other rulers of the world. But first I would like to make a little digression. Your Serenity and you, distinguished gentlemen, know that the sultan is a great ruler, who appears at this time to have no superior in the size of his lands, the amount of his wealth, the number of his subjects, or the size of his armies. Nevertheless, you should also keep in mind that he is not invincible. If you compare him with the other powers individually, he looks stronger than each of them, but it is very clear that if all Christians joined together against him, he could never hold them back. When the time comes that he must fight on land and sea at the same time his weaknesses will be very apparent. But the price we pay for our sins is that something we all agree should be done at all costs is almost hopelessly impossible. The real foundations of the Turks' power is the disunion of the Christian countries and

25. The Venetian ambassador in Constantinople was called a *bailo*.

47. Village on the Dardanelles.

(Detail from Camocio, Isole, famose porti, *1573, pl. 13.*
From an original in the Free Library of Philadelphia.)

their suspicions of each other. We must beseech God to remove these obstacles and give his people the grace to lose their fear of the infidels.

The Great Turk knows he is powerful, and he actually believes himself stronger than he really is. This is why he does not care about having the friendship of any other power, and why he says, with such remarkable arrogance, that his Porte is always open just as wide to would-be enemies as to would-be friends. His insolence arises partly from the natural pride of that people, who call themselves "The Shadow of God, the Granter of Empires and Crowns," and other arrogant names of that sort. It also stems from seeing that no ruler in the world, no matter how powerful he is, fails to send to the Porte to ask for the sultan's friendship. They regard that as a tacit confession that they are greater than every other power. This in turn makes the Turks believe that even if they betray those who consider them friends, as they will always do when it suits their purpose, the betrayed allies will always come back and seek to revive the friendship again.

Now, to begin with the Christian rulers, I think I can safely say that the Turks are deadly enemies of them all. They do maintain a "friendship" with some, but this is more apparent than real. The difference in religion counts too much for it to be otherwise, especially with those people. That is the reason they hate the pope more than anyone else. They consider his military forces negligible, but they believe he could be the force to unite the other Christian rulers against them, and so they hate him fiercely.

They think very little of the emperor,[26] knowing how weak his armies are. Despite this they periodically renew their treaty with him because of the profit it brings them. His Caesarian Majesty sends them 45,000 thalers a year, which the Turks call harac [tribute], because he is required to give it each year. He also gives other presents to the Grand Signor, the pashas, and various officials of the Porte, and these amount to 60,000 thalers a year.

With France the Turks have had a special understanding for a long time. This was particularly true during the life of the emperor Charles V, because with the French and the Turks equally hostile to the emperor it was easy for them to unite against their common enemy. The same motive has kept alive their alliance down to the present, because they are both still hostile to the Spanish even though the circumstances have altered somewhat. Since the Turks don't share any borders with the French or have any other grounds for conflict, it seems unlikely they will ever fight each other. Quite the contrary, if the Spanish decided to attack the French, the sultan would probably help France, not so much out of friendship as to keep the king of Spain from becoming more powerful than he now is. The Turks tend to underestimate France, believing the recent wars[27] have weakened it to the point where it counts for little. The French ambas-

26. I.e., the Holy Roman Emperor, Rudolf II (1576–1612).
27. The Wars of Religion, which racked France in the latter sixteenth century. See Part III, on France.

48. Pera, Suburb of Constantinople and Site of Venetian Embassy.

(Detail from Braun and Hogenberg, Civitates orbis terrarum, *I, pl. 51. Rare Book Division, New York Public Library.)*

sadors don't command much respect in the Porte, and French merchants who trade in Turkish lands are treated as badly as others, if not worse.

As for the Catholic King [of Spain], the Turks are extremely hostile to him and consider him their worst enemy. They know how powerful he is, however, and how hard it would be to hurt him, and they would not object to improving relations with him. They would like very much to have an ambassador come from His Catholic Majesty to negotiate peace.[28] If this happens neither the French nor anyone else will be able to stir up trouble between them, because the Turks are very determined to have peace. I grant you that if

28. In this same year (1585) Philip II and the sultan formally ended the war which had begun in 1570 and had really come to an end in 1581.

the Turks agree on a truce, they won't hesitate to break it when it suits their purposes, just as I am sure the king of Spain would do. But with one fighting a war in the Netherlands and the other fighting one with Persia, the result could be a temporary peace between them. That they can ever be on genuinely good terms, however, is hard to believe.

About myself, Serene Prince and illustrious gentlemen, I will say nothing. I am sure your goodwill is such that you realize, without my telling you, that I have done all I could and spared neither my energies nor my purse in your service. If my accomplishments at any time fell short of the good intentions I always had, I beg you to call on your boundless reserves of kindness and forgive my many failings. I can honestly say that neither illness of body, nor anxiety of mind, danger of plague, threats of imprisonment or death, endless wearisome negotiations, nor anything else has ever even slightly delayed me in serving you. I know very well how great are my debts to Your Serenity, and I freely admit that not even with the sacrifice of my life could I pay back a small part of them.

May it please God, the source of every blessing, to reward, preserve, and continually prosper this Serene Republic until the day of the Last Judgment.

10 "ITS DECLINE
MAY NOW BE UNDER WAY"

Lorenzo Bernardo, 1592

Bernardo had served a few years earlier as ambassador to Constantinople. In 1591 the Venetian government again sent him to Turkey, this time to bring back as a prisoner the current ambassador, Girolamo Lippomano, who had been discovered to be swindling Venice of funds sent him to buy grain. (This is the same Lippomano whose dispatches on the Spanish Armada appear earlier in this book.) When the ship was within sight of Venice Lippomano jumped overboard and drowned himself. Bernardo proceeded home and within a few days read the customary report of a returned ambassador. Toward the end of it he offered this analysis of the reasons Venice could expect a decline in Ottoman power. Like other ambassadors who discussed this topic, he stressed weaknesses in the empire's leadership, luxury and dissipation, loss of control over the armed forces, and the failure of Turkish will or spirit.[1]

Three basic qualities have enabled the Turks to make such remarkable conquests, and rise to such importance in a brief period: religion, frugality, and obedience.

From the beginning it was religion that made them zeal-

From a report by Lorenzo Bernardo, 1592, Albèri, III, 2: 366–77.

1. Bernardo's discussion is infused by his profound belief in the "lessons" of ancient history.

ous, frugality that made them satisfied with little, and
obedience that produced men ready for any dangerous campaign.

In an earlier report[2] I discussed at length these three
qualities, which were then and always had been typical of
the Turks. Now I plan to follow the same order, but to discuss whether any changes have taken place subsequently
that might lead us to hope that empire will eventually
decline. For nothing is more certain than that every living
thing (including kingdoms and empires) has a beginning, a
middle, and an end, or, you might say, a growth, maturity,
and decline.

In former times, Serene Prince, all Turks[3] held to a single
religion, whose major belief is that it is "written" when and
how a man will die, and that if he dies for his God and his
faith he will go directly to Paradise. It is not surprising,
then, that one reads in histories about Turks who vied for
the chance to fill a ditch with their bodies, or made a human
bridge for others to use crossing a river, going to their
deaths without the slightest hesitation. But now the Turks
have not a single religion, but three of them. The Persians[4]
are among the Turks like the [Protestant] heretics among
us [Christians], because some of them hold the beliefs of
Ali, and others those of Omar, both of whom were followers
of Mohammed, but held different doctrines.[5] Then there are
the Arabs and Moors, who claim they alone preserve the
true, uncorrupted religion and that the "Greek Turks" (as
they call these in Constantinople) are bastard Turks [i.e.,
bastard Muslims] with a corrupted religion, which they
blame on their being mostly descended from Christian renegades who did not understand the Muslim religion. As a
matter of fact, I have known many of these renegades who

2. Delivered after his earlier embassy in Constantinople.
3. By "Turks" he means here not only the Ottoman Turks but also
all of their Muslim subjects.
4. The Ottoman Turks had conquered three western Persian provinces in the period 1577–90.
5. In effect the ambassador means that some Persians belonged to
the Sunnite (orthodox), others to the Shiite sect of Islam.

So Deruis Religioſo Turco.

49. Dervish, Member of a
Muslim Religious Order.

(From Nicolay, Navigationi, *1576,
fol. 203. Collections of The Library
Company of Philadelphia.)*

had no religious beliefs, and said religions were invented by
men for political reasons. They hold that when the body dies
the soul dies, just as it does with brute beasts, which they
are.

The belief that one's death is "written" and that one has
no free will to escape dangers is declining in Turkey with
each passing day. Experience teaches them the opposite
when they see that a man who avoids plague victims saves
his life while one who has stayed with them catches plague
and dies. During my time there as *bailo* I even saw their
mufti flee Constantinople for fear of plague and go to the
garden[6] to live, and the Grand Signor himself took care to
avoid all contacts with his generals. Having learned they can
escape from plagues, they now apply the same lesson to

6. By "the garden" he may be referring to the gardens of the sultan's seraglio.

wars. Everybody shirks war service as long as he can, and when he does go he hangs back from the front lines and concentrates on saving his own life. When the authorities announce a campaign in Persia there are outcries and revolts, and if the sultan wants to send janissaries there he creates new ones who are so glad to have the higher pay that they are willing to risk dangers which the regulars dread and flee. In short, nowadays they all look out for their own safety.

As for frugality, which I said was the second of the three sources of the Turks' great power, this used to be one of their marked characteristics. At one time the Turks had no interest in fine foods or, if they were rich, in splendid decorations in their houses. Each was happy with bread and rice, and a carpet and a cushion; he showed his importance only by having many slaves and horses with which he could better serve his ruler. No wonder then that they could put up with the terrible effort and physical discomfort involved in conquering and ruling. What a shameful lesson to our own state, where we equate military glory with sumptuous banquets and our men want to live in their camps and ships as if they were back home at weddings and feasts!

But now that the Turks have conquered vast, rich lands they too have fallen victims to the corruption of wealth. They are beginning to appreciate fine foods and game, and most of them drink wine. They furnish their houses beautifully and wear clothes of gold and silver with costly linings. Briefly, then, they become fonder every day of luxury, comfort, and display. They are happy to follow the example provided by the sultan, who cares nothing about winning glory on the battlefield and prefers to stay at home and enjoy the countless pleasures of the seraglio. Modeling themselves on him, all the splendid pashas, governors, and generals, and the ordinary soldiers too, want to stay in *their* homes and enjoy *their* pleasures and keep as far as possible from the dangers and discomforts of war. The pashas make use of their wives, who are related to the Grand Signor, to persuade him to keep their husbands at home. They do this not only to satisfy the men but also because they know that if they stay in Constantinople their husbands can win more favor by serving and fawning on the Grand Signor. If they go to war their rivals find it easier to slander them and they run a greater risk of losing the sultan's favor. And right behind the great men are all the lower ranks of soldiers, following in their footsteps, and trying to avoid being pulled away from the comforts of home.

Obedience was the third source of the great power of the Turkish empire. In the old days obedience made them united, union made them strong, and strength rendered their armies invincible. They are all slaves by nature, and the slaves of one single master; only from him can they hope to win power, honors, and wealth and only from him do they have to fear punishment and death. Why should it be surprising, then, that they used to compete with each other to perform stupendous feats in his presence? This is why it is said that the Turks' strict obedience to their master is the foundation of the empire's security and grandeur. But when the foundation weakens, when the brake is released, ruin could easily follow. The point is that with those other state-preserving qualities [of religion and frugality] changing into state-corroding qualities, disobedience and disunion could be the agents which finally topple it.

This is all the more likely now that the chief officials have no other goal but to oppose each other bitterly. They have all the normal rivalries and ambitions of ministers of state, but they also have unusual opportunities for undercover competition with each other, because many of them have married daughters, sisters, and nieces of the Grand Signor. These women can speak with His Majesty whenever they want and they often sway him in favor of their husbands. This practice throws government affairs into confusion and is a real source of worry to the first vizier, who fears to take the smallest step without notifying the sultan. He knows that his rivals' wives might sometime find the Grand Signor in the right mood and bring about his ruin, something the *caiacadin* [matron of the harem] did to the first vizier Sinan when I was there.

When I was *bailo* [four years ago] I found the Turks less obedient than they had earlier been, and I mentioned this fact in reporting here to the Senate. This time I learned that the situation had deteriorated still further, as was clear from four notable acts of disobedience which had taken place in the years since my earlier departure. The first was the revolt against the beglerbeg of Greece and the defterdar [treasurer], when the spahis boldly entered the council room and demanded that the Grand Signor execute those two and give them their heads. No gifts of money, no command from the sultan would shut them up until they had had their way. They took the heads and brutally hurled them along the city streets with horrible cries. Another act of extreme disobedience took place when the janissaries set fire

So *Li Ebbriachi.*

Azamoglan.   Leuenti.   Azappi.

50. Drunken Turkish Soldiers.

(From Nicolay, Navigationi, 1576, fol. 152. Collections of The Library Company of Philadelphia.)

to the houses of Jews in several places in Constantinople and burned down a quarter of the city. They also sacked the Jews' homes with terrible cruelty. For all this they were never even threatened with punishment.

The third incident took place when the ulema[7] rose up against a man who had devised a new tax imposed by the Grand Signor and looted and burned his house so that he was fortunate to escape with his life. And the fourth event was one which took place in these recent months while I was in the Porte. The janissaries took advantage of a fire which broke out in the vineyards of Pera, near my residence, and attacked, looted, and burned the house of Ibrahim, the brother of the *caiacadin*. Their grievance against him was simply that while pasha he had publicly executed two janissaries at Diyarbekir! If they dare to commit crimes like this in the city, before His Majesty's eyes, what won't they do in their camps when they are armed? Surely they will be beyond what they did while I was there to Osman, the pasha general in Persia: to force him to raise their pay they slashed the ropes on his pavilion to collapse it on top of him, and with other insults like that they actually made him do what they wanted. If the Grand Sultan decides to revive the war against Persia there is real danger of outright rebellion; this possibility will have to be a major consideration when he makes up his mind.[8]

Just as obedience to a prince creates a spirit of unity, so disobedience causes discord and strife. I have already said how much the pashas who are in office hate each other. In the same way, the *massuli* or dismissed pashas think of nothing but ruining the ones in office so they can return to their former posts. The beglerbegs and sanjakbegs resent having to pay good money for their positions not only to the pashas but to those inside the seraglio and in the Grand Signor's personal staff. Then there are the common people, who hate the judges, sanjakbegs and beglerbegs because

7. The body of scholars of Muslim religion and law.
8. He did not resume the war with Persia, but began one with Austria (1593).

they tyrannize and victimize them beyond bearing. (The only way these men can hold their jobs is by spending and bribing on a large scale, so they have to rob and murder the common people in order to raise the money. This is so customary in that empire that anyone who does otherwise simply doesn't know his trade.)

The Grand Signor himself stirs up hatred and indignation among his subjects by making himself the heir of those who die rich, and grabbing their goods from their children. His avarice and penny-pinching are subjects for loud grumbling in every tavern and gathering place in the empire. This public talk is resulting in widespread scorn for the sultan, whom they consider a Sardanapalus[9] who was raised in the seraglios among jesters, dwarfs, and deaf-mutes. They know that he refuses to take part in military campaigns the way his ancestors did. Those men used to take the field with their armies and set examples of personal bravery; each one tried to outdo his predecessor in conquering kingdoms and winning fame and glory. What they accomplished is stupendous; no other series of emperors ever did anything like it. In most empires there have been one or two or at most three brave and able rulers in a row who have expanded their empires, but these have invariably been followed by an equal number of inferior ones who have lost much of the conquered land and started their empires on declines. In the uninterrupted succession of thirteen Ottoman rulers, however, the Turkish empire has been remarkably fortunate. If one was great, the next tried to surpass him, and if one conquered lands, the next tried to conquer much more. None of them ever lost so much as an inch of the land his predecessors had won; it seems that their religion forbids them ever to give up any land once they have recited their prayers on it. I find there is only one place which the Turks have lost and never recovered, and this is the island of Cephalonia, which the bravery of General Pesaro and Gonzalo Fernán-

---

9. Sardanapalus was an Assyrian king who, according to legend, burned himself on a funeral pyre with his favorite concubine while the Medes were besieging his palace.

dez [de Córdoba] won for our Most Serene Republic in 1500, and which we have retained ever since.[10] That is the only example in Ottoman history.

It seems reasonable to say that if the Ottoman Empire rose so remarkably fast in a short time because the Grand Sultan went on the major campaigns and because his men hoped and struggled for rewards, then its decline may now be under way. Sultan Selim, the father of the present Grand Signor, was the first to hold that a king or emperor's real satisfaction is not to be found in brave deeds on the field of glory but in peace and quiet, in gratifying all his physical senses, in enjoying the pleasures and comforts of the seraglios in the company of women and jesters, and treating himself to jewels, palaces, loggias, and every other human creation his heart desires. Sultan Murad has followed his father's example—in fact, he has gone further, because at least Sultan Selim occasionally left the seraglio and hunted as far away as Adrianople, but the present Grand Signor, as I said, hardly ever goes out.

We can hope that his son Mohammed will do the same. As I said earlier,[11] he is a spirited boy with an aptitude for military life, but he is following his mother's advice, which is to avoid raising any suspicions in his father.[12] He too now lives in seclusion in his seraglio and spends his time enjoying the pleasures of the flesh. We can hope that he will become so addicted that he will never be able to leave them, even if he should want to, and that he will pass on this inheritance to his successors. It seems quite possible that this would mean that no sultan would ever go in person on campaigns, but that they would leave them to their slaves, which would certainly start their empire on a downward path.

Anyone who studies the histories of the kings of Persia

10. Cephalonia is an Ionian island, off western Greece. The war in question was really won by the Turks, and while the Venetians won Cephalonia, they lost several other possessions in the peace settlement.

11. In a part of the report not included in this excerpt.

12. Eighty years earlier Sultan Bayazid II had been deposed by his son, the great-grandfather of Murad III.

51. Sultan Selim II ("the Sot").

(*From Stirling-Maxwell*, Don John
of Austria, *1883, I, 452. Libraries
of the University of Pennsylvania,
Philadelphia.*)

SULTAN SELIM II.

and the kings and emperors of Rome will find that the
Xerxeses, the Caesars, and the Trajans personally led their
campaigns and as a result enjoyed victory after victory. But
when kings and emperors preferred a life of ease and luxury
and sent their generals out to conquer, either the campaigns
went badly or the generals developed a taste for ruling, kept
the conquered lands for themselves, and turned against their
lords. That could easily happen in the Ottoman Empire, and
it might prove to be the beginning of a decline. Of course,
it's true that while the Grand Signor did not go out with his
troops he pushed his borders eastward three hundred miles
to Tabriz by conquests in Georgia, Shirvan, and Armenia[13]
during the war with Persia. But the change in the government was already reflected in this war, because it took
twelve long years, the lives of countless men, and an incredible amount of money to win this territory. When Suleiman
was sultan it took him only one year to carry out the same
campaign.

My conclusion, distinguished gentlemen, is that the three

13. More correctly, in Azerbaijan.

basic qualities which made the Turks a great power—religion, frugality, and obedience—are vanishing. If this trend continues, and if the sultan's successors follow his example of remaining in the seraglios and letting others lead campaigns, then we can hope for the decline of the empire. Just as it rose to great strength very rapidly, it seems logical to expect it to decline very rapidly, in the same way that those plants which quickly mature and produce fruit are also quick to wither.

Even if the Turks have enormous armed forces, this does not mean their state will not decline. If armed might guaranteed that an empire would last forever, think how many examples one can find of powerful Greek and Roman empires, especially the Roman one (the world has never seen a mightier power), and yet it was totally ruined in little more than two hundred years.[14] If having more money, more land, and more inhabitants always made one country more powerful than the others, the world would not have seen so many of those reversals in which countries with smaller but better armies wiped out larger ones. It is good government, not armies, that conserve an empire; fine laws and institutions have maintained our republic, with God's help, in a world where many states are more powerful.

This is a law of nature, that the same forces which caused a thing to grow must also keep it alive when mature. If the Turkish empire rose so high with the aid of the three qualities I have discussed, then when it lacks its wings it will surely fall.

14. The poor syntax of this sentence accurately reflects that of the original, and is typical of much official Venetian prose.

11 "FITS OF IDIOCY,
WITH LUCID INTERVALS"

From the dispatches of various ambassadors,
1595–1601

The most visible aspect of the rapid decline of the Ottoman Empire at the end of the sixteenth century was the
lowered caliber of the sultans. This change had already
been apparent when Selim the Sot (1566–74) replaced
Suleiman the Magnificent, but Selim had at least been
fortunate in his very able grand vizier, Sokolli. Murad III
(1574–95) and Mohammed III (1595–1603) lived in a
ghastly world of servile viziers, grasping concubines,
opium dreams, and capricious violence. These dispatches
suggest the way this environment destroyed the capacity
for government of Mohammed III.

JANUARY 21, 1595

[In cipher] *This is the third dispatch of this post, but it is
to be read first because the news it contains will not brook
delay. I made use of every means in my power to find out
whether the sultan [Murad] were really dead; and among
other steps, I sent Borisi to Memi Pasha, who assured him
that the sultan died on Monday the night of the sixteenth-*

From the dispatches of various ambassadors, 1595–1601, *Calendar
of State Papers . . . Venice . . . ,* vol. 9. The dispatches of 1595 and
1596 are by Marco Venier; 1597 and 1600, Girolamo Cappello; 1601,
Agostino Nani. Translation by Horatio F. Brown. Minor changes have
been made in Turkish titles, etc.

*seventeenth of this month, at the hour of the first cry.
Ferrad[1] wished to send Memi Pasha in his galley to bring
back the prince Mohammed. But the sultans declared that
this sudden departure would waken suspicion.[2] Accordingly
they resolved to send the* bostanji pasha *[chief gardener] in
the middle-sized caique, as he was accustomed to go every
day to Akbunar [Akbaba] to fetch water for the sultan's
use. His caique has a double relay of rowers, and so it is
expected that he will be back in seven or eight days.*

JANUARY 27, 1595

[In cipher] *The rumor of the sultan's death has spread
down to the very children; and a riot is expected, accompanied by a sack of shops and houses as usual. I have hidden
the embassy archives and brought armed men into the house
to protect it and to see that it is not set on fire.*

*The new sovereign [Mohammed III, 1595–1603] arrived
this morning at the hour of salaam. I saw him arrive and
disembark at the Kiosk. In the eleven days which have
elapsed since the death of Sultan Murad, several executions
have taken place in order to keep the populace in check.
Inside the seraglio there has been a great uproar, and every
night we hear guns fired—a sign that at that moment someone is being thrown into the sea.*

*As regards the death of Sultan Murad, I must repeat that
he was attacked by his old epilepsy while receiving the*
kapudan *[admiral] in audience. He was carried inside and
suffered all night. Next day he began to mend and progressed so favorably that they almost thought him out of
danger, when a second fit came on; this kept him for two
days and two nights languid, feeble, like one dead. It was
followed by a retention of the urine which caused him to call
out in pain, and on top of the other illness carried him to the
grave. He refused all medical attendance and all medicine;
even when in health his habit of life was strange; and they*

1. A former grand vizier, temporarily governing Constantinople in
the absence of the current grand vizier, Sinan.
2. The death of a sultan was not announced until his successor had
arrived in Constantinople and was ready to assume power.

*say, though it is hardly credible, that he ate no bread, but
lived on solid meats, thick soups, sheep's marrow, and other
aphrodisiacs, for he lay immersed in lust. . .*

JANUARY 31, 1595

[In cipher] *The new sultan seems to be a resolute man,
and terrible. The moment he arrived at the seraglio he went
to look on his father's corpse; then his nineteen brothers
were brought before him, one by one. They say that the
eldest, a most beautiful lad and of excellent parts, beloved by
all, when he kissed the sultan's hand exclaimed, "My lord
and brother, now to me as my father, let not my days be
ended thus in this my tender age"; the sultan tore his beard
with every sign of grief, but answered never a word. They
were all strangled, all the nineteen;*[3] *and that same day late
in the evening the dead sultan was carried to the tomb with
less pomp than usually accompanies persons of even low
degree. The new sultan, dressed in purple cloth, followed the
corpse to the first door of the seraglio; Ferrad and the other
pashas, dressed in black, attended it farther. On the bier,
which in this country is borne head first, was placed a small
turban with aigrettes. The bier was covered with cloth of
gold with a jeweled belt of gold across it. It was placed on a
piece of ground near Saint Sophia under a great magnificent
military tent; and round it will soon arise the mortuary
chapel, where the coffin will repose on a lofty platform in the
middle, and all round it lower down will lie the nineteen
sons, who were not carried in the procession that day owing
to the late hour, but were taken out the day following. At
present they are all in plain wooden coffins, but later these
will be covered and adorned.*

*The day of his brothers' funeral the sultan placed in divan
his tutor, Mohammed of Mecca; a man held in high esteem,
wise, and not avaricious. Ferrad*[4] *is in great favor with the
sultan for the way in which he kept the city quiet during so*

---

3. A number of female slaves, pregnant by some of the older of
these brothers, were thrown in the sea.

4. Mohammed made Ferrad his grand vizier but soon had him
strangled.

52. Turkish Pallbearers.

(From C. Vecellio, Costumes anciens, 1859, II, 393. Libraries of the University of Pennsylvania, Philadelphia.)

many days of interregnum. The sultan has given his seal to no one yet. Sinan will soon be here, in spite of a false rumor of his death. His Majesty has made great changes in the seraglio; he has expelled all the buffoons, the dwarfs, the eunuchs, and the women; they were all sent to the old seraglio; the amount of goods they carried out with them was incredible; the carriages, chests, and baskets of the whole city hardly sufficed. The present to the janissaries[5] is one hundred and twenty purses of ten thousand sequins per purse.

The sultan is about medium height, strong and well made, and wears a black beard and two huge moustaches.

JUNE 6, 1596

It has been found impossible to delay much further the departure of the sultan for the [Austrian] war. The sultana mother, enraged at seeing him leave her,[6] after attempting in vain many means of stopping him, persuaded a girl of singular beauty, with whom he is desperately in love, to beg of him as a favor that he would not go. She did so one day when they were together in a garden; but the sultan's love suddenly changed to fury, and drawing his dagger, he slew the girl. Since then no one has dared to approach the subject.[7]

MARCH 29, 1597

The doctors have declared that the sultan cannot leave for [i.e., return to] the war on account of his bad health, produced by his excesses in eating and drinking.

MAY 10, 1597

The sultan's eldest son is dead, and the sultan is grown so fat that they say he will make no more.[8]

JULY 29, 1600

The Grand Signor has retired to Scutari, and public rumor has it that for three days he had been subject to one of his fits of idiocy, with lucid intervals.

---

5. A new sultan always made a gift to the janissaries to win their support.

6. She feared that she might lose her influence over him.

7. The sultan went in splendor to the battlegrounds in Hungary, timidly watched the fighting, and never again went to war.

8. And he did not. By this time, however, he had fathered five sons, of whom the third eventually succeeded him as sultan.

JANUARY 21, 1601

. . . The sultan, on the persuasion of his mother, has refused to sign any more documents; instead the grand vizier in the presence of the other viziers writes out the sultan's replies, as used to be done in the days of Sultan Suleiman.

In this way the sultana and the chief eunuch hope to obviate the danger which threatens them from the insolent soldiery, and to free themselves from the charge of turning the sultan round absolutely; all the same owing to their secret influence with the grand vizier, everything is arranged to suit their views.

III.

The Most Christian Kings of France— In Travail and Triumph

12 "THE FRAGILITY OF EARTHLY GREATNESS"

Michele Suriano, 1562

Suriano wrote the report on Spain with which this book begins. Hardly returned from his tour of duty at Philip's court, he was then sent to France just as that country began the series of internal religious and factional wars which made the latter sixteenth century so tragic for her. In this report on France he devotes half of his time to a discussion of the "pillars" on which French *grandeur* had always rested: strong religious traditions, geographical advantages, a large population, stable political institutions, good warriors, ample revenues, and the like. Then he sorrowfully discusses the forces which were racking this admirable state.

Kingdoms and city-states are like men: their health and vigor do not last forever. First they flourish, then they grow old, and finally they disappear. Everything God creates, large or small, he marks with impermanence and uncertainty so that every man will bow down and acknowledge that he owes all his blessings to his Lord. The man who governs others will learn not to trust his continued luck so much that he fails to use caution, which is the only thing which will preserve a great state, or make a minor one rise to greatness. Every age has seen examples of rising and

From a report by Michele Suriano, 1562, Albèri, I, 4: 105–49.

falling fortunes—ancient kingdoms and wealthy republics, some of which had ruled the world, have vanished without leaving a trace except in the history books, while many of the mighty kingdoms of today hardly existed not so long ago.

But where is there a more vivid example of the fragility of earthly greatness than the kingdom of France? Only yesterday her power and smiling fortunes made her a bulwark to her friends and the terror of her enemies, but the truth is that today that great engine rests on weak supports. Not only is she unable to help others, but she herself is in such danger that every little noise makes her tremble with fright.

Since my task here is to describe France and report what I saw and heard in fourteen months at the French court, I will try to paint as lifelike a portrait as I can of the kingdom as it was and as it is. I will not offer a history, but rather a simple commentary on the reasons for France's [former] greatness and the mishaps that made her stumble into her present dangers. I know I won't delight my readers[1] with the charm of my subject matter, since most of it really deserves our tears, nor with a polished literary style, which is something I never developed. Just the same, what I have to write about is so important and so instructive to anyone who governs groups of people or entire kingdoms that I think he will not be wasting his time if he reads it, and the same will be true of others who read and reflect about it.

Let me begin by saying that it used to be generally acknowledged that France was the most respected of the Christian kingdoms, that she was the strongest of them, and that her king had the most absolute power.

The respect in which she was formerly held arose partly from the fact that she was an independent country from her very beginnings, and has never known any other overlord than God himself. Many other kingdoms can make the same claim, but not all. For example, at one time England paid homage to the Church, just as the kingdom of Naples does at

1. Suriano evidently polished his report so that it could be circulated in written form.

53. Paris, Left Bank and Île de la Cité, by Franz Hogenberg.

(Detail from view of siege of Paris. Prints Division, New York Public Library.)

this time, and Bohemia and Poland were under the [Holy Roman] Empire. In addition to that, France is older than any other extant kingdom, because she dates her beginnings from slightly over four hundred years after the birth of Our Lord Jesus Christ. Before any of the others did it, she escaped the yoke of the Roman Empire, of which she had been a part, and under the leadership of Pharamond, her first king, began to draw up her laws, and govern and defend herself. In the reign of Clovis, some eighty years later, she became the first kingdom to accept Christianity. This is why she deserves her title of "Oldest Daughter of the Church." Except for the pope, who is the head of our religion, and the signory of Venice, which from its very beginnings has always been Christian, no ruler, no emperor, no kingdom can boast of having accepted Christianity before the kingdom of France.

After laying the foundations for her preeminence among kingdoms in nobility and respect, France added something more. As she became a strong and successful country, her very able King Charles, who performed such deeds that he was called "The Great," was honored with the rank and dignity of emperor, and his descendants used the title for generations. He also won the title of "Most Christian," which is still used for kings of France. Another thing which many consider significant is that the French began the practice of anointing their kings with holy oil over a thousand years ago. This is a ceremony which God ordained in the time of the kings of the Jews. Only three or four Christian kings use it, and it is generally considered a mark of a first-rank country. They keep the holy ampulla, which is used in anointing all their kings, at Rheims, and everyone believes it can work miracles.

For all these reasons France has always held an uncontested place as the most universally respected among the Christian kingdoms. The king of Spain may believe he deserves to be rated first, but the fact is that none of his kingdoms compares with France in grandeur, or in long and splendid history, or in titles and prestige.

54. Sixteenth-Century Map of France.

(From Ortelius, Epitome, *1602, fol. 15. Rare Book Division, New York Public Library.)*

As for French military power, there is no doubt that it is very great. The kingdom is large, and has more people, arms, and wealth than any other in Europe. She contains eleven big provinces, which function together like eleven parts of a single body, lending each other strength and skill. In the center, like a heart, is the province of [Île-de-] France, which gives its name to the whole kingdom, while the other ten encircle it like a crown. Two of them, Normandy and Brittany, are bordered by the Atlantic Ocean; and two others, Gascony and Languedoc, by the Pyrenees, while Provence extends to the Mediterranean. Dauphiny runs to the borders of Savoy, and Lyons and Auvergne[2] touch upon Bresse. Burgundy has the Swiss and Germans on its borders, while Champagne and Picardy reach to Lorraine and the Netherlands (except for the tongue of land in Picardy including Boulogne and Calais which faces toward England). Each of these provinces used to have its own lord,

2. Lyons is here understood to be part of Auvergne.

who, however, conceded the higher authority of the king of France. But now they have all been taken over by the crown, which inherited some of them and conquered the others. This has caused a steady increase of the king's power and prestige. . . .

The kingdom of France lies in the center of Christendom, better situated than any other to join or to break up the armies of the greatest rulers and most warlike peoples. Italy is in front of her, while England is behind, and Spain is on her right, while Germany, Switzerland, and the Flemings [of the southern Netherlands] are on her left. In addition, she fronts on two oceans, the Atlantic and the Mediterranean. As a result, both by sea and by land she can help or interfere with the plans and campaigns of every king and emperor in the world. And yet her own borders are as safe as nature and human effort can make them, because mountains protect her from Spain and Italy, oceans separate her from England and other kingdoms that are farther away, and rivers flow between her and the Netherlands and Germany. At the same time all the important passes on her borders are guarded by forts, and throughout the kingdom she has great stores of arms, cannon, and every kind of war matériel, and many skilled soldiers who can put them to the best possible use. . . .

The chief asset of a great and powerful kingdom, however, is its men, because their bravery and hard work are more important both when attacking and when defending than any amount of artillery, other weapons, or fortresses. For this reason I will briefly discuss the French people— their number, their social divisions, how the king uses them, and what conditions made it possible for them to earn such a high reputation for their country.

The population of France is very large.[3] The kingdom has

3. Probably between 15,000,000 and 20,000,000 in the mid-sixteenth century. The states that made up "Italy" had populations totaling about 11,000,000, while England and Wales had just over 4,000,000 inhabitants, and Spain had 7,000,000 or 8,000,000.

over 140 cities big enough to have bishops, and a vast
number of estates, fortresses, and villages, which are packed
with people. Paris alone is thought to have 400,000 or
500,000 inhabitants.

There are three social orders, or estates, for which the
three Estates-General of the kingdom are named.[4] The first
estate is called "the clergy," and the second "the nobility,"
but the third has no special name. Since it is made up of
various groups and professions, it might be called simply
"the people." The clergy, in fact, includes many who rightly
belong to the third estate and a large number of non-French-
men (who have performed services for the king, or in some
way earned his favor, and were rewarded with this privi-
lege). On the other hand, a third of the clergy are noblemen.
This comes about because the younger sons of nobles and
gentlemen inherit only a small part of their fathers' estates,
which usually go to oldest sons, so they enter the Church in
order to gain both wealth and high social standing.

The noble estate includes free men who pay no tax of any
kind to the king, and have no obligation except to serve in
the army in person in time of war. The nobles are both
barons and princes, and the latter group includes the princes
of the blood, who are ranked higher than the others because
they are in the line of succession to the throne. Some of them
are too poor, however, to live on the splendid scale fitting
their high standing. Eighty years ago there were many
princes of the blood, but by now all of them—the houses of
Orléans, Angoulême, Anjou, Burgundy, Alençon, and Bourbon (which includes the Vendôme, Montpensier, and La-
Roche-sur-Yon)—have succeeded to the throne or died out.
There remain only the Bourbons, who once were the last in
the line of succession, but have had the good luck to end up
first in line after the king's brothers, Monsieur d'Orléans
and Monsieur d'Anjou, so that they have never been so

4. In other words, the French parliamentary body, or Estates-
General, had three subdivisions, each representing one of the social
divisions or "estates," and named for it.

important as they are now. The head of the house of Bourbon is Anthony the king of Navarre,[5] who has an eight-year-old son.[6] The next in line is [Anthony's youngest] brother [Louis], the prince of Condé, because the cardinal [Charles, Anthony's immediately younger brother] is ineligible, as a member of the Church. The duke of Montpensier has only one son, and his brother La-Roche-sur-Yon has none. As for the other princes, who are not of the blood, and the barons, I won't try to mention them all, because there are so many that it would be long and boring. Suffice it to say that among the princes the richest and most powerful is [Francis], the duke of Guise,[7] and among the barons the most important is [Anne de Montmorency] the constable of France.[8]

The estate of the people comprises men of letters, who are called "men of the long robe," merchants, skilled workmen, and the lowest classes in the towns and countryside. Those "men of the long robe" who reach the rank of president, or councillor, or anything of that level, receive the privileges of nobility, and are treated as nobles for the rest of their lives. The merchants control a great deal of money these days, so they are courted and made much of, but they do not enjoy much respect and they are not given high positions, because in France any kind of trade is considered ignoble.

As a result, the merchants are lumped together with the lowest classes, and they pay their taxes right along with the plebs and peasants, who are as badly treated by the present government as they were under the Franks. The emperor Maximilian used to say that the king of France is the king of asses, because his subjects will bear every kind of burden without a complaint.

5. Navarre was a little kingdom in the southwest corner of France.
6. The son was the future King Henry IV. The fact that he was prince and then king of little French Navarre is incidental, but his leadership of the Bourbons, his place in the line of succession, and his powerful personality were to make Henry a major figure through much of the period covered in these ambassadors' reports.
7. Francis and his brother Charles, cardinal of Lorraine, were the heads of the very wealthy and Catholic Guise family.
8. Anne de Montmorency was the head of the religiously divided Montmorency family.

55. French Doctors Consulting and Preparing Medicines,
by Jean Perissin and Jacques Tortorel.

(Detail from Death of Henry II. *Philadelphia Museum of Art.
Photograph by A. J. Wyatt.)*

The king uses the three estates in several different ways.
Either by law, or custom, or because the nobles consider
these posts beneath them, four kinds of government offices
are always filled by commoners of the third estate. One is the
post of the grand chancellor, who attends all the councils
and keeps the Great Seal; nothing important may be decided
and put into practice without hearing his views. Another is
the secretaryships. Each secretary carries out decisions
which have been made in his particular section of the government, and guards the important secret documents. A
third is the presidents, councillors, judges, lawyers, and
others who run both the civil and criminal law courts
throughout the country. And the fourth is made up of the
treasurers, customs officials, and tax collectors of all kinds,
through whose hands pass all the crown's revenues and

expenditures. The people of the third estate then fill all of these offices, which are the routes to fame and wealth. Two of these, the chancellorship and the many posts in the judiciary, go to university-trained "men of the long robe."[9] This is why every father tries to have one of his sons complete his studies, and that in turn explains why there are so many students in France—more than in any other country. There are more than fifteen thousand in Paris alone. For a while now the nobles too have been sending their sons to the schools, especially the second and third sons, not in order to prepare them for these [government] jobs but to place them in the Church. This is happening because there are now some scruples about giving bishoprics to unlettered men. God knows it would have been a good thing for Christianity if they had thought of this long ago.

The running of the state is entirely in the hands of nobles and churchmen. The churchmen serve as councillors but not executives. The nobles fill both roles, but often they have been willing enough to let the ecclesiastics have all the honor of deliberating, knowing they themselves would put the decisions into effect. This suits everybody because the nobles are not usually very rich and if they had to stay at court, where prices are very high, they would bankrupt themselves paying for servants, horses, food, and clothes for their entire households. Living more simply in their own castles, they can do very well with what they have, and can save on liveries, fancy clothes, high-priced horses, banquets, and all the other things expected of a courtier. For this reason the custom began that a courtier must serve the king at court only three months a year. The rest of the time he may stay at home and economize enough so that he can afford to live in suitable splendor during his three months of service. . . .

The natural sphere of the nobility, and the one most useful to the king and the rest of the people, is warfare. One can fight on land or sea, but there is not much to be said

9. The ambassador's wording is ambiguous but the meaning is clear: some of the offices are especially desirable because they confer privileges of nobility.

about the navy, because France lacks ship timber, armaments, oarsmen, and captains, and therefore has never put
together a navy large enough for successful attacks on other
powers. This is why King Francis began the policy of using
the Turkish fleet in their wars. However, they have never
needed foreign help to defend their kingdom, because they
have shown that in the Atlantic they can assemble as many
as two hundred boats (which they call "ships" even though
the largest carries no more than three hundred *botti*) [10] and
in the Mediterranean off Provence they have maintained up
to forty galleys, though the number is now down to eight.
Sometimes they have used these galleys in the Atlantic, but
chiefly to carry troops to Scotland or to worry the king of
some other country.

The backbone of the French forces is the army, and here
the cavalry are more important than the infantry. The
French do not like to put arms in the hands of their own
peasants and townspeople, and can easily recruit Swiss and
German infantry. As a result they depend more on their
cavalry, which consists entirely of noblemen and therefore is
very brave and effective, unlike the horsemen of other countries, who are drawn from every social level. There are two
kinds of cavalry—some of them are paid while the others,
who are usually called the *arrière-ban,* serve because of an
obligation [of vassalage]. The latter are forces provided by
those noblemen who are obliged to fight for the king in
person along with a number of horsemen proportionate to
the size of their fiefs. Since there are many nobles, there is a
great number of these horsemen. However, they do not
amount to much, partly because the noble vassals are stingy
and undutiful and all they have to do is provide so many
horsemen, good or bad, and partly because the best of these
horsemen are assigned to the regular paid cavalry companies and fight with them instead of the *arrière-ban.* So
when they call up the *arrière-ban* it is a sure sign that the
kingdom is in trouble but not that the army will now become

10. About two hundred tons. A Venetian round warship was six or
seven times as large.

much stronger. The real strength lies in the mercenary light
and heavy cavalry; these are usually fine soldiers, well
armed and well mounted (because even if the country
doesn't produce its own war-horses they spare no expense to
import them from other lands). . . .

Turning now to the foot soldiers, the Gascons are said to
be the best. They are the most cautious, and they bear up
best under the strains and hardships of war and have much
of the Spaniard in them. The French can raise six or seven
thousand of these Gascons. If they wanted to they could
recruit a great many infantrymen in other parts of the
kingdom, and once they were trained they would be good
soldiers, especially those from the border regions, since they
are already used to fighting. When he was king, Louis XII
ordered the formation of legions, and then after him King
Francis I did the same, with the intention of organizing a
militia of forty or fifty thousand infantry, in order to avoid
being continually dependent on the Swiss. But the plan was
then cancelled by decision of the Estates-General and only
noblemen are allowed to train themselves in the use of arms.
There are many reasons for this, one of which is that if the
common people were armed they would rebel against the
nobles and rulers (partly out of envy and partly for revenge
for the oppressions they suffer). The judges would not be
able to hold them back, and they would leave their jobs, stop
working the land, become robbers and, in short, throw the
kingdom into wild confusion. They have always found that
as soon as one of them is made a soldier he turns overbear-
ing and tries to order his father and brothers and everyone
else around. However, this decision by the Estates-General
and all of these considerations are swiftly forgotten if a
king really wants to have his way.

As for army commanders, France has always produced
great numbers of very gallant, skilled, and lucky men. For
many years the French kings have hired German and Italian
officers and even an occasional Englishman or exiled Spaniard, but they have always insisted that the commander in
chief of their armies be a Frenchman. Of those alive today

56. Francis, Duke of Guise.

(From Montfaucon, Collection, 1750, pl. 276. Libraries of the University of Pennsylvania, Philadelphia.)

the most powerful are the king of Navarre, the king's lieutenant general; and my lord the constable, who is commander in chief of the kingdom. But neither of them is the equal of the duke of Guise in courage, judgment, or battlefield experience. This nobleman is more gallant than all the famous figures of today and many of the past as well. . . .[11]

With armed forces like these, former kings of France not only assembled a great deal of land and defended it against

11. Concerning the three great noble families (Bourbon, Montmorency, and Guise) to which the king of Navarre, the constable, and the duke of Guise belonged, see pp. 181–182, 220–222.

the armies of countless rulers, they also fought Germany, Hungary, and Spain, conquered Italy, made their influence felt in Asia and Africa, and caused the whole world to tremble. By nature the French are proud and haughty. They throw themselves into whatever they tackle and when things go their way they are unbearable. They work hard in their own interests but as allies they are undependable and often untrustworthy. The general rule of France is: whatever suits my convenience is also noble and honorable. An old proverb, which you can find in all the history books, runs "Have a Frenchman for a friend but try not to have him for a neighbor." It is true, as the old writers used to claim, that at the start of a battle they are more than men but at the finish they are less than women; however, it is also true that many times the beginning of an attack is so crucial that it determines the outcome, and anything that goes wrong at the beginning can start a chain of failure. If the French are so proud and fearsome that it is dangerous to attack them, it must also be very hard [for their leaders?] to restrain and control all of that frenzy and drive which make them so proud and bold.

That is all I have to report about the size and quality of the French armed forces, and the services the crown gets from the estates. When the three estates[12] have cooperated together and each has done its work and contributed in its own way to the general welfare, and each has helped the king (some with advice, some with money, some with life itself), they have made that kingdom unconquerable and universally feared. But now that the curse of the new sects has pitted the clergy against the nobles, the nobles against each other, and the people against everybody, confusion reigns and everyone suffers as a result, as I will explain when I reach the subject.

Now that I have discussed the kingdom of France and the condition of the people, I must still report on resources and money, because if you lack those two things you cannot

---

12. Here he means the three broad subdivisions of French society—not the Estates-General.

57. Huguenot Soldiers Making a Sortie, by Franz Hogenberg.
(*Detail from* Siege of St. Jean-d'Angély. *Prints Division, New York Public Library.*)

provide for your needs in war or keep order during peacetime.

France has always been considered very rich and comfortable and overflowing with all the goods needed to sustain human life. She is almost in the center of the finest part of the globe, which is Europe; the weather is temperate and benign, with none of the bitter cold spells you get in Germany or the terrible heat of Spain. Although there is considerable wind, the air is healthy and not heavy or marshy, as it is not far away in Flanders. The countryside is very pleasing and full of rivers (all of them navigable). The mountains are not rugged, except at the farthest borders, and the middle consists of plains and hills, which are all fertile and cultivated. They produce so many crops and so much wine, flax, hemp, dyestuffs, and other things that I cannot name them all, but there is enough not only for the home market but also for export to Spain, Portugal, the Netherlands, England, Scotland, Denmark, and even more distant countries. There are no gold or silver mines in France, and yet there is never any lack of money, because it is brought there from other places which import French goods. The borders of Portugal, for example, are always open and that country alone provides France with quantities of gold and silver. Spain does the same, even though the laws against it are very strict, and the profit from there is at least fifteen or twenty percent. I remember that even during the war with the Catholic King trade with the Netherlands and Spain never stopped, because they rely so much on French goods. It's not surprising that in wartime their troops, not only in Italy but inside the kingdom as well, were paid in Spanish escudos and silver reals.

Because there is so much of everything in France, it is estimated that the yearly value of all the products of the soil averages fifteen million in gold. Of these, six go to the Church, one and a half go to the king from his own particular possessions, and the rest belongs to the princes, lords, and others who have lands and incomes, so that the Church gets two-fifths of the country's annual product. The king, however, in addition to what he gets from his own possessions (this is the regular income of the crown, but much of it has now been sold or mortgaged), has revenues from excises and the taille,[13] which for a long time have been regular sources of income, and he levies at least two-tenths a year on the clergy. [These sources provide] four and a half million in gold. In all, therefore, he has a regular income of six million. . . . As if it weren't bad enough to have to pay all the treasurers and tax collectors, everyone cheats, both the collectors and taxpayers, and it is widely believed that the king is cheated of a large part of his revenues.

What is collected goes for household expenses, servants, and other needs of the king; advisers, governors, officials, and other employees of the courts and the government; cavalry, bowmen, forts, guns, warships, and galleys to guard the kingdom—all of which are customary expenses—and

13. The main direct tax, from which the wealthy and important were usually exempt.

thousands of others which are considered irregular expenses
and yet are continuous. As a result, since the time of King
Francis I, who left almost a million in gold when he died,
they have not been able to save anything. But in an emergency such as a war, they have always managed to collect
what they need either by raising the taille, or by raising
more tenths from the clergy, or by collecting grants that the
walled cities must make in time of need (otherwise they are
untaxed), or by borrowing. The monarch is in debt for
fifteen million in gold, counting what has been mortgaged
from the royal domain. For this reason they are now cutting
down on expenses as much as they can and collecting funds
to get out from under this weight of debt, as they hope to be
able to do in a few years if peace continues.

That's enough on the power and might of the kingdom of
France. I will turn now to the question of the way the
country is ruled, which was the third topic I listed at the
beginning of my report.

This huge and powerful kingdom, thickly populated and
rich and productive, is completely subject to the will of the
king, who is a "ruler by nature," invested with absolute
power, and loved and obeyed by his people. The king of
France is a "ruler by nature" because the monarchy is not
new but very old, and for more than a thousand years the
country has known no other form of government. The king
does not succeed to the throne by choice of the people, and
therefore he does not have to curry their favor, nor does he
succeed by force, and so he does not have to be cruel and
despotic. Instead he inherits the throne, which goes by
natural succession from father to firstborn son, or to the
person who is most closely related, except that bastards and
women are ineligible.

The firstborn inherits the throne, or if there is no firstborn
son, then the one who is most closely related by birth, so that
the kingdom is not divided but goes always to one man alone.
This is the custom in France not only for the royal family
but in all the important families: the firstborn inherits
everything, while the others get only enough to live in a

manner suitable for their position. This practice conserves
the wealth and power of the families and the state, because
if they divided everything equally, as is done in Germany,
they would quickly be reduced to nothing at all. This is why
Saint Bernard said that of the three classes of men in the
active life, kings and other rulers should all succeed by
primogeniture, the middle class and those who live on rents
should divide in equal shares, and common people and peasants should hold everything in common.

Women are excluded because of the Salic law—so they
say[14]—or because of a custom which has the strength of law.
As a result the king of France is always French and can
never be from another country. It never happens, as it has in
other countries, that with a woman succeeding to the throne
no one is sure who will be king and often the one who is
made king[15] comes from an enemy land. . . .

All these reasons are the root and foundation of the
French people's love for their king. They have been ruled
this way for so long that they are used to it and wouldn't
want any other kind of government. Having accepted the
fact that it is their lot to obey a king, they willingly serve
the man who was born to rule them. They know he has not
had to use force or fraud to reach his position and that he
does not have to hurt any of his subjects because of suspicions about them, but that he will rather look out for them in
the interests of his own greater glory and power. The
French king is so close to his subjects that he treats them all
as comrades and never excludes anyone from his presence.
Even the lackeys, the lowest kind of people, think nothing of
entering his chambers and watching what he does and listening to everything that is discussed. Anyone who has
important business to discuss with him must bring it up in
the presence of all sorts of people and has to speak as softly
as possible so as not to be overheard. This informality does

14. The ambassador doubts the old claim that it is because of an
ancient law of the Salian Franks that women are kept off the French
throne.
15. In other words, the queen marries a foreign prince, who in effect becomes the ruler.

58. A French Courtier.
(*From Deserps,* Recueil, *1562. Prints Division, New York Public Library.*)

make the people too familiar and impudent but it also makes them more loyal and devoted to the king.

However, the most important reason why they love him is that each person hopes to gain some personal advantage. The king of France has the patronage of an enormous number of titles, offices, judgeships, Church benefices, grants, pensions, gifts, and other good jobs and honors, which are innumerable in France, and he assigns all of them to his own subjects. It is not the same in France as it is in other kingdoms, especially Naples, where the subjects are dissatisfied because titles and jobs which ought to go to native subjects go instead to foreigners. Sometimes the king favors an Italian or some other alien, but not very often and only because they have earned a reward through service to the monarchy.

This is why the French have never revolted against their king in order to subject themselves to another one. Rebel-

lions have been very rare, and no conspiracies have come to
light except the recent one of Amboise. Frenchmen rarely go
abroad to serve other rulers; instead they love and even
worship their own king. Anyone of them will readily spend
his money and if need be his life in the king's service, and
will put up with hard work, suffering, and danger instead of
enjoying a life of ease, comfort, and pleasure. Some do this
out of a sense of duty, others to set an example, others in the
hope of reward.

It is just because his people love, obey, and serve him so
well that the king enjoys absolute power. It is he who
decides whether to make war or peace, what taxes and levies
to raise, and who will get favors, benefices, government
offices, judgeships, and other jobs throughout the kingdom.
The king is considered to be lord and master of everything.
No council or official, no matter how important, may put any
limit on his freedom of action, nor is there any prince or
noble daring enough to stand in his way. Compared to the
king, the princes of the blood and other important nobles are
so relatively poor and weak that if they rose against him
they would have no followers. The reason they are poor is
that at one time or another the crown has taken over the
lands and other wealth of the great families of the kingdom.
This has happened because of a lack of male heirs, as was
the case in Provence, Anjou, Berry, Alençon, Guienne, and
Brittany; or because the family inherited the crown, as
happened to the houses of Orléans and Angoulême, and
earlier with that of Valois; or because of confiscation, which
happened to Bourbon during the reign of Francis I. They
lack power because no prince in the kingdom has jurisdiction over the people except the king. It's true that one
brother of the king has the title of duke of Orléans and
another is duke of Anjou, but in fact they have only the
titles and the incomes, and the king has all the power.

As far as councillors and officials are concerned I will only
say this: that the king chooses and handles them just as he
wishes. The Council of Affairs, where matters of state are
handled, is made up of just a few men who are very close to

the king. Sometimes it consists of only one man, such as the constable during the reign of King Henry and the cardinal of Lorraine in the time of Francis II. . . .

If there is any authority in France which can put a limit on the king's absolute power it is the assembly of the three estates [Estates-General], which represents the whole of the kingdom, as the parliaments do for England and Scotland and the diet for Germany. It used to assemble almost yearly, and was sure to meet if there was business to be settled. This was the method: In each province, in each bailliage, and, as we would say, in each district, each of the three estates (clergy, nobles, and people) elected a certain number of representatives. These men assembled in the presence of the king, in what was like a public audience, to form a high council. Here they considered the burdens of the common people, the quarrels of the nobles, and the needs of the kingdom, and decided, as the case might be, to raise troops or money, increase or cut down expenses and taxes, straighten out offenses done by the army, reform morals and customs, decide what portions to give sons or brothers of the king, correct problems in the country and the government, and delegate authority when the king was a minor. In short, they deliberated everything pertinent to the peace and welfare of the kingdom. Any decision that body made had the force of law and bound not only the people but the king as well.

The kings had no objections to "summoning the Estates," as it was called, when the world was not yet overrun with pride and ambition and when it was felt that a king's task was to rule his people justly and simply, not to expand his kingdom by force, as they do today. But after a while the kings began to lack those real virtues and each one wanted to have more than he was entitled to by right. So they began to discontinue the custom of summoning the Estates, and started slowly to shake this yoke off their necks. By the time of King Louis XI anyone who wanted to revive it was treated as a rebel; the king used to say that he was no longer a page or a schoolboy and he no longer needed a guardian.

Since that time they have assembled the Estates only twice: once in 1483, when King Charles VIII inherited the throne and arrangements had to be made for governing the kingdom during his minority, and again a year ago, in 1560,[16] when they were summoned while King Francis II was alive on the advice of the cardinal of Lorraine for reasons I will explain presently. When that king [Francis II] died and was succeeded by the present King Charles IX, who is a little boy, they decided they would still summon them, but the Estates caused fully as much turmoil as they used to bring law and order. I imagine, therefore, that they will stop once and for all summoning the Estates, and the power of the king will continue to grow.

These are the foundations and the columns which until now have supported that great machine which is the kingdom of France. The size of the country, its many cities and provinces, the natural strength of its setting and its frontiers, the number, unity, and obedience of its people and soldiers, the supreme authority of the king, and the absolute power of the government are the chief reasons why that monarchy has endured so long, fought so many glorious wars, won such fame and territory, kept her friends, terrified her enemies, and earned a reputation in recent times as the only refuge of the oppressed. She could have done even more and better if only certain misfortunes, which I will discuss, had not taken place, because these have weakened those moral qualities which used to hold this kingdom together in its pursuit of glory and grandeur.

I must now discuss weaknesses and diseases in France which are certainly of the greatest importance. If it is true, as common sense and experience show us, that any change in kingdoms and seigniories is dangerous, then what country was ever in greater danger than this one, where at the same time—almost in the same instant—there have been changes in the head, the limbs, and the whole body? In the head, because when King Francis, who had the authority of a king,

16. The ambassador apparently wrote this report in 1561. He read it in the Senate in 1562.

59. Royal Family and Officials
at the Estates-General of
1560–61, by Franz Hogenberg.

(*Detail from* The Estates-General in
1561. *Prints Division, New York
Public Library.*)

died he was succeeded by King Charles, who has nothing
kingly about him but the title. In the limbs, because the
government of a large kingdom has fallen into the hands of
inexperienced men and women. In the whole body, because
of the appearance of this curse of new sects that have sown
confusion throughout our religion, which is the only thing
which holds people together and obedient to their rulers. I
suspect you will be eager to hear more about this topic of
religion, so I will discuss that first. I will have nothing to say
about beliefs and doctrines, because this is not the place for
that. Instead I will limit myself simply to what gave rise to
this great movement, which has progressed so far, and the
evils it has brought into the world.

PART TWO

The beginning of any great evil is always insignificant,
and has some beneficial look about it which deceives men in
the same way that a poison mixed with delicious food deceives the sense of taste. There is a great deal of truth in the
old saying that you must look sharp at the beginnings of

things, because when an evil is small no one considers it dangerous and when it has become great there is nothing to be done about it.

I don't think I need to exert myself telling you how small this evil was at the beginning. Everyone knows that the first to revive the old heresies and introduce the new sects of our own times was a single, insignificant man, and yet the disease spread to many parts of the world in few years, and changed the religion not only of Germany, where it began, but also Denmark, Sweden, Prussia, Poland, and all the northern countries. It damaged England and Scotland, corrupted France and the Netherlands, threw Italy and Spain into confusion, and reached even to the Indies [South America], so that there is no part of Christianity which has been spared from this plague.

Out of this evil root grew a tree with three branches— Lutherans, Sacramentarians,[17] and Anabaptists—and there are now more than thirty sects, all different. But they all started with that one man.

All the creators of these new doctrines rely on two points, which serve as a cover or mask for lies and as starting points for attacks on the ancient truths. One is to stress the "purity of the Gospels," which they say anyone can interpret for himself,[18] and the other is preaching "Christian liberty." Claiming that the Gospel is sufficient and anyone can interpret it for himself, they destroy the true meaning of the Scriptures, take away the authority of the teachings of the Church fathers, and undo the decretals of the pontiffs and councils, which they say have no scriptural authority. As for "liberty," a popular word with a pleasing ring to it, it opens the way to lust and sensuality, and leads by easy steps to a kind of licentious living which corrupts the morals and the old statutes of towns and provinces and weakens the authority first of the Church's laws and courts, and later of the civil ones. With all this changing of religious beliefs, each man wants to decide on his own beliefs by himself. As a

17. Followers of the Swiss reformer Huldreich Zwingli.
18. A reference to the Protestant position that each man can find the truth for himself in the Bible, without the aid of pope or priest.

result doubts and uncertainties arise in men's minds; they don't know which is the true faith and, not satisfied with any of them, they end up believing in none. And that is what comes of the "purity of the Gospel" and the "Christian liberty" which they boast that they are preaching and teaching to the world.

This plague was first brought into France twenty years or more ago by means of a hoax. Sheets of paper called placards were posted at the street corners and these bore proclamations or rather "excommunications" of the mass. This method of ridicule spread the thing through much of the kingdom. But what had a stronger effect were some contacts of the French with foreigners, especially with Germans and Swiss who were hired in 1536 by King Francis I to help defend the kingdom against an attack by the emperor Charles V. These were the kind of men who want to be free to do and talk and believe just as they wish, and so the force of their arguments and the example of their way of life contaminated almost all of Provence and all the land around it—not just the soldiers but ordinary people and even whole cities. When the king realized that his subjects were in this mess he had to cope with it by means of stern measures, including harshly putting many to death. In numerous cases where he could not get his hands on people, he confiscated their belongings and sometimes he had houses torn down to the ground and drove the inhabitants out to wander over the land.

The kingdom lived in fear of this kind of thing until the reign of Henry [II], who was busy with a war and in any case was a spiritless man who was more pleasure-seeking than was suitable for a king. Henry neglected the problem and didn't take such pains as his father had done to keep the kingdom purged of the disease. As a result the poison spread secretly and even infected many important men at the court, so that when it was discovered it already had deep roots[19] and was very hard to extirpate. By the time the king

---

19. It is the ambassador, not the translator, who mixed his metaphors for spreading Protestantism—a plague, a poison, a deep-rooted plant, and (below) a fire and the choleric humor.

60. Henry II Dying of Joust Wound, by Tortorel and Perissin.

(Detail from Death of Henry II. *Philadelphia Museum of Art.*
Photograph by A. J. Wyatt.)

finally realized the danger, the people, who once were very
compliant, had become downright insolent. They were not
only ignoring his decrees and his threats but, almost as if
they wanted to spite him, they were listening to preachers
everywhere and men and women of all ages and every social
class were attending mass meetings. In order not to lose
control completely he had to make peace with King Philip,
agreeing to very harsh terms, so that he could give all his
attention to putting out the great fire which was burning on
all sides. Just as he was starting, however, he died.

He was succeeded by King Francis II, who was first
despised because he was so young and spiritless, and then
hated because he put himself and the whole kingdom in the
hands of the Guises and had nothing to do with the other
great nobles. Francis's reign gave this humor the chance to
reach its climax, since the big men of the kingdom supported

61. Surrender of Château de Noizy during the Conspiracy of Amboise, 1560, by Tortorel and Perissin.

(L'Entreprise d'Amboise. Philadelphia Museum of Art. Photograph by A. J. Wyatt.)

it out of contempt [for the king], or [religious] fickleness, or, in many cases, hope of reward. And at the same time every malcontent joined them in the hope that with a religious pose he could pick up followers and some support and then do what he wanted in the government and the kingdom. The results could be seen in the Amboise conspiracy and the risings in Orléans, Lyons, Provence, Normandy, Guienne, Poitiers, and other parts of the country. Emboldened by the backing they enjoyed, the rebels confidently demanded the use of churches and other public places for their meetings, and threatened that if these were not given to them they would take them by force. They were so insolent that they claimed the king had no right to stop anyone from practicing any religion he pleased, or to act as the ruler of their consciences. As if the king was required to change the laws and customs of his kingdom whenever it suited anyone's pleasure!

Confronted by all this impertinence, the king, who was haughty and severe by nature, could hardly fail to lose his temper. With the advice of those who were running the government he made a decision which, if he had only had time to put it into effect, would have purged the country and set the world an example for all time. He resolved to turn completely against the leaders of the uprisings and punish them without fear or favor, which is the only way to put out a fire once and for all. But he faced two problems. One was that these leaders were influential and powerful, partly because they were great aristocrats and princes of the blood and partly because they had large numbers of armed followers in many places. The other problem was that His Majesty did not have enough forces in being so that he could fight, nor enough money to hire them. Furthermore, he was not sure whom he could trust and suspected many of those who were closest to him, as well as a number on the council, such as the admiral; Cardinal de Châtillon; Marillac, the archbishop of Vienne; Montluc, bishop of Valenza; Mortier, father of the ambassador in Rome; and others. So he decided to keep his plan secret until he had collected some troops and found a way to split up his enemies' forces, the better to rout them.

The movement that was under way had two chief aims: one was to change our religion, and this was fairly widely supported and well known; but the other was to drive out the Guises, and this was something of a secret. With both of these in mind, therefore, they [the king and his advisers] decided on two steps to take, not so much perhaps because they wanted to do them as to cool off the rebels and gain some time. One was to summon the Estates-General for a meeting at the end of a month and the other was to hold a national [Church] council a month after that. The council was intended as a sop to those who wanted to change the religion. (The question of whether or not to have a council was discussed without telling the pope, and the decision was opposed by His Holiness and the king of Spain, who did all they could to thwart it because they were not in on the secret.) The summoning of the Estates gave the impression that they planned to reorganize the government since, as I explained, in the assembly of the Estates-General everyone is allowed to air his grievances and ask for redress, which may be granted with general consent by the majority of those voting.[20]

General expectations about the council and the Estates-General proved very effective in calming things down, and those who had taken up arms for religion or politics laid them down again, so that the plan of the king and his advisers worked perfectly. To make things look even better, they asked the constable (who seemed to be behind all the uprisings) to stay at court and take part in all the councils, so that it would look as if they wanted to restore him to his earlier prominence. All of this was the work of the cardinal of Lorraine, who is absolutely unequaled when it comes to dissimulation. But the constable was not "in favor" long because while these things were being arranged the king collected his own army, sent for 4,000 German *landsknechts*[21] and an equal number of Swiss, demanded that the city of Paris lend him 500,000 francs to pay them, and got pledges of help from Spain, the Netherlands, and Lorraine (though he never took advantage of these promises). As soon as he felt that his forces were strong enough and his enemies were sufficiently divided and disarmed that he no longer had to fear them, he took off his mask and suddenly declared war on the rebels, without, however, naming any specific individuals. He sent Marshal de Termes with an army to the area of Guienne, which he distrusted; ordered the arrest of the *vidame* of Chartres—a man of the noblest blood—and the *bailli* of Orléans, a powerful figure who led the events there:

20. The ambiguity is the ambassador's: *"con consenso universale per i voti della maggior parte."*
21. Infantrymen.

and had Maligny and Montbrun, the leaders respectively of
the conspiracies of Amboise and Provence, beheaded in
effigy. He summoned the king of Navarre and his brother,
the prince of Condé, both of whom are princes of the blood,
to answer in his presence to charges against them, and as
soon as they appeared he arrested the prince and commanded the king not to leave the court.

His firmness terrified everyone so much that for the remaining few days of his life the commotion of the kingdom
was replaced by a miraculous calm. There was no more news
of uprisings and rebellions, or of Huguenots (as they call
the heretical sect which rejects the Blessed Sacrament).
Where there had been thousands of preachers who had come
from Geneva (the spawning ground for that kind of fish),
now not one of them felt so safe that he did not head for
safety outside the borders. The king of Navarre, who along
with his brother the prince had been considered a leading
Huguenot supporter, began attending mass and—to show
that he was a true Catholic—wrote to His Holiness in Rome
to assure him of his obedience, and took other steps for the
same purpose. And finally, every man, woman, and child,
especially the ones who were most suspect, made a great
show of their opposition to the new beliefs.

This shows how much their respect for the king influences
the French. If he had lived a little longer he would not only
have confined but actually extinguished the fire that is now
burning up the country. Clearly it has that trait that it
grows or fades away according to how much the princes and
other big men foment it. If we didn't have so many other
proofs that this business is mere vanity and not the will of
God, this would be enough, because something that grows
when men support it and shrinks when they do not could
never have been willed by God.

That is all I will say about the causes of this great evil.
Since the death of King Francis it has spread far and wide
because the measures which King Henry carelessly failed to
take and which Francis did not complete because of his
untimely death, the present King Charles IX has not been

62. The Burning of Anne du Bourg, Huguenot Councillor, 1559, by Tortorel and Perissin.

(Philadelphia Museum of Art. Photograph by A. J. Wyatt.)

able to attempt. This is because he is so young that he must rule under the guidance of others, which has caused worse confusion than before. While they were arguing about who would run the government the fire began to rage as furiously as before, and there was no one to get it under control. When they finally chose the king of Navarre it burned all the harder and within a few months it reached its peak. Partly because of some of the king of Navarre's schemes, which I will mention later, and partly because (it must be said) he is basically a frivolous person, this king likes anything new. As for the queen mother, she lacks the self-confidence to resist [the Huguenots], and the chancellor, who is an avowed enemy of Catholicism, provides every means he can devise to bring it to ruin. Meanwhile, all the other great men of the kingdom taken together have less power than the king of Navarre has by himself. As a result a number of mistakes have been made which have gradually gotten the country deeper and deeper into trouble.

The first of these was the proclamation of a general pardon of all those who were charged with religious crimes. This should never have been done, not only because laymen have no authority in this kind of Church business, but because it was not right to abruptly undo the work of earlier kings, or to corrupt men by giving them a guarantee of impunity, or to allow them free rein to upset the kingdom. This measure led directly to the return of all the exiles, and for every one who had fled ten now arrived. As if there weren't enough Frenchmen among them to ruin the country, men also came from England, the Netherlands, Switzerland, and Italy, with the latter group including a lot of Florentines and Luccans and even a few Venetian subjects. They all began to preach here and there throughout France and while most of them were ignoramuses and had to give their sermons outdoors, still each of them had his following.

Another mistake was to allow men to speak publicly against Catholicism in the Estates and in open meetings in the presence of the king and his council. It was even worse to reduce the authority of the Church and worse still to accept disgraceful petitions and to discuss giving the heretics places where they could hold their services and meetings in their own way, and to permit them to propound their beliefs in the bishops' colloquies, as if a government ought to encourage discord and division! Of course there are times when it seems best for rulers to close their eyes and not be too strict and harsh, but there is no greater mistake than to allow men to discuss and set in motion things which can lead to dangerous changes. They soon found out how serious that mistake was because now many people who had been afraid to speak out before openly declared that they

63. French Cardinals at the Estates-General of 1560–61, by Franz Hogenberg.

(*Detail from* The Estates-General in 1561. *Prints Division, New York Public Library.*)

were members of that sect. Soon things which were freely discussed in the king's presence at court were discussed even more boldly in other places. All over the country, in every town and village, men seized images of Our Lord Jesus Christ and the saints and threw them to the ground, plundered churches, thrashed bishops and priests, broke open the prisons, insulted governors and royal officials and finally even the queen. Of many examples I could give I will only tell about one which happened at Saint Germain in full view of a crowd of people several months ago. An edict dealing with these religious matters was supposed to be issued in Rouen, and one of the Huguenot leaders had gone to the queen to urge her not to issue it. When he found that he could not change Her Majesty's opinion, he had the effrontery to put his hand on his sword and say, "Madame, if it is decided to post this edict, this sword and many others will prevent it." Even though there is a custom that anyone who puts his hand to his sword in a ruler's presence is immediately killed, this man was not punished. And what is more, the edict was not published. . . .

. . . This plague [Protestantism] has won too much ground against too little resistance. Those who could suppress it don't want to, and those who would like to suppress it cannot. That is why it has spread so far so fast and given

rise to the same evils which other countries have gone
through. I will discuss these now—not all of them, because
that would be long and boring, but the three most important
ones.

The first is that it makes men lose their fear of God, which
should be the most important form of respect they have
because it ensures order in our daily life, peace among men,
and the survival of governments and all that is important.
How can there be fear of God where men ignore divine law
and disobey the civil and religious authorities? And where
everyone dares to imagine that God is as he wants him to be,
and interprets the Holy Scriptures not according to the
ancient teachings of the Church and the Fathers but according to his own interpretation, just as if someone who could
see only a hand's breadth away wanted to measure things
that are thousands of miles away.

Another harmful effect of tampering with religion is that
it wrecks law and order and good government because it
gives rise to changes in customs and living habits and causes
scorn for laws and the authority of judges and finally even
of kings. They have already fired the judges in some parts of
France and installed new ones chosen by the rebels, and in
other places they have prevented the publishing of royal
edicts. They have started to spread the idea among the
common people in some areas that the king derives his
authority from the people, and that subjects are not obliged
to obey their ruler if he orders them to do something which
is not taught in the Bible. They are on their way toward
reducing the country to a popular government like Switzerland, and destroying the monarchy and the kingdom.

There is a third evil in addition to the other two, and this
is internal strife, rebellion, and civil war, which always
grow out of religious controversy. Many of you remember
the revolt of the German peasants against the nobles, when
more than fifty thousand people were put to the sword, and
you all know about the turmoil the Anabaptists caused in
that country more recently. We all know about affairs in
England and how much blood has been spilled in that king-

dom because of religion. And in Scotland recently the queen has had a very hard time getting her subjects to allow her to worship as a Catholic. All of which shows how the arrogance of these rebels is so great that it reverses the order of nature, and where the head once ran the parts of the body, now they give orders to the head.

Things have not yet reached such a state in France, but every day there is news of deaths and injuries and other violence all over the country. It is clear that this sect is united and has links with the Netherlands, England, Scotland, Switzerland, and other countries, and that it spends money freely and counts among its members not only preachers and ministers but also many princes and other important men who give it their support. As a result it becomes bolder with each passing day, and harder to suppress. The violence itself is all the work of the poor, who envy the wealthy and want to take over their riches. Consequently everybody is uneasy, business is coming to a halt, people don't trust contracts, and none of the merchants of Paris, Lyons, or any other place feels safe these days even in his own home. . . .

Up to now I have been dealing with the problem of religion, which has caused turmoil and confusion throughout the whole body of the kingdom. Now I will turn to two lesser developments which have happened at the same time, one in the head of this body (the king) and the other in its limbs (those who run the government). It seems as if all the ills which usually lead to the destruction of kingdoms had conspired together to ruin France.

Regarding the first, everyone knows that when one king succeeds another, changes in the kingdom always result, because it is very rare that a new king has the same ideas as the old one. In France we have seen that sons use different methods from their fathers, and lack close ties to the men who served them; the result is confusion in public affairs and resentment among private citizens. With respect to government policy what had been done is undone, and what had been started is left unfinished, and what had been planned one way is carried out differently. As for private persons, one is moved up and another is dropped, this man is favored and that one maltreated, one person raises his hopes while another loses all of his. The hopeful one always looks for ways to profit and the fearful one tries to save himself, and this kind of situation often gives rise to plots and uprisings. The less ability and power a new king has, the greater the change, and what happened with other kings because of their foolishness has happened to the present King Charles because of his tender years, and because he is like an innocent lamb who must be watched over by his guardians. It has always been considered disastrous for a kingdom to have a child king, and this is proved by the saying "Woe to you, O land, when your king is a child,"[22] which was written by one who can never lie.[23] How much worse is it, then, when that kingdom is wracked by quarrels and uprisings, weighted down with debts and poverty, and exhausted by a long and costly war, and when one child has been followed by another after their father died too early to teach them or show them how to govern.

When Francis became king he was just fifteen years old. The present King Charles was only ten [when he came to the throne], and is now twelve and a half. He certainly has a fine, noble character, behaves modestly and seriously, speaks sweetly and kindly, and has a cheerful and gracious face. He has all the qualities of a king. We can have great hopes for His Majesty if he lives long enough and does not change, and if he takes charge before things are in such a mess that he has to resign himself to a state of affairs which was produced by other men's negligence or malevolence. I said "if he lives long enough and does not change" because there are worries on both scores. Many people think he will not live long because his health is fragile and his diet is not supervised the way it should be. What is just as disturbing is a

22. Bible (Revised Standard Version), Ecclesiastes 10:16.
23. The writer of Ecclesiastes claims that he was "the son of David, King in Jerusalem," which can only mean Solomon. However, the ambassador presumably means that the whole of the Bible was inspired by God.

64. Queen Catherine de Medici, by Jacques Granthomme.

(*Museum of Fine Arts, Boston, Harvey D. Parker Collection.*)

prediction made by Nostradamus, the astrologer who for many years has foretold disasters in France, so that many have faith in him. Nostradamus has said that the queen will see all of her sons become king. She has already seen Francis and Charles do this, and there are two others, the dukes of Anjou and Alençon, respectively ten and seven years old. If she is to see them become kings of France[24] Charles will have to die soon, and that would bring the total ruin of the country. If they continue to have child kings (guided by regents until maturity) as long as that it will be too long to wait, [because they need] a king who has absolute power, is feared by his subjects, respected by neighboring countries, and well thought of by all, who could carry out some dramatic exploit that would restore the reputation and greatness of the monarch. . . .

But now I must discuss the faults of the people who are really in charge, by which I mean the queen [Catherine de Medici] and the king of Navarre. I will take up the queen

24. Some of the rest of the prediction of Nostradamus (Michel de Notredame, 1503–66) came true. When Charles died in 1574 Catherine saw the duke of Anjou (Henry III) crowned (in fact, she lived through almost his entire reign). The duke of Alençon, however, died in 1584.

first. It might seem bad enough that she is a woman, but one has to add quickly that she is a foreigner, and what is more, a Florentine and a commoner,[25] born in surroundings very different from the great kingdom of France. She does not have the prestige and personal authority that she might have if she had been born in France, or had more aristocratic blood. On the other hand, no one can deny that she is a courageous and spirited woman and if she had more experience in government and felt a little surer of herself she could accomplish a great deal. But while her husband King Henry was alive she was kept out of things, and even after King Francis took the throne it only looked as if she was ruling, while in fact the cardinal of Lorraine ran everything by himself. Her Majesty needs guidance, but because of the religious quarrels and the rivalries between the important men there is no one she trusts that she can turn to.

There are differing opinions about Her Majesty's religious views. Some importance is attached to the strong influence which Marshal Strozzi had on her—he claimed to have no religious beliefs at all. It is known that some ladies with whom she is very friendly are suspected of heresy and loose morals. It is also known that the chancellor, on whom she relies a lot, is an enemy of the pope and the Catholic Church, and that she has not shown as much goodwill toward Catholics as she should have. On the other hand, while I don't know Her Majesty's personal religious opinions, I can say that I noticed definite signs that she is not happy about the disorders in the kingdom. If she has not been as energetic about suppressing them as we would like to see, this is because she is afraid that if she uses force this will lead inevitably to civil war. I also know that she has always been glad to hear the urgings of others on this matter, especially what the signory of Venice has had to say, and has been so receptive to them that they were by no means ineffective. She tries to keep her sons Catholics and good Christians and

25. The ambassador says she was born *"in fortuna privata."* Actually her father was duke of Urbino, but the Medici were, by the standards of French royalty, parvenus.

often gets into vigorous discussions of this. So on balance I think we can approve of Her Majesty. If she does not appear to be all we would like, perhaps the reason is that she does not have as much prestige and experience as she needs. That is all I have to say about the queen.

The king of Navarre, to speak freely, is a feeble specimen. He is indeed a courteous, charming, and goodhearted prince, but he does not have the experience and common sense that are needed to meet the responsibilities of such a government. As far as experience is concerned, he had never held a government post before; all he ever tried to do is lead a life of pleasure. And as for his common sense, I think I should tell you that he wears rings and earrings, like a woman, even though he is not young any more and his beard is white; that on important matters he accepts the advice of the hoards of sycophants and fools who surround him; and that he is dominated by his wife, who can make him do whatever she wants. On the religious question he has been very shaky, leaping first one way and then another, sometimes favoring the Catholics so as to stand in well with the pope, sometimes the Huguenots so as to win a following in France, and sometimes the Lutherans in order to keep Germany friendly. True, there is a plan behind these shifts, but it betrays a character that is weak and indecisive. It doesn't pay to try to sit on more than one stool at a time. . . .

So that is how conditions are at present in France. The king is a child with no experience or power; the Council is thoroughly disorganized; and ruling power is in the hands of two people: the queen, who may be clever but is also a woman and fearful and indecisive, and the king of Navarre, who is highborn and affable but also vacillating and inexperienced. The people are obviously divided and agitated, and there is a good number of plotters and bullies who have used religion as a pretext to disturb the peace, corrupt morals and customs, ruin discipline, interfere with justice, attack the authorities, and finally endanger the king's authority and the general welfare. Compared with the way it used to be, when the greatest kings and emperors feared her,

France today is weak and ailing, and no part of the country is sound.

But now that you have heard about internal problems with respect to both the rulers and the ruled, you should also know something about the relations between this kingdom and the rulers of other countries. I will first discuss the ones that are most closely involved, who are the king of Spain, because of his nearness, and—for different reasons—the pope, the emperor, the queen of England, and the duke of Savoy. The pope is concerned because his authority and his relationship with France is threatened by this business of the religious sects. The emperor is involved because of Metz, the queen of England because of Calais, and the duke of Savoy because of the towns in Piedmont.

The king of Spain is a very powerful ruler and arbiter of the world. His lands border France in so many places that you might almost say that he surrounds it. If he had his father's spirit, and [or?] if his father had had the same opportunity he has, there would no longer be a France. This is because while those who run the government distrust him, those who hate the present regime long for him, especially the bishops and the rest of the Catholic party, who cannot look to any other quarter for help, so that if the king attacked he might well find more Frenchmen supporting than opposing him. Some believe that the duke of Guise, who has so many friends and dependents, is partial to that side [Spain] and this would be important because the duke is not only powerful and courageous, he also has a large following among the better kind of Frenchmen. Because His Catholic Majesty has shown great favor to the duke for some time now, the court distrusts him and they watch his comings and goings carefully, although nobody would dare to oppose him openly. When there was talk recently that the king of Spain was going to attack France from all sides, there was also a rumor that the duke had tried to have himself made the leader of the French Catholics so that he could fight the Huguenots. The queen, therefore, sent a gentleman to the duke's lands to ascertain whether this was true. The duke answered that it was indeed true that he had been asked to do it, but that he had declined. It may be that this has made them more suspicious of him.

So they fear the Catholic king both because he is powerful and because they think he has his own supporters in the country. It was for this reason that they decided several months ago to keep a supply of money ready for any emergency. But someone reminded them that this plan could have just the opposite effect from what they wanted, since someone in the kingdom might get his hands on the money and use it to support those it had been readied against. They dropped the idea of preparing the fund, therefore, because they did not know where it could be safely kept. They continue to irritate His Catholic Majesty by not crushing the heresy he detests so much and which he has urged and then threatened them about so often. And yet there is no sign as yet that they are making any significant [defense] preparations to use when needed. However, I have heard that the heretics have threatened that if the king of Spain makes a move they will make the whole Netherlands revolt within one day, and that they can easily do this because the area is full of members of their sect. That is all I need to say about the king of Spain. . . .[26]

26. After the next paragraph (which concerns the papacy) the report ends abruptly.

13 "NOW I WILL TURN
TO THE CAUSES OF THESE WARS"

Alvise Contarini, 1572

On a Sunday in March of 1562 the duke of Guise permitted his retainers to kill or wound a large group of Huguenot (Protestant) worshipers at Vassy in northeastern France. Civil war broke out, and though this one soon ended, two other such wars followed in the 1560s. These were fought with increasing savagery, and the intervals were scarred by plots, assassinations, and massacres of both Protestants and Catholics. Here Alvise Contarini looks back over a decade of turmoil and explains with considerable dispassion how it was that understandable—even admirable—feelings motivated the kings, the Guise, Montmorency, and Bourbon families, the lesser nobles, the Catholics, and the Huguenots, and impelled them to ever greater violence. Pervading Contarini's report is a sense of the tragedy in the sundering of a mighty Christian bulwark.

. . . Your Excellencies know, and all the histories tell us, that the French have always been among the most devoutly religious of peoples. Even before they were converted they never fought against Christians, and since they became one of the first of the distant lands to accept Christianity, more than a thousand years ago, they have constantly guarded it, more than any other kingdom or people, and preserved it

---

From a report by Alvise Contarini, 1572, Albèri, I, 4: 241–52.

65. Peasant of Champagne.
(*From Deserps,* Recueil, *1562. Prints
Division, New York Public Library.*)

without any taint of heresy. In fact, the English, Germans,
Spaniards, and other nearby peoples have often reformed
their religion on the model of French Catholicism. The
French have also proved their devotion in countless wars in
the Holy Land, Egypt, the Barbary Coast, and elsewhere
against infidels and heretics and enemies of the Church and
the authority of the popes. Proofs of their piety are easy to
see in France, because property left to the Church amounts
to more than a third and nearly a half of the wealth of that
very wealthy kingdom. And then there are the magnificent
churches and monasteries that can be seen—and there were
more before the wars—all over that enormous country. In
view of these deeds performed inside and outside of the
country on behalf of Christianity, their kings certainly
deserve their title of "Most Christian."

Now that this plague of heresy has entered the country
every province has been infected to some degree. The worst
are Guienne, Gascony, and Poitou, while the least infected
are Burgundy, Champagne, and the Île-de-France (which is
the area around Paris). As for social classes, those who live
in the countryside are almost entirely free of this sickness.

(I mean those who are free, because people in the lands of the queen of Navarre and around La Rochelle and such places all share the same religion because of fear of the authorities or other reasons. All the other [country people] are loyal to traditional, uncontaminated Catholicism.) Concerning the nobility, those who know the situation best reckon that a sixth of them or perhaps even less are Huguenots. The majority of the people who belong to this sect are artisans, such as shoemakers, tailors, and other uneducated people, because that kind of religion opens the way to liberty, or I should say license, and the way is wide open, so that there are plenty who want to follow it. Everyone is ready to listen to someone who tells him that he does not have to recognize or obey religious authorities—or maybe even temporal ones—or that he may seize the property of the churches, or that he does not have to confess things he is ashamed to mention (but was not ashamed to do), or that he may forget about vows of chastity, poverty, and obedience, or that he may eat whatever he wants at any time, or that our deeds have nothing to do with whether or not we receive God's grace.

Most of the French heretics are Calvinists[1] but every one of the infected provinces, cities, families, and even persons has at some time had some other opinion, because anyone who leaves the straight and narrow path wanders from one belief to another, and finally falls headlong to the ground. In France things have reached such a point that many who have been infected have passed from believing what is true to believing what is false to believing nothing at all. History shows that this is what has always happened to heresies.

What caused this changing of religion? I think we can blame it on bad government, and God's righteous judgment on that bad government. The heart of the matter is the distribution of Church benefices, which are all handed out by the king. This is done as badly as you can imagine. In order to have a benefice in France, all you have to do is to be the first to ask for it. Frequently they are given as rewards to

1. I.e., Huguenots.

soldiers, and many go to women. The assigning of bishoprics, which carry responsibilities for human souls, is
handled by giving them to whichever men are satisfied with
the least profit.

I think we can say that another cause has been the contacts which have always existed between France and Germany, which is very near and almost completely infected. By
"contacts" I mean the usual trade in goods that always goes
on between a country and its neighbors, but also and particularly international relations. The kings of France have
always tried to counterbalance the power of Austria and
especially of Charles V[2] by stirring up the German princes.
This may even have extended to encouraging heresy in
Germany and thwarting meetings and councils which might
have succeeded in getting that country back on the right
road. The French are afraid that if the emperors could unite
and control Germany, France would not be strong enough to
resist them. For the same reason they maintain friendly
relations with the Turks; it is not a question of goodwill but
of wanting to have a means and a tool with which to ruin an
enemy. Many souls have been lost for this reason, and we
can be sure that all those voices crying out to God have
provoked his just wrath against the kingdom of France.
This is what has led to the religious upheaval and all the loss
and destruction. More than 300,000 are believed to have died
in these civil wars, and so many churches and houses have
been destroyed that it will take hundreds of years to rebuild
them.

So that is the present state of religion in France. From
the root [of bad government] the tree of religious upheaval
has grown, and we can see the ruins which civil wars have
produced in that land. Now I will turn to the causes of these
wars.[3]

Different groups in France account for the wars in different ways. The Huguenots claim that they took action for

2. Charles had been not only king of Spain but also archduke of
Austria, Holy Roman Emperor, etc.
3. Presumably he distinguishes between a divine cause (God's
wrath, mentioned immediately above) and more visible earthly ones.

religious reasons, especially their desire for freedom of
conscience. The other side, however, claims that the Huguenots were not motivated by religion but by a thirst for
power. It will be easier to understand the truth if we make a
very important distinction. There is a difference between a
cause and an *occasion*. The *cause* is the principle which
results in the making of plans, while the *occasion* is the
opportunity to put them into execution. We can say that
there were two real causes of this uprising. One was the
hatred between the two families of Guise and Montmorency,
the latter of which is very closely related to the Châtillon
family, which the admiral belongs to.[4] The reason for the
quarrel is that the proud and powerful never get along with
each other. Just as the Roman civil wars took place because
Caesar would tolerate no one equal to him and Pompey
would have no one superior to him, so these civil wars in
France broke out because the cardinal of Lorraine wanted
no one to be his equal and the admiral and the Montmorency
family wanted no one to be above them. The other cause of
the uprising is a very important political question. The
leaders of the recent rebellion belong to the most important
families and have leading French nobles among their followers. [They knew that] a century ago the French nobility,
which guards its privileges very carefully, had rebelled
against their king in the name of the "public weal."[5] Now, it
seemed to these leaders, the kings were [again] assuming
too much authority, and they made many complaints about
this. The nobility wanted France to be a well-ordered republic, with the king serving as the head, but with his powers
carefully defined and limited by the laws of the kingdom and
the regional courts, so that he could do nothing without their
prior approval. The nobles complained that King Francis I
and King Henry especially had violated this constitution,

4. Gaspard de Coligny, admiral of France, was now virtual head of
the Montmorency family, and the Huguenot cause as well.
5. The League of the Public Weal, a conspiracy formed against
Louis XI in 1465.

particularly in the matter of gifts. And among many possible examples they singled out the cases of two gifts to women, one by King Francis to Mme. d'Étampes of more than 80,000 *écus,* and the other by King Henry to Mme. de Valentinois of more than 120,000, which he gave her on a single occasion. They also had a number of other complaints which it would take too long to mention. So these men made themselves spokesmen for the nobility and said they wanted to reform what they called "abuses" and "irregularities."

Those were the real *causes* of the rebellion, but they might not have had any effect if it had not been for two *occasions* which developed at just the right time. One was the matter of religion, which had already been causing problems for many years but now put force and courage into their opposition to the Guise family (which was their main target). There are a great many churchmen among the Guises and they have vast wealth in Church property. In the Montmorency family, on the other hand, even though there were six brothers and even though their father, the constable, had complete control of the country for a long time, he would never permit any Church property in his family. The other *occasion* was the fact that two kings, one after the other, were small boys and the queen [mother][6] was a foreigner without any real backing. This gave [the rebels] an opportunity to attend to their second objective, which was to limit the king's authority. So they took advantage of these occasions by assuming leadership both of the Guises' enemies and the religious converts, and with the excuse of the "public good" they took up arms. Seeing that they were the objects of the hostilities, the king and some generals chosen from the Guise family and their supporters naturally headed the Catholic side. The other side was led by relatives of the Montmorencys, while the heads of that family shrewdly kept themselves out of it. In order to get more support for their side from the common people they needed to have a prince of the royal blood, and they easily attracted first the prince of

6. Catherine de Medici.

66. The Shooting of Louis, Prince of Condé, on the Battlefield of Jarnac, 1569, by Tortorel and Perissin.

(Detail from Le rencontre des deux armées. *Philadelphia Museum of Art. Photograph by A. J. Wyatt.)*

Condé and his sons and then the prince of Navarre.[7] These men had already been contaminated by the new religious beliefs and they were all the more willing to join when they were reminded that they would be in line to inherit the throne after the king and his brothers.

In these wars there were Huguenots on the king's side and Catholics on the admiral's. This is because there were both "Catholics of religion" and "political Catholics," just as there were "Huguenots of religion" and "political Huguenots." The "Catholics of religion" were those who were really fighting for the Catholic faith because they wanted no

7. Louis, prince of Condé, and his older brother, Anthony of Navarre, belonged to the third great French noble family of this period, the Bourbons. They were princes of the blood, i.e., heirs to the throne should the reigning family die out.

other religion to be allowed in the country. The "political Catholics" were men who may in fact have had some heretical opinions but could not support an uprising or virtual rebellion against their great monarchical institutions[8] and felt that as loyal servants of the king they had to fight for His Majesty. By the same token, on the admiral's side the "Huguenots of religion" were those who were fighting for freedom of religion and conscience, while the "political Huguenots" were the ones who hated the Guise family and the way the king ruled, and wanted a change.

So much for France's illness and the reasons for it. In order to cure it they have tried two completely opposite kinds of remedies. One is force, by which I mean the use of iron and fire to amputate the diseased limb; the other is skill and loving care to heal it and bring it back to health. Each of these remedies has been used three times, which is why there have been three wars, followed by three peace treaties. Up to the last one (which I will discuss presently) all the wars and the peace treaties have had very little effect.

People objected to the treaties because, for one thing, they dishonored God by allowing a second religion in the kingdom beside the true Catholic one. And furthermore they dishonored the king because they were negotiated with rebellious subjects who were actually under arms, had done terrible damage to the country, and had tried to grab the king's crown from his head and even his head from his body. (On one occasion they had attacked him in the countryside).[9] Furthermore, it seemed that the hatred between these enemy families and the wrongs each had done to the other would make the treaty useless. For the king to make peace with them could only strengthen this enemy within his borders and it would be like keeping a viper under his shirt. Since the king had a just cause and more men, money, and contacts with other rulers who could help him, it seemed fairly sure that he could beat his enemies. A judge who does

---

8. This seems to be the sense of *"contra il loro re così grande."*

9. Probably a reference to an attempt to seize King Charles near Meaux in 1567.

not punish an assassin or murderer is himself guilty of an even greater crime, and by the same token the king, who was ordained by God to help the good and punish the bad, could do no less than to strike down those who rebelled against God and himself. If he did this he would be obeying God, and since God is the Lord of armies, he would surely help the king's cause. Foreign rulers—particularly the pope and the king of Spain—urged all these arguments on the king, and so did the Guises. This family had been gravely offended when the other side had killed the duke of Guise and in addition to that they wanted to stay in the government, which would have been impossible if peace was made. So they did all they could to keep the treaty from going into effect and to stir up the fighting. A number of other important nobles did the same, and so did many cities, including major ones like Toulouse and Paris. Since these cities, especially Paris, provided much of the money the king needed for fighting the Huguenots, it seemed wise to respect their wishes.

For these reasons they have fought three cruel wars. Neither side spared buildings or had any mercy on either sex or any class of people. [The Catholic side] denounced the Huguenots in speeches and proclamations as traitors and rebels against the crown, and they seized their goods, razed their houses, took away their jobs, and killed those they could get their hands on. (They hung the others in effigy.)

However, there were some who pointed out that while the king was winning victories, these had little effect, and his generals might find the future harder to control and victories harder to win. There was a great deal of dissension in the king's camp and no one could agree with anyone else. Furthermore, nothing was discussed in the royal council without the enemy learning about it immediately. The king had larger forces, but smaller armies win twice as many battles as larger ones,[10] and in this case the soldiers on the other side were a desperate, determined, and warlike lot. They had less money than he did but they used it better and managed to raise what they needed both among themselves

10. This wild generalization is probably supposed to mean only that underdogs often win.

67. Part of the Royal Army in the Battle of Jarnac, 1569,
by Tortorel and Perissin.

(Detail from Le rencontre des deux armées. *Philadelphia Museum of Art.
Photograph by A. J. Wyatt.)*

(because they had decided rather to pawn all they had than
to scant on war expenses) and from foreign rulers. (It is
known that they got money from England, Genoa, and
perhaps some places in Germany.) The king's side recognized that even if they could beat the Huguenots in future
battles they could not get rid of them, because they held
fortresses where they could take refuge. To completely wipe
them out would have been a long, hard task which would
cover the land with blood and fire and leave it so empty that
there would be a real danger that France's neighbors would
move in to occupy the vacant nest. And it did not look as if
there was any hope that the death of one of the leaders, such
as the admiral, would bring the troubles to an end, because
that same hope had been raised when the prince of Condé
died, and yet it proved vain.

In addition to seeing all these obstacles in their path, they

realized how dangerous it would be for the king and the
kingdom if a battle were lost, because it was obvious that
many would then have revealed their true feelings and
turned against His Majesty. And if the Huguenots were so
proud and confident and high-spirited when times were
tough, imagine how arrogant a victory would have made
them! Everyone knows how reluctantly the victor goes back
to taking orders from the man he has just beaten.

And here is another point. The war period produced
something which was very destructive and insidious. The
common people on both sides picked up habits of disobeying
the king, disregarding his courts, slighting his authority,
and using brute force to accomplish their ends. They enjoyed this taste of what they thought was freedom and even
started forcing changes in the form of government. In fact,
they were on their way to breaking the country down into
cantons, such as they have in Switzerland. As for the big
men of the country, the long war had the effect of pushing
certain leaders forward and aggrandizing them so that they
got big reputations among the ordinary people and too much
influence over them, as well as considerable fame in other
countries. As a result they felt much too free vis-à-vis their
king. This is a very dangerous business for a state, and can
be the seed for other civil wars, especially when you consider
the ages of the king and his brothers.

These arguments were supported by men who, either for
selfish reasons or out of genuine conviction, held that peace
would be the best thing for the country. They said, in effect,
that if there is no hope of curing a rotting leg, then of course
the surgeon has to amputate, but if there is any hope at all
and he still amputates instead of trying to heal it, then he is
a murderer. They tried to persuade the king that the sickness of the Huguenots was not incurable, since they did not
refuse to obey His Majesty, and that as far as the religious
problem was concerned, skillful management and the passage of time could accomplish a great deal. If a man has two
sons who are quarreling, they said, he doesn't urge them to
fight so as to get rid of the one he loves less and then profit
from the winner after the fight; no, he tries to make peace

between them and see that they get along together, so that they may both support him in his old age. In the same way, they said, the king should act like a loving father, and for the safety of the kingdom he should lead the wanderers back to the straight and narrow path.

All these reasons combined on two occasions and especially this last time to make them conclude a peace, except that in France they don't like to picture it as a peace between the king and his subjects. Instead they like to say that His Majesty induced his people to make peace among themselves. This is why in the peace treaty the king calls the rebels his "Good, loyal, and faithful subjects," declares them free of blame, gives them back their property and their jobs, states that the money they took from him was properly taken and was spent in his service—and consequently pays the rest of their salaries to the soldiers who served against him, and thanks the rulers who aided them. Anyone who compares the edicts and proclamations which this king issued in wartime with the ones he publishes in a time of peace will be stupefied by the contrast between them.

As I said, only the omnipotent hand of God can provide the medicines that would really help that kingdom. At present the people at court are just doing what a good physician does when he sees that a malign humor has spread through the nobler parts of a sick man's body and that he cannot completely purge it without endangering his patient's life. He tries to produce the proper condition in the man. What he hopes is that the proper foods, a change of air, and careful supervision of all the man's living habits will sap the strength and the malignity of the humor and that eventually, when his patient is healthy, he will be able to rid him completely of the humor. The court's experience seems to show that they don't have the military might to rid themselves of these religious humors. To try it would be like pitting the right arm against the left; whichever won, the king would lose, since he is the head of the body. So now they are devoting all their skills to the uses of peace, and they hope to win over one man after another and eventually get things to settle down. The approaching marriage of the

king's sister with the prince of Navarre should help, and if
the admiral or the queen of Navarre should die that too
would certainly help a great deal. In the meantime, too, the
king is getting a little older, wiser, richer, stronger, and
more popular. This is going to increase his enemies' fear of
him and his friends' respect, and one day he will carry out
the good intentions he clearly has. (I'm convinced there is no
better Christian or stauncher Catholic in France.) This will
bring to an end one of the two "occasions" of the rebellions
which I mentioned, namely the age of the king.

68. Gentleman Fowling.

(Detail from de Serres, Le théâtre d'agriculture, *1600, p. 815.
The Houghton Library, Harvard University, Cambridge, Mass.)*

Concerning the other occasion, which was religion, I'm
sorry to say that no remedies at all are being prepared. The
same abuses still exist, and may even be getting worse,
particularly because the priests (especially the bishops) are
not exhorting the people to lead the good life, and are not
setting an example for them. That is the only thing which
would keep the Catholics firmly attached to the right beliefs
and win over some of those who hold the wrong ones. It is
true that if the Catholic churchmen are not what we should
like, those on the other side—they call them "ministers"—
are much worse; they are ignorant, immoral, and self-seek-

ing. For us Catholics it is not enough not to lose ground, we must move ahead, and if the best we can do is to stay in the saddle, then we are losing. If those who once lived as Catholics cannot be gotten back on the right road, how much harder it will be to save those who are being born every day and who have never heard of the sacraments of the Church, or the mass, or the obedience we owe to religious authorities! The longer an evil exists, the harder it is to cure it. It is true that many people who used to belong to that sect are leaving it now that they realize that the admiral and the other leaders are only looking out for their own interests. Now that their ardor and fury have died down, they are losing their zeal.[11] They have resorted to paying people to go to their services in order to make it look as if they are more numerous than they really are.

The other two factors I mentioned were the hatred between the Guises and the Montmorencys, and the nobility's wish to correct what they consider to be wrongs in the way the country is ruled. As far as the second of these is concerned, the men who made an issue of it now are mostly in the government, so they are keeping quiet about that. As for the first, they are trying to handle it by reconciling the two families. That will be hard to do, but if they succeed it will certainly be a very good thing for France.

The last part of this report should be a prognosis for this illness, but as I said earlier, I want to leave that task in the hands of this wise and serious Council. You have heard me discuss the causes and the present state of the illness and the remedies that are being tried; now you will be able to draw your own conclusions. I shall certainly pray to God, as every good Christian should lovingly do, that he restore France to health. If that powerful, staunchly Christian country should change religion, all her neighbors would be in grave danger because, as I said, she is the heartland of Christianity.

11. The meaning seems to be that with the coming of peace the Huguenots had lost the sense of religious exaltation they had had during the fighting.

14 "THE WHOLE THING WAS THE WORK OF THE QUEEN"

Giovanni Michiel, 1572

During late August of 1572 there took place in Paris and elsewhere in France the slaughter of Huguenots called the Saint Bartholomew Massacre. The Huguenot leader, Admiral de Coligny, had hoped to promote internal peace in France by uniting his divided countrymen in a national war against Spain. The vigorous queen mother, Catherine de Medici, genuinely believed the plan a dangerous one for France and was also jealous of Coligny's influence over the young King Charles. Most historians agree with the ambassador Michiel that Catherine planned both Coligny's murder and the general massacre, though it seems likely that she arranged for the latter only after the first attempt to kill Coligny had failed, and when it appeared that the angry Huguenots might revive the civil wars. When word of the massacre reached Philip II he wrote to Catherine that "to hear of it was the best and most cheerful news which at present could come to me," and Michiel's government voted its congratulations. But part of the interest of the ambassador's account lies in the somberness of his assessment of this act of statecraft.

Turning to the queen [mother],[1] Admiral de Coligny said, "Madame, the king refuses to involve himself in one

From a report by Giovanni Michiel, 1572, Albèri, I, 4: 285–99.

1. All references in this section to "the queen" concern Catherine de Medici, mother of King Charles.

war. God grant that he may not be caught up in another which he cannot avoid."

By these words he meant, some say, that if they abandoned the prince of Orange[2] things might go badly for him, and there would be a danger that if the prince failed to win or was actually driven out by the Spanish or for some other reason, then he might enter France with his French and German followers and it might be necessary to drive him out by force. However, everyone understood his words in a very different sense, namely that he was giving notice that he planned to stir up new storms and renew the rioting and civil war. When the queen carefully pondered this it became the chief reason, taken together with the other considerations, why she hurried to prepare that fate for him which he eventually met.

Now that it was settled at court that the king would not make war, the admiral was confused and worried. In time of war he had all the power that went with his position and lorded it over everyone (because no one was his equal in conducting a war), and he could find jobs for all his men, let them profit from the purchasing and the booty, and help the careers of those he liked. But if there was to be no war he had to leave the court because he could not cope with his enemies, especially the queen and Monseigneur, the king's brother,[3] who had a mortal hatred for him. In contrast to the admiral, the queen was and is strongly opposed to war, not just by nature but because of her own interests; she knew perfectly well that she would have no place in a council of war and would have to stay out of the discussions. In this way she would lose her control of the government and her dominant influence over the king, which would be taken over by generals and other military men. Once she lost this power, God only knew whether she could ever regain it. This is why she has been and always will be strongly opposed to war.

2. Coligny wanted France to join the Netherlands leader, William of Orange, in fighting Spain.

3. He was the older of the king's two brothers and became King Henry III.

So now that it was certain that the king did not want war, thanks to the queen [mother's] advice, they immediately prepared for the wedding of the prince of Condé to the third daughter of the late duke of Nevers. Her mother is a sister of Cardinal Bourbon and his brothers [so that the bride] is a first cousin of the groom. These marriages were performed in the Huguenot way, and they made no attempt to get a dispensation because of the close relationship of the bride and groom. . . . After this marriage had been performed the king of Navarre[4] was married to Lady Marguerite, the king's sister, even though they had not succeeded in getting a dispensation from Rome. This took place in the cathedral of Notre Dame in Paris with all the pomp customary in weddings of kings' daughters and sisters. The groom's uncle, Cardinal Bourbon, married them using the Catholic service, but the groom refused to attend the mass and stayed in the sacristy while it was sung. Regal and magnificent banquets and festivities were held in the great Parlement building and they were attended by crowds of nobles and commoners, with as many women there as men. I had been present before at the marriages of the other two sisters,[5] the duchess of Lorraine and the late queen of Spain,[6] and if there was any difference, this wedding of the king of Navarre was even more splendid than those. . . . The wedding and the parties and balls went on for four days without stopping, from Monday to Friday, and there were still several kinds of tournaments to be held.

Then, at the dinner hour on Friday, while the admiral was returning on foot[7] from the court to his lodgings and reading a letter, someone fired an arquebus at him. The shot came from a window which faced a bit obliquely on the street, near the royal palace called the Louvre. But it did not strike him in the chest as intended because it so happened

4. Young Henry of Navarre, a Huguenot and a possible heir to the throne.
5. I.e., of King Charles IX.
6. Elizabeth, who died in 1568.
7. The ambassador's account disagrees on this point with the contemporary artist who engraved the illustration on page 233.

69. The Attempted Assassination of Coligny, by Franz Hogenberg.

(*Detail from view of Saint Bartholomew Massacre. Prints Division, New York Public Library.*)

that the admiral was wearing a pair of slippers which made walking difficult and, wanting to take them off and hand them to a page, he had just started to turn around. So the arquebus shot tore off a finger on his left hand and then hit his right arm near the wrist and passed through it to the other side near the elbow. If he had simply walked straight ahead it would have hit him in the chest and killed him.

As you can imagine, news of the event caused great excitement, especially at court. Everyone supposed it had been done by order of the duke of Guise to avenge his family,[8] because the window from which the shot was fired belonged

8. Henry, duke of Guise, believed Coligny responsible for the assassination of his father in 1562.

to his mother's house, which had purposely been left empty after she had gone to stay in another. When the news was reported to the king, who happened to be playing tennis with the duke of Guise, they say he turned white and looked thunderstruck. Without saying a word he withdrew into his chambers and made it obvious that he was extremely angry.

Great numbers of Huguenots and the admiral's friends and followers were in Paris at this time for the marriages of Condé and the king of Navarre. (I should mention that to be in Paris is the dream of every Frenchman, as if Paris were—as indeed it is—the leading city of Europe and perhaps the whole world. Frenchmen feel that life is not worth living if they cannot go there, and for years now many had not dared to go because of the disturbances.) They all hurried directly to the admiral's lodgings and even though it was not yet known whether the shot was fatal or whether he would lose the arm, they yelled and threatened that that arm of the admiral would cost more than forty thousand other arms. Some of their leaders went to where the king was dining and complained violently and bitterly. They demanded swift and stern justice and said that otherwise there was no lack of men who would provide it. Among them was a certain Captain Briquemault, who was later dragged out of the English ambassador's house, where he had hidden, and was jailed and ultimately hanged. According to what Briquemault revealed, the Huguenots assembled that same day bearing arms and came very close to carrying out a plan to march on the Louvre (where the king lives and also the duke of Guise), overpower the royal guards and any others who blocked their way, and kill the duke in his apartment. If it had come to this there would have been great danger of an all-out battle in which most of the nobility would have been killed, because there were a great many of them in both factions. In their fury the Huguenots might not have spared even the king's brothers or the king himself. But Briquemault persuaded them not to do it, or so he claimed.

To return to the admiral, after dinner the same day the king, the queen [mother], and Monseigneur paid him a visit and urged him to move to the palace, where he would be safer and more easily looked after. The king told him that he had had some of the duchess of Lorraine's rooms prepared for him. But he thanked His Majesty and said he was quite comfortable where he was. They say that after the king left the admiral told those who were with him about this offer of rooms in the palace and said, "Only a fool would let them lead him between those four walls!" But as we shall see, as long as he was in any building in the city he was already in the king's power.

All of the above happened on Friday. On Saturday the admiral's dressings were changed and the word was given out—which may or may not have been true—that the wound was not a mortal one and that there was no danger even that he would lose the arm. The Huguenots only blustered all the more, and everyone waited to see what would happen next. The duke of Guise knew he might be attacked, so he armed himself and stuck close to his uncle, the duke of Aumale, and as many relatives, friends and servants as possible.

But before long the situation changed. Late Saturday night, just before the dawn of Saint Bartholomew's Day, the massacre or slaughter was carried out. The French say the king ordered it.[9] How wild and terrifying it was in Paris (which has a larger population than any other city in Europe), no one can imagine. Nor can one imagine the rage and frenzy of those who slaughtered and sacked, as the king ordered the people to do. Nor what a marvel, not to say a miracle, it was that the common people did not take advantage of this freedom to loot and plunder from Catholics as well as Huguenots, and ravenously take whatever they could get their hands on, especially since the city is incredibly wealthy. No one would ever imagine that a people could be armed and egged on by their ruler, yet not get out of control once they were worked up. But it was not God's will that things should reach such a pass.

The slaughter went on past Sunday for two or three more days, despite the fact that edicts were issued against it and

9. The ambassador discusses this question below.

the duke of Nevers was sent riding through the city along
with the king's natural brother to order them to stop the
killing. The massacre showed how powerfully religion can
affect men's minds. On every street one could see the bar-
barous sight of men cold-bloodedly outraging others of their
own people, and not just men who had never done them any
harm but in most cases people they knew to be their neighbors and even their relatives. They had no feeling, no mercy
on anyone, even those who kneeled before them and humbly
begged for their lives. If one man hated another because of
some argument or lawsuit all he had to say was "This man
is a Huguenot" and he was immediately killed. (That happened to many Catholics.) If their victims threw themselves
in the river as a last resort and tried to swim to safety, as
many did, they chased them in boats and then drowned
them. There was a great deal of looting and pillaging and
they say the goods taken amounted to two million because
many Huguenots, including some of the richest of them, had
come to live in Paris after the most recent edict of pacification. Some estimate the number who were killed as high as
four thousand, while others put it as low as two thousand.

The killing spread to all the provinces and most of the
major cities and was just as frenzied there, if not more so.
They attacked anyone, even the gentry, and as a result all
the leaders who did not escape have been killed or thrown in
prison. It is true that Montgomery[10] and some others who
were pursued by the duke of Guise escaped to England, but
they are not major figures. And the king has terrified them
enough so they won't make any trouble.

In birth and rank the chief [Huguenot] leaders are Condé
and the king of Navarre, but they are boys who have no
followers. What's more, they are in the king's power and
might as well be in prison. It will be a long time before they
will be allowed away from the court, and they will be lucky
if they are not treated worse than they are now, especially

10. The captain of the Scotch guard who mortally wounded King
Henry II in a tournament in 1559. He led a wildly eventful life which
ended when he was beheaded and quartered in Paris in 1574.

Condé. I must not forget to tell Your Serenity that after the wounding and the murder of the admiral someone told the king that Condé was going around and making threats, so the king had him brought to him and said, "I hear you are making threats. All right! I'll have you put on the block and tell the executioner to chop off what little you have in the way of a head!" So then Condé bowed humbly and begged for mercy. This Condé is a young fellow sixteen or seventeen years old, with a face which looks proud, but also scowling and gloomy; we [Venetians] would say he has a "threatening brow." And his manners are as bad as his looks, the result of growing up during the rioting and civil wars. He looked on the admiral as an idol and a father. But there is no danger now that he or any others will raise the banner again. The Huguenots, reduced in number to two thousand, have taken up arms so as not to be slaughtered and they have gathered in their old refuge of Sancerre on the Loire River. But it won't be hard for the king to besiege them and starve them out. . . .

At present, sermons, meetings, and all other activities of the new sect are forbidden. Both nobles and commoners are returning to the Church, especially since the leading families are showing them the way. The prince of Condé and his wife have publicly abjured, and so has Mme. de Crussol (a great friend of the queen) and many other ladies. The king of Navarre has recanted and ordered that Catholicism be reestablished in his lands, monasteries set up again, and the churches allowed to have their revenues. And that's not all. The Huguenot ministers themselves, including the most important ones, want to become Catholics again! But with these men they will handle the abjurations more carefully than they did with the others.

There were two kinds of Huguenots in France. One group was made up of rebels and atheists who used religion only as a pretext and encouraged the growth of the sect because it led to wars in which they profited from the plundering and the looting and the good pay they got as soldiers and officers. These men would fight against anyone, even the king. The other kind had flocked to the new sect only because they wanted to enjoy more freedom and license, but they kept out of the riots and rebellions and obeyed the king. There is nothing to fear now from the first group because the leaders and others who could disturb the peace are all dead or being killed. The second group may not change their real beliefs but they have no choice but to continue to obey the king if they want to enjoy the presents and favors and titles he distributes. The king is an absolute ruler and just as he can shower rewards on those he likes, so he can ruin and make life miserable for those he despises and chooses to forget. The French are so constituted that they cannot and will not live anyplace but in France; they would never dream of it. They have no God but the king, and the common people fall on their knees and worship him when he passes by, just as if he were God. So we can state this as a general proposition: everywhere, but especially in France, whatever religious beliefs the king holds, his subjects must do the same.

Serene Prince, there are different opinions as to whether the death of the admiral and what was done to the Huguenots was spontaneous or planned. I think I should tell Your Serenity what I have managed to learn from some very important people who are in on the secrets of the government. I can state to Your Serenity that from start to finish the whole thing was the work of the queen. She conceived it, plotted it, and put it into execution, with no help from anyone but her son the duke of Anjou. She first had the idea a long time ago, as she recently reminded her cousin, Monsignor Salviati, who is the nuncio there. She told him not to forget and to bear witness (as he does) concerning a message she sent to him secretly to carry to the late pope. The message was to the effect that he and the king would soon see themselves avenged on the Huguenots.

This was the reason, moreover, why the queen worked so hard to arrange her daughter's marriage to the king of Navarre and passed up important marriage offers from Portugal and other quarters. She wanted to have the marriage take place in Paris, calculating that the admiral and

70. King Charles IX, by Jacques Clouet.
(*Kunsthistorisches Museum, Vienna.*)

the other important leaders on that side would attend, and that there was no better way to get them there. They say that the people who conducted the marriage arrangements had to warn her not to look so anxious to complete them, because she was giving in easily on everything the Navarre group asked for, whereas her people thought they could easily get the Navarre people to reduce their terms to whatever she wanted. But the queen answered that she did not want to quibble about details as long as they insisted firmly on having the wedding at Paris. To make sure of this point she had her daughter herself tell the king and her other brothers several times that if they wanted the marriage to take place they must not allow her to be treated as if she counted for less than her sisters. Daughters of kings, she told them, are married in Paris, and if this was not part of the agreement she would not consent to the marriage. As soon as this point was agreed on (with no opposition) the queen went ahead and planned the rest.

As for the arquebus shot, which I said was thought to have been the work of the duke of Guise, he knew nothing about it. He would never have dared to do such a thing against the king's will, because His Majesty would have

71. Henry, Duke of Guise.

(From Montfaucon, Collection, 1750, pl. 288. Libraries of the University of Pennsylvania, Philadelphia.)

taken offense, and while he might have concealed his anger for the time being he could later have done Guise and his family grave harm by keeping the duke out of his service and his favor. But as things now stand others have amply carried out Guise's vengeance for him without his giving any thought to it, and his standing and favor at the court rise higher with each passing day. He is an attractive person who is very popular with the king and everyone else, and his ardor and bravery on the battlefield have shown him to be a worthy son of his father.

They say, therefore, that the attempt with the arquebus was plotted by the duke of Anjou and the queen. And they also say, but in a whisper (and it would be best if we kept it to ourselves), that there was no Frenchman they trusted for the job, so they had it done by a Florentine officer named Piero Paolo Tosinghi. Everyone who has lived in France knows about Tosinghi, who has an outstanding reputation as a soldier, and it is known that a few days after the shooting he boasted about it to one of his cronies. The official story, however, is that it was done by a Frenchman named Maurevel, a professional marksman who once killed a famous Huguenot officer named Muy with an arquebus shot. But nothing was seen of him and he never turned up as one would have expected.

After the arquebus shot on Friday they had to arrange the rest of the business, so the queen and the duke of Anjou closeted themselves in the royal study with the king—just the three of them were there—and told him how matters stood. The queen showed him that the rebels were virtually caged within the walls of Paris, so that he had a perfect opportunity to get his revenge on them safely and easily. She pointed out that he could make up for the shame he had incurred by making peace with them and that since he had only done that out of fear and compulsion he was not obliged to live up to the treaty. Then she made him see how deceitful and treacherous the admiral had been in advising him to make war, when this would have meant ruin for a kingdom which was already exhausted and debt-ridden. She also pictured the disgust other rulers would have for him if he went to war without the slightest justification against a king with whom he had such a close family tie.[11] And she made him consider the most important point of all, that if the admiral survived, the civil war would surely resume because he and his followers would be determined to have their revenge. In short, they had to forestall him before it was too late.

With these and some other well-grounded arguments it was easy for the queen to convince the king she was right. Her task was helped by the fact that on that same day a Huguenot leader named Bouchavannes (now dead) had come to them secretly and revealed a secret Huguenot battle order. They were to assemble with all their infantry and cavalry on September 5 at Melun, which is thirty miles from Paris, and then attack the unsuspecting king and have their revenge for the injury to the admiral. So [Bouchavannes

11. Philip II of Spain had married Charles's sister Elizabeth, who, however, had died in 1568.

had said] they had better make careful preparations. This is the conspiracy which the king later told the Parlement had been discovered against the queen, his brothers, and himself, and he added his brother-in-law [Condé] and the king of Navarre [to the list of intended victims] to make the plot even more shameful.

As soon as the king had been won over by his brother and the queen, they called in the provost of the merchants, an able man named Marcel whom they knew they could rely on. They asked this Marcel how many Parisians the king could count on to help him in a time of need, and he answered that it would depend on how much time there was to get them together. "Suppose there was a month," they said; "then you could have 100,000," he told them, "or more than that if the king needed them." "If there was a week?" they asked. "A proportionately smaller number," he said. "And what if there was only one day?" "At least 20,000," he told them. They swore him to absolute secrecy and commanded him to give the same oath to the chiefs of the parishes and tell them that that same night they must order one man in each household to stay on the ready with arms and a torch. This command was carried out so carefully and secretly that no one even knew what his neighbor was doing; and precisely because no one knew the reason for the orders everyone stayed alert to see what would happen.

After they dismissed Marcel they called in the duke of Guise and gave him and his uncle (the duke of Aumale) and the king's natural brother the assignment of murdering the admiral, his son-in-law Teligny, and any followers who were with him. They told Marshal Tavannes and the duke of Nevers, both of them trusted men and great enemies of the Huguenots, to do the same to the count of Rochefoucauld (despite the fact that he was a favorite of the king) and some other important men. (I mention these details because I imagine Your Serenity will be happy to hear them.) You can imagine how delighted the duke of Guise was to be given this task, and how enthusiastically he carried it out. Since I wrote dispatches to you about this I won't go into details

72. St. Bartholomew Massacre (upper right: Admiral Coligny is thrown from window), by Franz Hogenberg.

(*Detail. Prints Division, New York Public Library.*)

about the death of the admiral—how [Guise's men] found him, and stabbed him, and, thinking he was dead, threw him out the window as the duke and the others insisted so that they could see him. The first to strike him was a German who used to be a page for the late duke of Guise, and when the admiral saw him coming near he said, "Young soldier, have pity on an old man!" I will also leave out the details about how after his murder the common people savagely defiled and abused the corpse, and how his head, hands, and genitals were cut off and he was hung by his feet at the public scaffold outside Paris called Montfaucon. You have read about all these things.

All the leaders and important men I have mentioned who lived near the court were killed at daybreak, and the ordinary people knew virtually nothing about it. But then they heard the news, and the king gave the order that all the other Huguenots in Paris should also be murdered and robbed, and things began to happen with all the fury I have described. However, many nobles and other prominent people who could pay money or promised to pay it later were rescued and hidden in the king's brothers' residences with their consent, and even in the lodgings of the duke of Guise himself. The same happened to a lot of others who were in good standing or were friends or relatives of the king's men. As for [Huguenot] noblewomen, their houses were sacked but great care was taken to spare their lives, and none of them were killed. As a matter of fact, the queen sent coaches to bring them to court and sheltered them there. The king wanted to know who were being protected and commanded that everybody report them or pay severe penalties. When he heard that two of his officers had taken a payment of twenty thousand francs to shelter a man named Cavagnes (the chief secretary of the admiral, later hanged), he ordered them to bring him the man immediately. In the presence of a crowd of people he told them, "If you don't bring him you'll pay with your own heads." So they brought him! Those who were reported were taken from their hiding places and put in several prisons, as if they were in storage, and every night they took ten or so to the river and drowned them. And that's not all. Army officers and others were sent into the countryside to kill some of the better-known Huguenots who happened to be in their houses there and plunder their belongings. It makes one think of Sulla and his proscriptions.[12]

This procedure added to the general terror, even though the king went to the Parlement after the massacre in Paris and promised that he would respect the recent edict of pacification, stop the looting and killing, and obey the country's laws and customs by prosecuting the guilty with the customary forms of trial and punishment. This was not done, however, nor is it being done now, and this is why all the Huguenots who have the means have gone to live outside France until the frenzy subsides and they can see how things will turn out. The fact is that the Catholics are just as angry as the Huguenots, not so much about the fact of the massacre, they say, as about the way it was done. That a man can be alive in the evening and dead the next morning seems to them something foreign and they say this way of doing things—using naked power and ignoring the forms of justice—amounts to tyranny. They blame this on the queen, saying that she is an Italian from Florence, and a Medici at that, and therefore she has tyrant's blood in her veins.

12. Sulla was a Roman general and dictator, 138–78 B.C., famous for his pitiless methods, which included proscription (outlawing by fiat a potential enemy, who could then be summarily executed, and his estates added to the treasury).

15 "WHAT IS HOLDING
THIS COUNTRY TOGETHER?"

Lorenzo Priuli, 1582

The Saint Bartholomew Massacre (discussed in the preceding section) provoked the fourth War of Religion, and
this was followed in dreary succession by a fifth, sixth,
and seventh before the interval of peace in which Priuli
wrote this report. What the ambassador[1] here discusses is
not the wars but the accompanying deterioration of the
monarchy, army, Church, currency, and relations between
the social classes. He nevertheless closes by stressing the
underlying strength and resilience of France. Some of his
observations seem superficial or inconsistent, but there is
much that is interesting in Priuli's attempt to explain the
apparent paradox that a country so weakened by its
internal problems could yet survive. His general optimism
was not ill founded, but France had still to undergo a
decade and a half of war before she could fully demon-
strate her powers of recuperation.

Serene Prince, it was not so many years ago that the
happiness of the people of France was proverbial everywhere—and rightly so. It wasn't just that the French had so
many natural resources and other blessings that other countries lack. Anyone who studied France more closely also

---

From a report by Lorenzo Priuli, 1582, Albèri, I, 4: 407–21.

1. Priuli served the Venetian government for many years, then
became patriarch of Venice (in 1591) and a cardinal.

discovered that it was founded on good, pious laws which were carefully obeyed. And he saw that although it was ruled by one man alone, his power was considerably regulated by the authority of the judges, especially those in the parlementary courts, and—on vital issues—by the authority of the Estates-General (the clergy, nobility, and people) ; these institutions provided an evenhanded justice and looked out for the interests of all subjects. Religion flourished in that country better than in any other part of the world, and the kings were admired and loved so much that you might almost say they were worshiped. And lastly, people of every social class and profession got along together perfectly. No one was oppressed, everyone enjoyed his property and his freedom, and there was widespread happiness and contentment. It was perfectly clear why the kingdom was so rich and powerful and it couldn't have surprised anyone to learn that the monarchy had endured for a period of nearly twelve hundred years. That's a claim that cannot be made by any empire of the past or present except the very well regulated government of this Serene Republic, which, by the grace of God, in this respect equals and perhaps surpasses France.[2]

But anyone who sees what a tragic catastrophe has taken place and how different things are from what they used to be would surely be astounded. The same form of government still exists and there are still judges just as before and the same laws and the same ordinances can still be enforced. And yet justice, government, and religion are just the opposite of what they should be, and it seems as if everything has been thrown into the worst kind of confusion. They used to blame all these woes on the civil wars that wracked the country and of course such wars always do a great deal of

2. Apparently the ambassador means that the legendary founding of Venice in 421 A.D. would make its government older than the French one started by Clovis. The implied point of the last two sentences of the paragraph is that the well-regulated, constitutional governments of the Venetian republic and the French monarchy were more durable than the usually despotic, unregulated, unconstitutional governments of empires. Of course, Venice herself ruled an empire, but the ambassador says that her type of government made her an exception to the usual rule about the governments of empires.

harm. But for several years now there has been no fighting
in most of the kingdom, and even where the war has continued to rage it seems not to have had a great impact. And
yet there continue to be serious disorders, so one has to
conclude that these problems must have other underlying
causes. For this reason I think it will be a good thing if I
spend the first part of my report telling Your Serenity about
the true state of affairs in France, and about the problems
and what has caused them. But as it becomes apparent that
there are a great many of these, and they are very serious,
everyone will wonder how a country with such problems can
stand on its feet. So I plan also to devote part of this section
to discussing the reasons for France's stability and firmness. . . .

To start with the first subject—her power—I would say
that this seems to be quite considerable. Nature showered
gifts on France, so that she has plenty of everything and can
also easily supply her neighbors. Just how well endowed she
is was never so apparent as it was during the civil wars. She
bore up so well under them that even though they lasted so
long they never hurt France the way such wars have usually
done to other countries. No place in the kingdom was ever
deserted or left unfarmed for so much as a year. It is a fact
that even though the armies always tried to lay waste the
countryside as they passed through, when several different
armed forces came along the same road during the same
year they always found ample stores of everything—just as
much the second time as the first, and just as much the third
time as the second. The same point can be made about
the tremendous wealth of the kingdom, which has always
managed to fill and refill the different kings' coffers; during
the civil wars this meant providing about ten million a year.
The provincial governors also raised money during those
wars for their needs, and soldiers applied raw force in a
variety of fantastic ways to squeeze a great deal more out of
the people. When you consider all the huge outlays the
French people have paid for and then you see how prosperous they still remain, you realize what a powerful kingdom France is.

And you will be even more impressed when you take into account how many people there are in France and what kind of people they are, because there are more than sixteen million subjects and a great number of them are bold, skilled, and seasoned fighters. These include a large number of valorous nobles whom the king can always call upon when he needs them. The kingdom can also put together large naval fleets, especially in the Atlantic, because the coasts of Normandy, Brittany, and Guienne are full of ships and bold sailors. The Mediterranean shore would also be in good shape if they put forth an effort, because there are plenty of

73. Harvesting Grapes and Making Wine.

(*Detail from de Serres,* Le théâtre d'agriculture, *1600, p. 141. The Houghton Library, Harvard University, Cambridge, Mass.*)

materials there for building galleys. [All] these assets do a lot more to make the kingdom strong than those walled fortresses which have been built on all the land and sea frontiers to block invasions by her Spanish, German, Flemish, and English neighbors.

But while France has a lot of "inherent strength" (as I would call it), it is weakened by a number of difficulties. The first of these is the king's [Henry III's] lack of concern about matters of war. He neglects all the military preparations which his predecessors used to keep up even in peacetime to protect their safety and prestige. For example, the four thousand men at arms, who in effect amount to ten thousand

74. King Henry III, by
Thomas de Leu.

*(Museum of Fine Arts, Boston, Gift
of Horatio G. Curtis.)*

horsemen,[3] are maintained on paper only; the king pays
only a small number of them and puts the money he collects
from his subjects for this purpose to other uses. There used
to be artillerymen stationed throughout the country but
these don't amount to anything now, and there are very few
soldiers in his garrisons and on the frontiers, despite the
fact that the people pay him enough money annually to
maintain fifty thousand infantrymen. Something which also
helps to lower the reputation his forces enjoy is the big
problem of money, and there are two chief reasons why this
problem has arisen. One is the king's wastefulness and the
other is the enormous number and the untrustworthiness of
the officials who handle the funds. I will make only two
points about the king's wastefulness. One is that for the past
four years His Majesty has followed the practice of putting
a million in gold in his personal coffers each year, and he
spends this just as he wants without letting the treasurers
keep any record or account of it. (The kings who preceded
him used to take at most twelve thousand *écus* and spend
them that way.) All of this money is considered entirely

3. The men at arms (heavy cavalry) were customarily accompanied
by a larger number of light cavalry.

75. Favorite of King Henry III.

(From Montfaucon, Collection, 1750, pl. 293. Libraries of the University of Pennsylvania, Philadelphia.)

given[4] to him and the treasurers keep no records of it. The other point is that it has been calculated that during these same four years His Majesty has given more than four million in gold to just four of his favorites—and only two of them are in good standing with him now! As for the problem caused by his officials, this has gone so far that it is said to be a fact that the king receives only half his revenues. The other half trickles into the officials' hands by various means, some legal and some not. This grave situation causes the kingdom considerable harm; in order to provide for the king's regular and special expenditures they have to raise new, unprecedented taxes and create new offices which they can sell. . . .

The other thing which lowers the country's strength are the rivalries and quarrels and the fact that the people have

4. A very unsure translation of: *"e questo denaro è donato tutto."*

little love for their king. When I say "little" I mean in comparison to the great devotion they used to have for his predecessors. It's easy to understand why this is the case in the light of the difficulties I have just finished discussing and also what I will be talking about when I discuss matters of government and justice.

Concerning the rivalries and quarrels in the kingdom I can report this: While it is true that the civil wars and the disturbances resulting from them have ended, the religious disagreement is still very much alive. Furthermore, the Huguenots still control some important places in the kingdom and this could sometime lead to real trouble. Another important point is that there are many vendettas between the great families, among which the most important is that between the Guises on one side and Condé and Navarre on the other.[5] And in addition to that there are now very bad relations between the nobility and the common people, who are tyrannized and oppressed by a great number of poor gentlemen who want to feed and dress themselves and live an easy life at the people's expense. This abuse has spread wildly, especially in places far from the court, and there is not much hope of doing anything about it. There are great numbers of these poor gentlemen in France because first-born sons inherit the major portions of the estates. To some extent they are forced to live this way because they can't make a living in the companies of men at arms now that these are no longer paid. But during the civil wars they also got used to living a very easy life with all the expenses heaped on the back of the poor—on the "good man," as they say in France.[6] But despite all these evils the people never hold back whenever they have a chance to show their ancient, heartfelt affection for the French crown. Whenever they have had an opportunity to help the cause of the monarchy they have shown that they are ready and willing and obedient to the king.

5. Condé and Henry, king of Navarre were the leaders of the very important Protestant Bourbon family. Seven years later Henry became King Henry IV of France.

6. "Jacques Bonhomme" (James Good Man) is a personification of the French peasant.

Those are my observations about the strength of France. I have left out a number of other points which I consider superfluous.

Now I come to the subject of religion. To begin with the clergy, I can report that their temporal affairs are in excellent shape. They collect all their temporal revenues (except those from the Béarn area, which is under the king of Navarre, so that the revenues go to him) and these revenues have increased a great deal because the value of goods all over France is at least double what it used to be. However, it can't be said that the spirituality of the clergy has doubled. There are many abuses and a great deal of confusion which result from the fact that they have no interest in doctrine, or morality, or living in residence and caring for souls. Bishoprics, abbacies, priorships, parish churches, and every other kind of Church appointment have all been made venal and are publicly bought and sold. Although this abuse is at its peak now, it began not recently but many years ago. This was the reason why it was so easy for the ministers sent from Geneva and elsewhere to import so many new and heretical ideas into France—the Catholic clergy had lost their public esteem. To tell the truth, it's amazing that

76. Prior of a Monastery.

(From Deserps, Recueil, 1562. Prints Division, New York Public Library.)

things are not worse than they are. They have given very
little attention to the problem, and yet by the grace of God
the number of Huguenots has decreased by seventy percent.
And the Catholics are showing a religious zeal and fervor
that is amazing to see; in Paris particularly the churches
are packed with people from morning to night. But it is the
common people who are pious, not the aristocrats. (The
truth is that it would be a good thing if the aristocrats were
more generally respected than they are.)

The main cause of the difficulties is said to be the im-
proper distribution of bishoprics and abbacies, which the
king and other people who have his permission casually
assign to completely unqualified people, including as many
women as men, and as many Huguenots as Catholics. These
bishops and abbots enjoy the incomes and hire poor priests
to carry out their spiritual duties for them, and they give the
priorates and churches to their servants, who sell them
openly and without the slightest embarrassment. It's no
surprise that the poor priests who carry out the actual work
of caring for souls are forced to earn their livings by publicly selling the administration of the sacraments.

This abuse has gone so far that they say it would be very
hard for the king to correct it even if he wanted to. There
are people at court who for years have been waiting to be
given various positions and titles which they were promised
as rewards for service to the crown. If the king should
decide to change the way these posts are awarded they would
raise a terrible outcry and call it unfair to abolish the old
pattern of rewards and payments. . . .

That part of the system of justice that has to do with the
distribution of jobs, honors, and salaries,[7] and which is all
in the king's hands, is very unfairly handled and gives rise
to a great deal of dissatisfaction. While he has been enriching and aggrandizing a few of his best-loved courtiers and
their followers, the king has virtually forgotten about all the
others. Even though the kingdom is badly pinched for funds,

7. The ambassador is speaking of "distributive justice," a phrase
little used today.

he is determined at any cost to get money to lavish on these [favorites]. So he has had to cut down on the pay of the cavalry, thus vitally affecting the interests of a great many French gentlemen. He has held up payments of funds to many people who are supported or salaried or pensioned by the crown . . . and he has suspended payments to many of the crown's creditors. And finally he has levied a number of taxes and is having to neglect many of the country's needs in order to keep up his enormous extravagances.

Now let us turn to the subject of ordinary justice. I would like to ask Your Serenity and Your Excellencies to imagine what it must be like when all judicial positions, large and small, are bought and sold, and when the number of officials has multiplied until there are sixty thousand of these harpies scattered through France. These judges and their assistants have increased their salaries, bribes, travel expenses, and such things twenty or thirty times over, and they have turned their positions into business ventures and squeeze the maximum profit out of everything they do. There is no doubt that anyone in France who wants to make a good investment with his money invests it in an office.

77. Judge of a French Court.

(From Deserps, Recueil, *1562. Prints Division, New York Public Library.)*

In former times the poor, long-suffering people could turn to the courts when they were treated unjustly or when the government behaved criminally. And there they found well-born men with high principles who would help them if they were oppressed, and who would serve as go-betweens to take care of those problems that often arose when trusted counselors gave harmful advice to the kings. The ancient customs of the government require that any decisions the king makes about serious and important matters must be approved by the Parlement [of Paris] before they can be put into effect. But now that the offices are sold, persons of quality don't want to buy their way into these parlements and as a result they are filled by baseborn men who have neither the courage nor the personal authority to stand up to the king's chief ministers and serve the common good. It used to be, too, that when the kingdom was wracked by really serious disorders some relief could be obtained by the summoning of the three Estates-General (the people, the nobility, and the clergy), where subjects could tell the kings about their sufferings and have their needs taken care of. For their part, the kings made skillful use of these meetings to get what they needed from the people, so all in all this was a very effective instrument for preserving the affection between the kings and their subjects. But the periods between meetings have grown longer and longer and this is especially so now that so many abuses have crept into the government of the country and particularly because of the taxes which have been levied on the people in violation of their rights. It seemed to be a waste of time, and even dangerous, to listen to all the people's complaints when there was nothing [the king and his ministers] could do or would do about them. Now that the abuses have gotten so bad that they are to be found throughout the whole body of the country, the [government] dreads the Estates and people who talk about them are considered to be rebels. Many of the king's chief ministers claim that if the Estates assembled they might be so zealous to put matters in order that they would put the king under their supervision, but no doubt it is their own involvement in past and present wrongdoings that makes them talk this way. A meeting of the Estates would probably result in steps to prevent corrupt ministers from enriching themselves so easily in the future. The Estates would also force the usurpers to return what belongs to the crown and they would demand a detailed accounting of their administration from the men who have managed the finances and the royal treasury. (A number of men have made large fortunes this way in a period of very few years.) . . .

The king badly lacks good counselors. This is partly because most of them are looking out chiefly for themselves and partly because the king seems uninterested in employing capable, wellborn men who could do good work for him. He has formed the habit of discussing all important questions only with his mother and the government secretaries. The members of the Council of Affairs—cardinals, princes, and others—meet in the same room at the same time but they usually take no part in the discussions. The king and the queen mother sit together in one part of the chamber and none of the councillors comes near to them unless he is summoned, which happens very rarely. But it isn't only them that he leaves out; sometimes he does the same thing to his mother by reversing decisions which were made in her presence—and doing this without even consulting her. They say he does this partly because he is by nature very daring about making decisions and has a lot of confidence in his judgment, and partly also because his favorites have a lot of influence with him and he privately discusses all his affairs with them in his chambers. The queen has complained to him about this several times with no success and realizes he won't change, so now she hides her feelings and deals with the king very cautiously in order not to irritate him.

Serene Prince, I have sketched a true likeness of the kingdom of France as it is today, and the picture is filled with so much confusion and wrongdoing that it must seem as if no part of the country is sound. I know Your Excellencies will be asking, What is holding this country together, if it is threatened on all sides by disaster? It will be a good thing if I try to satisfy your curiosity on this score.

I can report on the basis of observations I made during

my embassy that there are several general reasons why the
kingdom still stands and several particular ones. The first of
the causes is the great size of the kingdom, since experience
shows us that large, inherently strong apparatuses will hold
together even if they are beaten and subjected to terrible
strain. The second general cause is the self-interest of all
these people involved in the wrongdoing I talked about. They
do for the kingdom what ivy does for a wall: once it has
broken it and worked its way all through it so that the wall
can no longer stand alone, the ivy itself holds it and keeps it
from falling down. And that is what these people do who
have brought all her troubles on France; having ruined the
country with all the crimes they have committed, now they
try to keep it going in their own interest. The third and final
general cause is that apparently the country cannot be
ruined either by her own people or by the rulers of other
countries. I say not by her own people because we know
from experience that even though the French have done all
they could for many years to ruin their country, they have
not succeeded. The chief reason for this is that although they
are very quick to revolt to achieve their individual purposes,
they still want to have a great monarchy, because that is
what their own importance as individuals depends on, and
they want to be ruled by a great king. As for foreign rulers,
the country is so large, so united, and so strong that there is
no king in the world who would dream of invading it. The
French are peculiarly hostile not simply to foreign rule, but
even to the very mention of foreigners.

Now I will turn to the specific reasons why the kingdom
still stands. These have the effect of counteracting the specific difficulties that I mentioned above. For example, while
the king pays little attention to military questions, this is
made up for by the natural strength of the country, the fact
that it contains as many soldiers as there are in all the other
parts of the world,[8] and the fact that the nobles find it in

8. This is of course a gross exaggeration, but we should keep in
mind that by "the world" the ambassador means Europe, and that
the population of France was more than twice as large as that of
Spain, three or four times as great as that of England and Wales,
and as large as all the "German" states put together.

78. Peasant Woman Going to Market.

(From Deserps, Recueil, 1562. Prints Division, New York Public Library.)

their own interest to stay prepared for cavalry warfare. The financial difficulties are compensated for by the country's enormous wealth and the great obedience and respect the people have for the king, which leads them to pay him all they are commanded to.

As for the Catholic religion, one thing that keeps it going is the French aristocracy's involvement with the Church's worldly property; many of them support Catholicism in order to preserve this property. This tendency is complemented by the Frenchman's ancient and inborn attachment to the Catholic religion. And lastly there is the example set by the king, who loves and supports the Catholic religion just as his predecessors have always done.

The divisions in the kingdom are counteracted by the king's wishes and his power, because he wants to do and is doing all he can to bring peace to the whole country. While the people don't love the king, this is made up for by his power over them and the fact that everyone for one reason or another respects him.

And lastly, the people manage to put up with all those corrupt ministers. This is partly because the king backs them up and wants them to be obeyed (since he sold them their offices and titles) and partly because there are so many of them and they have such control over the parlements (which are the country's high courts) that everyone is afraid of them.

So those are the supports that hold up the country. Without them France, which is wracked by so many problems, could easily fall in ruins.

There is one other item Your Serenity should know about so that you can deliberate on this first and very important topic. The king has been told many times that the people are dissatisfied with the present regime and that they have held secret meetings and threatened to rebel and use armed power to force him to summon the Estates-General and correct all the wrongs. It's quite true that the people have considered taking such a step and still are because they are very disaffected. So it will be worth our time to ask why it is that a people who have not only studied but mastered the art of rebellion don't take up arms to right their wrongs, especially since there is no other way they can get the reforms they want. I would say, Serene Prince, that the chief reason is the hostility between the Catholics and Huguenots, who could never reach agreement on a matter as serious as this and cannot trust each other. . . . A second consideration is that they have no leaders who could take charge of such a major undertaking. The Catholics, who are by far the larger group, would never put this kind of business in the hands of the Huguenot leader. As for Catholic princes who could take such a lofty responsibility,[9] the only ones who are talked about are Monsieur,[10] who, however, is too busy with affairs in the Netherlands, or a prince of the Guise family. But they have all stayed on very close terms with His Majesty even when they were exasperated with him, and they will never desert him because they consider it in their interest to have him on their side against the king of Navarre and the prince of Condé.

9. Presumably the leader of a successful revolt would become king.
10. The king's troublemaking younger brother, the duke of Alençon. At this time he was fighting on the Protestant side in the revolt of the Netherlands against Philip II of Spain.

There are a number of other reasons why the nobles and the people hold back from undertaking such a thing. One is that there are many who are sorrier for the king than the country, and feel that he inherited a lot of problems caused by the civil wars which he can't solve all at once. Others love the king because he is very goodhearted and neither vindictive nor cruel. Then there are many who are grateful to him because of past favors he has done for them and many others who hope to benefit in the future from his superabundant generosity. And finally there are those who don't have these concrete reasons but who just go on hoping that time will take care of the problems either by cutting short the king's life (astrologers have warned of this) [11] or by the passage of years, which usually change the lives and views of kings just as they do to ordinary men. From time to time the king has given some sign that he wants to change his outlook and his way of life and devote more effort to serving his kingdom.

11. See page 211 for the predictions of Nostradamus. A monk stabbed Henry III to death seven years after the ambassador read this report.

16 "HE ROSE LIKE A PHOENIX
FROM THE ASHES
OF THAT HUGE KINGDOM"

Pietro Duodo, 1598

The Valois dynasty, which had ruled so feebly for three decades, died out at the end of the War of the Three Henrys. Henry of Guise, leader of the Catholic party, had virtually deposed the weak King Henry III, whereupon the latter had Guise and his cardinal brother murdered, and took refuge in the Huguenot camp. There a monk who believed himself a divinely appointed agent stabbed him to death. Henry of Navarre now became King Henry IV of France, but it took him nearly a decade to defeat the Catholic League and to drive out the Spanish troops which King Philip II of Spain had sent to aid the Catholic side. To unite France behind him, Henry had meanwhile become a Roman Catholic. In 1598, when Duodo wrote this report, Henry had brought the wars to an end and issued the Edict of Nantes, which reconciled the Huguenots, his former coreligionists, to his rule. Duodo's report glows with satisfaction over the restoration of peace to a great Catholic land, and with admiration for the gallant and magnetic Henry IV. It suggests the vitality of the institution of monarchy in this period, and it foreshadows the major role a revived France would play in seventeenth-century Europe.

From a report by Pietro Duodo, 1598, Albèri, app., 76–205.

Ever since the house of Austria[1] rose to such power in the Christian world, France has been a country which weaker rulers have wanted to have as an ally. But while these lesser powers counted on her survival, the bigger ones aimed to destroy her in order to rid themselves of an obstacle on their road to universal monarchy.[2] This is why they have tried so hard for so many years to defeat and destroy her, both by attacking her from outside her borders and by [encouraging] internal civil wars. It may seem as if it is the fate of only that majestic kingdom which is at stake, but it is on that battlefield that it will be decided whether or not all the rest of Christianity is to sink into miserable subjection.[3]

Under her former kings France reached the point forty years ago where she was the protector of her friends and the scourge of her enemies. But the three brothers,[4] all of whom are now dead, left her in such a state that one could only weep over her fall, and never dream that he would ever see her rise again. It may have been because two of them[5] were such little boys when they came to the throne that they were easy victims for their enemies' schemes, or it may have been that an insatiable thirst for power excited many men to the point where they could think only of their own interests. But in any case this much is true, that by the time of Henry III's death (he was the last of that branch of the family) the kingdom was like a body torn into a thousand pieces, and nothing was left of its former splendor. There was nothing but war, fire, bloodshed, selfishness, contention, quarreling, suspicion, insolence, mutiny. Wherever one looked he saw horrible scenes of barbaric cruelty, and houses razed to the ground, castles burned, churches profaned, entire villages destroyed. In short, no evil had been left undone and there was nothing left for their fury to rage against.

1. The ambassador has in mind the two branches of the Hapsburg family, one in central Europe and the other in Spain.
2. *"Monarchia."* From the context it appears that he means "universal monarchy."
3. To the Hapsburgs—chiefly those of Spain.
4. Kings Francis II, Charles IX, and Henry III, who reigned from 1559 to 1589.
5. Francis and Charles.

Despite all of this, God chose not to abandon France. On the contrary, it was just when her miseries were at their worst and just when fears that she would sink under the storm-tossed waves of civil war were greatest—precisely at that point that she rose again. She had been given King Henry IV as her monarch and ruler.

He rose like a phoenix[6] from the ashes of that huge kingdom, abandoned by those who were near him and pursued by those who were far away and wept over by his friends and fought against by his enemies. With marvelous and incredible skill and luck, sometimes striking, destroying, and trampling, other times forgiving, embracing, and treating those who surrendered with kindness, humanity, and clemency, he has arrived in glory on the throne. Now it is he alone who can put power and wisdom to work to revive hopes—which had almost vanished for a while—of restoring his country to its former splendor.

God endowed France with such remarkably fine resources that I'm certain that if that land could enjoy them in peace there would be nothing like it in the world. But the French have never learned to live in peace with each other or with their neighbors, and they have fought countless foreign and civil wars. Often, perhaps, it was not so much a consuming drive to rule others that got them into these wars as it was their hope of winning honor and glory, and this is why they have been more valorous in acquiring lands than careful about holding on to them. However, if the torments they have gone through and the want and poverty they have fallen into have driven them to make peace with each other at present, it may be that they will remain at peace for a while—at least for as long as they still remember what they have suffered. Certainly there is not a house, not a man, not even a plant, a stump, or a rock which the evils of war have not struck, beaten, and trampled. At present virtually every-

6. The phoenix is a mythical bird of Arabia, the only one of its kind, which is fabled to live five or six centuries, then burn itself on a funeral pyre, rise renewed from the ashes, and go through another cycle of life.

79. Henry IV Entering Paris.

(*From Montfaucon, Collection, 1750, pl. 297. Libraries of the University of Pennsylvania, Philadelphia.*)

one wants peace, and the king more than anyone else, since
more than any he is still the target of his enemies' greed and
ambition. . . .

His Christian Majesty's father was Anthony de Bourbon,
a prince of the blood royal of France, who had married
Jeanne d'Albret, the only daughter and heiress of Henry,
king of Navarre, and Marguerite, the sister of King Francis
I. Anthony was entitled king [of Navarre], just as his son
was after his death. His Majesty was born on December 13,
1553, and is now in his forty-fifth year. He had an older
brother who died young, so his father, who blamed the boy's
death on the fact that his mother had raised him too deli-
cately, had His Majesty brought up in the kind of privation
that the son of the wretchedest subject might know, not at
all like the great prince that he was. Often he made him
walk with bare feet and go bareheaded in the wind and rain
and—as if he foresaw how much he would have to endure—
he hardened him so that now there is no one who can endure
more and mind it less than he does. He has reached the point
where he doesn't even have any special time when he sleeps;
he rests during whatever time is left from his other occupa-
tions and amusements. At any hour, whenever and wherever
he wants to, in bed or on straw or on the bare ground,
clothed or not, armored or not, before or after eating, he can
sleep perfectly soundly, and three or four hours are all he
needs. Often during the wars he had no bed to sleep on and
nothing to cover himself with. When that happened he put
his big cloak on the ground and had one page lie down
crosswise so that he could rest his head on him and two
others by his sides and the same number on top, and thus
equipped, he slept soundly.

He is not tall, but I wouldn't say he is short either, and he
is lean, which makes it easier for him to put up with discomforts. His face is grave and handsome, with an aquiline nose
and big flashing, piercing eyes which reveal his lively
spirits. It is this high-spiritedness which makes him impa-
tient with anything long and boring and especially fond of
anyone who tells him briefly and frankly what is on his

mind. With his keen intelligence he quickly understands the drift of a conversation and he suffers torments if the person he is talking to takes forever to finish what could be put into a few words. . . .[7]

He hates the work of ruling just as much as he loves that of making war, so he has had the constable[8] come to court so that he can unload it on him. As a result the ministers now have a great deal of authority, and many matters are left to them to settle, which was not true in former times. On the other hand, it's true that there was never a group of ministers more afraid of speaking freely before their master, because he often yells at them in his most pungent vocabulary when he doesn't like what they say. Many times the public interest and his own suffer for lack of good advice that could have been given him.

What His Majesty is most alert against is any little thing that could endanger what he has set his heart on, which is the peace of his kingdom. When he hears of plans for secret meetings, leagues, and alliances he uses a thousand different schemes and maneuvers to block them, no matter which of the parties[9] is involved. He never fails, however, to keep up the appearance of loving everyone. Without stooping from his kingly dignity (which he owes to God and nature and his own prowess), he nevertheless treats everybody so affectionately that at the same time that fear constrains them, love impels them to stay within bounds. . . . Almost by main force he has won over the stubborn souls of the rebels. The same men who were fiercely hostile to him, and shouted to the whole world that they had not been paid off[10] as they should, end up by saying, "Despite all these things we can't hold back from following him and serving him. It is as if we

7. The ambassador probably makes this point for the benefit of members of the Venetian Senate who might conceivably serve as ambassadors to France.

8. Probably a reference to the duke of Sully, Henry IV's very able minister. However, Sully never held the position of constable.

9. Catholic or Huguenot.

10. Probably a reference to Henry's practice of bribing powerful governors and military leaders to keep the peace.

80. "Henry IV, By the Grace of God King of the French and of Navarre, at the Age of 40," by Hendrik Goltzius.
(National Gallery of Art, Washington, D.C., Rosenwald Collection.)

are drawn by some mysterious hidden quality which we cannot resist and which compels us to join with him." All this despite the fact that there may never have been a king who rebukes the nobility as harshly as he does when they don't do what they should. It is just when they are moved and saddened by such rebukes that many of them say the things about him that I have mentioned.

When it comes to making war, which is the real calling of a great captain and king, he has no match in Christendom,

nor has there been one for a long time. You can't imagine
how fine and brave he is. What flutes and violins are to other
men, drums and trumpets are to him, and the field of battle
is his ballroom. Like a Lacedaemonian *agis*,[11] he has never
been known to ask how many of the enemy there are but
rather where they are. If he had his way and were rid of the
problems I have mentioned, he would stay continually with
his armor on his back and his sword in his hand, because
fighting is really his vocation. He moves fearlessly under
arquebus and cannon fire without giving it a thought and as
gaily as if he were going to a wedding, and he often takes
greater risks than he should [when you consider his impor-
tance] to Christianity and the preservation of his country.
Those who have seen it say that in battles and tournaments
he always arrives first, in a state of ecstasy, at the enemy's
front lines or at the place where the fighting is thickest and
the danger greatest. They say there is nothing more terrifying than the sight of His Majesty armed and mounted and
with his sword drawn in combat, for then he rises from his
stirrups, leans forward from his saddle until his head is over
that of his horse, and with his eyes flashing blood and fire
and his mouth frothing and his expression horrifying, he
thrusts and hurls himself against his enemies like a snake,
and when he leaves the battle he is always covered with his
enemies' blood. During the fighting he is merciless and
terrifying, but once it is over he is the kindest and most
humane of men—one who would not allow you to slap a page
or a lackey. A Spaniard who was in Rome after he had been
freed was asked what kind of man the king was. He answered, and rightly, that he was a God when pardoning but
a devil when fighting.

The fact that the king sets such [a warlike] example is
very important, but it is also true that it is something that
you look for and praise in a soldier or an ordinary officer,
but not in a great king like His Majesty. He knows this and
apologizes for it. But as he said to me at Lyon, the only coin
with which he can pay his soldiers is the example he sets for

11. The term for the ancient Spartan kings.

them, and if he did not provide it, he would lose his troops and be unable to defend his country. Nor would any noble put on his breastplate if he did not see that the king had already armed. So that is why the king has had to do this in so many of these wars and suffer even when he wasn't needed.[12] When you consider the necessity, and balance it carefully against the dangers, you have to give him great credit for doing what he does.

Never was there a commander who was better than he at choosing the field of battle, ordering his troops, and knowing where to attack at just the right moment to win the day. This ability especially has made him win many battles and succeed in a lot of risky ventures. He has always had really amazing good luck. Many Frenchmen claim they have seen a figure in white who hovers over him in battle and helps and protects him—certainly this much is true, that the things he has accomplished seem more godlike than human. On one occasion I remarked to Madame, the king's sister, that His Majesty performed deeds which not only put his life in danger but for which he would certainly never be honored, because the living, who know about them, can scarcely believe them, and posterity, who will read about them, will not believe them at all.

12. An apparent contradiction. Presumably the ambassador means that in these battles Henry was not needed to command the army but he was needed to set the necessary example for the troops.

SUGGESTIONS
FOR FURTHER READING

Readers whose interest in early modern Europe has been whetted by the Venetian ambassadors' reports may want to look further into some subjects. The books suggested below are both reliable and (in most cases) readable. For more comprehensive lists see the bibliographies in any one of these books: H. G. Koenigsberger and George L. Mosse, *Europe in the Sixteenth Century* (1968); J. H. Elliott, *Europe Divided, 1559–1598* (paperback, 1968); or Richard S. Dunn, *The Age of Religious Wars, 1559–1689* (paperback, 1970). All of them provide good narratives of the age of Philip II.

To know the Venetian ambassadors one must first know Venice. The third and fourth volumes of the English version of Pompeo Molmenti's masterly social and cultural history (*Venice* . . . , 6 vols., 1906–1908) offer a good survey of Venetian Renaissance society, while the paintings of Titian, Tintoretto, and Veronese tell a great deal about the physical appearance of the ambassadors' world and about their interests. (See Bernard Berenson, *Italian Paintings of the Renaissance, Venetian School* (2 vols., 1957, vol. 2.) The first chapter of James C. Davis, *The Decline of the Venetian Nobility as a Ruling Class* (1962) is a discussion of the structure and activities of the ambassadors' social class, or caste, in the sixteenth century. William J. Bouwsma's *Venice and the Defense of Republican Liberty; Renaissance Values in the Age of the Counter Reformation* (1968) is an excellent recent study of politics and ideas during the period dealt with in this book.

Garrett Mattingly's admirable *Renaissance Diplomacy* (paperback, 1964) enables one to see the Venetian ambassadors against the background of the general development of diplomacy.

Perhaps the most intellectually exciting and influential book on the latter sixteenth century is Fernand Braudel, *La Méditerranée et le monde méditerranéen à l'époque de Philippe II* (rev. ed., 1966; an English translation will be published by Harper & Row). Braudel is interested in physical geography, the destinies of social classes, changing "mentalities," and comparative history involving large areas, and he raises speculative question after question.

Of the books in English on what the ambassadors considered "The strongest and safest Christian land," perhaps the best is J. H. Elliott's *Imperial Spain* (*1469–1716*) (paperback, 1963), in which the author has fresh things to say about Spain's moment of greatness and the reasons for her later decline. John Lynch, *Spain Under the Habsburgs* (1964) is also good and R. Trevor Davies, *The Golden Century of Spain, 1501–1621* (paperback, 1954) is old but very readable. Garrett Mattingly's *The Armada* (paperback, 1962) reads like a novel and was awarded a Pulitzer citation. *Don Quixote,* by Philip II's great subject Miguel de Cervantes Saavedra, illustrates Spanish values unforgettably, as do the canvases of the painter El Greco (1541–1614). (See L. Goldscheider's excellently illustrated *El Greco,* 1954.)

On Turkey, Albert H. Lybyer's *The Government of the Ottoman Empire in the Time of Suleiman the Magnificent* (1913) still fully rewards a reader's investment of his time. Lybyer drew heavily on the Venetian ambassadors' reports. Edward S. Creasy, *History of the Ottoman Turks* (reissued, 1961) is old but a useful summary. H. A. R. Gibb and Harold Bowen, *Islamic Society and the West,* vol. 1, 2 pts. (1950–57) is authoritative but dry. Bernard Lewis, *Istanbul and the Civilization of the Ottoman Empire* (1963) is a brief, interesting survey by a distinguished historian. Ogier Ghiselin de Busbecq's *Letters to the Holy Roman Emperor Maximilian* (1962) are the charming and thoughtful work of the Holy Roman Empire's ambassador to Sultan Suleiman.

On France there is no counterpart in English to Elliott's and Lynch's excellent general books on sixteenth-century Spain. On political history there is James W. Thompson's *The Wars of Religion in France, 1559–1576* (1909) and J. E. Neale's little *The Age of Catherine de Medici* (paperback, 1962). On cultural history see Werner L. Gundersheimer, ed., *French Humanism, 1470–1600* (paperback, 1969), an anthology of articles. Donald F. Stone, Jr.'s *France in the Sixteenth Century: A Medieval Society Transformed* (paperback, 1969) aims to provide a historical background for French Renaissance literature. One should be sure to turn to the writings of a great contemporary of the Venetian ambassadors, Michel de Montaigne. His essays reveal the outlook on all aspects of life of an unusually warm, candid human being. They can of course be read as they stand, but Marvin Lowenthal has created from them a remarkably absorbing ersatz *Autobiography of Michel de Montaigne* (paperback, n.d.).

INDEX

Format by C. Linda Dingler
Set in Century Expanded
Composed by American Book—Stratford Press, Inc.
Printed and bound by Murray Printing Company.
HARPER & ROW, PUBLISHERS, INCORPORATED

Revised January, 1970

hARPER ⚜ ⊤ORCHBOOKS

American Studies: General

HENRY ADAMS Degradation of the Democratic Dogma. ‡ *Introduction by Charles Hirschfeld.*   TB/1450

LOUIS D. BRANDEIS: Other People's Money, *and How the Bankers Use It. Ed. with Intro, by Richard M. Abrams*   TB/3081

HENRY STEELE COMMAGER, Ed.: The Struggle for Racial Equality   TB/1300

CARL N. DEGLER: Out of Our Past: *The Forces that Shaped Modern America*   CN/2

CARL N. DEGLER, Ed.: Pivotal Interpretations of American History
     Vol. I TB/1240;   Vol. II TB/1241

A. S. EISENSTADT, Ed.: The Craft of American History: *Selected Essays*
     Vol. I TB/1255;   Vol. II TB/1256

LAWRENCE H. FUCHS, Ed.: American Ethnic Politics   TB/1368

MARCUS LEE HANSEN: The Atlantic Migration: 1607-1860. *Edited by Arthur M. Schlesinger. Introduction by Oscar Handlin*   TB/1052

MARCUS LEE HANSEN: The Immigrant in American History. *Edited with a Foreword by Arthur M. Schlesinger*   TB/1120

ROBERT L. HEILBRONER: The Limits of American Capitalism   TB/1305

JOHN HIGHAM, Ed.: The Reconstruction of American History   TB/1068

ROBERT H. JACKSON: The Supreme Court in the American System of Government   TB/1106

JOHN F. KENNEDY: A Nation of Immigrants. *Illus. Revised and Enlarged. Introduction by Robert F. Kennedy*   TB/1118

LEONARD W. LEVY, Ed.: American Constitutional Law: *Historical Essays*   TB/1285

LEONARD W. LEVY, Ed.: Judicial Review and the Supreme Court   TB/1296

LEONARD W. LEVY: The Law of the Commonwealth and Chief Justice Shaw: *The Evolution of American Law, 1830-1860*   TB/1309

GORDON K. LEWIS: Puerto Rico: *Freedom and Power in the Caribbean. Abridged edition*   TB/1371

HENRY F. MAY: Protestant Churches and Industrial America   TB/1334

RICHARD B. MORRIS: Fair Trial: *Fourteen Who Stood Accused, from Anne Hutchinson to Alger Hiss*   TB/1335

GUNNAR MYRDAL: An American Dilemma: *The Negro Problem and Modern Democracy. Introduction by the Author.*
     Vol. I TB/1443;   Vol. II TB/1444

GILBERT OSOFSKY, Ed.: The Burden of Race: *A Documentary History of Negro-White Relations in America*   TB/1405

CONYERS READ, Ed.: The Constitution Reconsidered. *Revised Edition. Preface by Richard B. Morris*   TB/1384

ARNOLD ROSE: The Negro in America: *The Condensed Version of Gunnar Myrdal's* An American Dilemma. *Second Edition* TB/3048

JOHN E. SMITH: Themes in American Philosophy: *Purpose, Experience and Community*   TB/1466

WILLIAM R. TAYLOR: Cavalier and Yankee: *The Old South and American National Character*   TB/1474

American Studies: Colonial

BERNARD BAILYN: The New England Merchants in the Seventeenth Century   TB/1149

ROBERT E. BROWN: Middle-Class Democracy and Revolution in Massachusetts, 1691–1780. *New Introduction by Author*   TB/1413

JOSEPH CHARLES: The Origins of the American Party System   TB/1049

HENRY STEELE COMMAGER & ELMO GIORDANETTI, Eds.: Was America a Mistake? *An Eighteenth Century Controversy*   TB/1329

WESLEY FRANK CRAVEN: The Colonies in Transition: 1660-1712†   TB/3084

CHARLES GIBSON: Spain in America †   TB/3077

CHARLES GIBSON, Ed.: The Spanish Tradition in America +   HR/1351

LAWRENCE HENRY GIPSON: The Coming of the Revolution: 1763-1775. † *Illus.*   TB/3007

JACK P. GREENE, Ed.: Great Britain and the American Colonies: 1606-1763. + *Introduction by the Author*   HR/1477

AUBREY C. LAND, Ed.: Bases of the Plantation Society +   HR/1429

JOHN LANKFORD, Ed.: Captain John Smith's America: *Selections* from his Writings ‡   TB/3078

LEONARD W. LEVY: Freedom of Speech and Press in Early American History: *Legacy of Suppression*   TB/1109

---

† The New American Nation Series, edited by Henry Steele Commager and Richard B. Morris.
‡ American Perspectives series, edited by Bernard Wishy and William E. Leuchtenburg.
α History of Europe series, edited by J. H. Plumb.
§ The Library of Religion and Culture, edited by Benjamin Nelson.
Σ Researches in the Social, Cultural, and Behavioral Sciences, edited by Benjamin Nelson.
° Harper Modern Science Series, edited by James A. Newman.
   Not for sale in Canada.
+ Documentary History of the United States series, edited by Richard B. Morris.
# Documentary History of Western Civilization series, edited by Eugene C. Black and Leonard W. Levy.
Λ The Economic History of the United States series, edited by Henry David et al.
¶ European Perspectives series, edited by Eugene C. Black.
** Contemporary Essays series, edited by Leonard W. Levy.
* The Stratum Series, edited by John Hale.

PERRY MILLER: Errand Into the Wilderness TB/1139

PERRY MILLER & T. H. JOHNSON, Eds.: The Puritans: *A Sourcebook of Their Writings* Vol. I TB/1093; Vol. II TB/1094

EDMUND S. MORGAN: The Puritan Family: *Religion and Domestic Relations in Seventeenth Century New England* TB/1227

RICHARD B. MORRIS: Government and Labor in Early America TB/1244

WALLACE NOTESTEIN: The English People on the Eve of Colonization: 1603-1630. † *Illus.* TB/3006

FRANCIS PARKMAN: The Seven Years War: *A Narrative Taken from* Montcalm and Wolfe, The Conspiracy of Pontiac, *and* A Half-Century of Conflict. *Edited by John H. McCallum* TB/3083

LOUIS B. WRIGHT: The Cultural Life of the American Colonies: 1607-1763. † *Illus.* TB/3005

YVES F. ZOLTVANY, Ed.: The French Tradition in America + HR/1425

American Studies: The Revolution to 1860

JOHN R. ALDEN: The American Revolution: 1775-1783. † *Illus.* TB/3011

MAX BELOFF, Ed.: The Debate on the American Revolution, 1761-1783: *A Sourcebook* TB/1225

RAY A. BILLINGTON: The Far Western Frontier: 1830-1860. † *Illus.* TB/3012

STUART BRUCHEY: The Roots of American Economic Growth, 1607-1861: *An Essay in Social Causation. New Introduction by the Author.* TB/1350

WHITNEY R. CROSS: The Burned-Over District: *The Social and Intellectual History of Enthusiastic Religion in Western New York, 1800-1850* TB/1242

NOBLE E. CUNNINGHAM, JR., Ed.: The Early Republic, 1789-1828 + HR/1394

GEORGE DANGERFIELD: The Awakening of American Nationalism, 1815-1828. † *Illus.* TB/3061

CLEMENT EATON: The Freedom-of-Thought Struggle in the Old South. *Revised and Enlarged. Illus.* TB/1150

CLEMENT EATON: The Growth of Southern Civilization, 1790-1860. † *Illus.* TB/3040

ROBERT H. FERRELL, Ed.: Foundations of American Diplomacy, 1775-1872 + HR/1393

LOUIS FILLER: The Crusade against Slavery: 1830-1860. † *Illus.* TB/3029

DAVID H. FISCHER: The Revolution of American Conservatism: *The Federalist Party in the Era of Jeffersonian Democracy* TB/1449

WILLIAM W. FREEHLING, Ed.: The Nullification Era: *A Documentary Record* ‡ TB/3079

WILLIM W. FREEHLING: Prelude to Civil War: *The Nullification Controversy in South Carolina, 1816-1836* TB/1359

PAUL W. GATES: The Farmer's Age: *Agriculture, 1815-1860* △ TB/1398

FELIX GILBERT: The Beginnings of American Foreign Policy: *To the Farewell Address* · TB/1200

ALEXANDER HAMILTON: The Reports of Alexander Hamilton. ‡ *Edited by Jacob E. Cooke* TB/3060

THOMAS JEFFERSON: Notes on the State of Virginia. ‡ *Edited by Thomas P. Abernethy* TB/3052

FORREST MCDONALD, Ed.: Confederation and Constitution, 1781-1789 + HR/1396

BERNARD MAYO: Myths and Men: *Patrick Henry, George Washington, Thomas Jefferson* TB/1108

JOHN C. MILLER: Alexander Hamilton and the Growth of the New Nation TB/3057

JOHN C. MILLER: The Federalist Era: 1789-1801. † *Illus.* TB/3027

RICHARD B. MORRIS, Ed.: Alexander Hamilton and the Founding of the Nation. *New Introduction by the Editor* TB/1448

RICHARD B. MORRIS: The American Revolution Reconsidered TB/1363

CURTIS P. NETTELS: The Emergence of a National Economy, 1775-1815 △ TB/1438

DOUGLASS C. NORTH & ROBERT PAUL THOMAS, Eds.: *The Growth of the American Economy to 1860* + HR/1352

R. B. NYE: The Cultural Life of the New Nation: 1776-1830. † *Illus.* TB/3026

GILBERT OSOFSKY, Ed.: Puttin' On Ole Massa: *The Slave Narratives of Henry Bibb, William Wells Brown, and Solomon Northup* ‡ TB/1432

JAMES PARTON: The Presidency of Andrew Jackson. *From Volume III of the* Life of Andrew Jackson. *Ed. with Intro. by Robert V. Remini* TB/3080

FRANCIS S. PHILBRICK: The Rise of the West, 1754-1830. † *Illus.* TB/3067

MARSHALL SMELSER: The Democratic Republic, 1801-1815 † TB/1406

TIMOTHY L. SMITH: Revivalism and Social Reform: *American Protestantism on the Eve of the Civil War* TB/1229

JACK M. SOSIN, Ed.: The Opening of the West + HR/1424

GEORGE ROGERS TAYLOR: The Transportation Revolution, 1815-1860 △ TB/1347

A. F. TYLER: Freedom's Ferment: *Phases of American Social History from the Revolution to the Outbreak of the Civil War. Illus.* TB/1074

GLYNDON G. VAN DEUSEN: The Jacksonian Era: 1828-1848. † *Illus.* TB/3028

LOUIS B. WRIGHT: Culture on the Moving Frontier TB/1053

American Studies: The Civil War to 1900

W. R. BROCK: An American Crisis: *Congress and Reconstruction, 1865-67* ° TB/1283

T. C. COCHRAN & WILLIAM MILLER: The Age of Enterprise: *A Social History of Industrial America* TB/1054

W. A. DUNNING: Reconstruction, Political and Economic: 1865-1877 TB/1073

HAROLD U. FAULKNER: Politics, Reform and Expansion: 1890-1900. † *Illus.* TB/3020

GEORGE M. FREDRICKSON: The Inner Civil War: *Northern Intellectuals and the Crisis of the Union* TB/1358

JOHN A. GARRATY: The New Commonwealth, 1877-1890 + TB/1410

JOHN A. GARRATY, Ed.: The Transformation of American Society, 1870-1890 + HR/1395

WILLIAM R. HUTCHISON, Ed.: American Protestant Thought: *The Liberal Era* ‡ TB/1385

HELEN HUNT JACKSON: A Century of Dishonor: *The Early Crusade for Indian Reform.* † *Edited by Andrew F. Rolle* TB/3063

ALBERT D. KIRWAN: Revolt of the Rednecks: *Mississippi Politics, 1876-1925* TB/1199

WILLIAM G. MCLOUGHLIN, Ed.: The American Evangelicals, 1800-1900: An Anthology ‡ TB/1382

ARTHUR MANN: Yankee Reforms in the Urban Age: *Social Reform in Boston, 1800-1900* TB/1247

3

ROBERT L. HEILBRONER: The Future as History: *The Historic Currents of Our Time and the Direction in Which They Are Taking America* TB/1386

ROBERT L. HEILBRONER: The Great Ascent: *The Struggle for Economic Development in Our Time* TB/3030

FRANK H. KNIGHT: The Economic Organization TB/1214

DAVID S. LANDES: Bankers and Pashas: *International Finance and Economic Imperialism in Egypt. New Preface by the Author* TB/1412

ROBERT LATOUCHE: The Birth of Western Economy: *Economic Aspects of the Dark Ages* TB/1290

ABBA P. LERNER: Everbody's Business: *A Re-examination of Current Assumptions in Economics and Public Policy* TB/3051

W. ARTHUR LEWIS: Economic Survey, 1919-1939 TB/1446

W. ARTHUR LEWIS: The Principles of Economic Planning. *New Introduction by the Author°* TB/1436

ROBERT GREEN MC CLOSKEY: American Conservatism in the Age of Enterprise TB/1137

PAUL MANTOUX: The Industrial Revolution in the Eighteenth Century: *An Outline of the Beginnings of the Modern Factory System in England°* TB/1079

WILLIAM MILLER, Ed.: Men in Business: *Essays on the Historical Role of the Entrepreneur* TB/1081

GUNNAR MYRDAL: An International Economy. *New Introduction by the Author* TB/1445

HERBERT A. SIMON: The Shape of Automation: *For Men and Management* TB/1245

PERRIN STRYER: The Character of the Executive: *Eleven Studies in Managerial Qualities* TB/1041

RICHARD S. WECKSTEIN, Ed.: Expansion of World Trade and the Growth of National Economies ** TB/1373

Education

JACQUES BARZUN: The House of Intellect TB/1051

RICHARD M. JONES, Ed.: Contemporary Educational Psychology: *Selected Readings* ** TB/1292

CLARK KERR: The Uses of the University TB/1264

Historiography and History of Ideas

HERSCHEL BAKER: The Image of Man: *A Study of the Idea of Human Dignity in Classical Antiquity, the Middle Ages, and the Renaissance* TB/1047

J. BRONOWSKI & BRUCE MAZLISH: The Western Intellectual Tradition: *From Leonardo to Hegel* TB/3001

EDMUND BURKE: On Revolution. Ed. by Robert A. Smith TB/1401

WILHELM DILTHEY: Pattern and Meaning in History: *Thoughts on History and Society.° Edited with an Intro. by H. P. Rickman* TB/1075

ALEXANDER GRAY: The Socialist Tradition: *Moses to Lenin °* TB/1375

J. H. HEXTER: More's Utopia: *The Biography of an Idea. Epilogue by the Author* TB/1195

H. STUART HUGHES: History as Art and as Science: *Twin Vistas on the Past* TB/1207

ARTHUR O. LOVEJOY: The Great Chain of Being: *A Study of the History of an Idea* TB/1009

JOSE ORTEGA Y GASSET: The Modern Theme. *Introduction by Jose Ferrater Mora* TB/1038

RICHARD H. POPKIN: The History of Scepticism from Erasmus to Descartes. *Revised Edition* TB/1391

G. J. RENIER: History: *Its Purpose and Method* TB/1209

MASSIMO SALVADORI, Ed.: Modern Socialism # HR/1374

GEORG SIMMEL et al.: Essays on Sociology, Philosophy and Aesthetics. *Edited by Kurt H. Wolff* TB/1234

BRUNO SNELL: The Discovery of the Mind: *The Greek Origins of European Thought* TB/1018

W. WARREN WAGER, ed.: European Intellectual History Since Darwin and Marx TB/1297

W. H. WALSH: Philosophy of History: In Introduction TB/1020

History: General

HANS KOHN: The Age of Nationalism: *The First Era of Global History* TB/1380

BERNARD LEWIS: The Arabs in History TB/1029

BERNARD LEWIS: The Middle East and the West ° TB/1274

History: Ancient

A. ANDREWS: The Greek Tyrants TB/1103

ERNST LUDWIG EHRLICH: A Concise History of Israel: *From the Earliest Times to the Destruction of the Temple in A.D. 70 °* TB/128

ADOLF ERMAN, Ed.: The Ancient Egyptians: *A Sourcebook of their Writings. New Introduction by William Kelly Simpson* TB/1233

THEODOR H. GASTER: Thespis: *Ritual Myth and Drama in the Ancient Near East* TB/1281

MICHAEL GRANT: Ancient History ° TB/1190

A. H. M. JONES, Ed.: A History of Rome through the Fifgth Century # *Vol. I: The Republic* HR/1364

Vol. II The Empire: HR/1460

SAMUEL NOAH KRAMER: Sumerian Mythology TB/1055

NAPHTALI LEWIS & MEYER REINHOLD, Eds.: Roman Civilization *Vol. I: The Republic* TB/1231

Vol. II: The Empire TB/1232

History: Medieval

MARSHALL W. BALDWIN, Ed.: Christianity Through the 13th Century # HR/1468

MARC BLOCH: Land and Work in Medieval Europe. *Translated by J. E. Anderson* TB/1452

HELEN CAM: England Before Elizabeth TB/1026

NORMAN COHN: The Pursuit of the Millennium: *Revolutionary Messianism in Medieval and Reformation Europe* TB/1037

G. G. COULTON: Medieval Village, Manor, and Monastery HR/1022

HEINRICH FICHTENAU: The Carolingian Empire: *The Age of Charlemagne. Translated with an Introduction by Peter Munz* TB/1142

GALBERT OF BRUGES: The Murder of Charles the Good: *A Contemporary Record of Revolutionary Change in 12th Century Flanders. Translated with an Introduction by James Bruce Ross* TB/1311

F. L. GANSHOF: Feudalism TB/1058

F. L. GANSHOF: The Middle Ages: *A History of International Relations. Translated by Rémy Hall* TB/1411

W. O. HASSALL, Ed.: Medieval England: *As Viewed by Contemporaries* TB/1205

DENYS HAY: The Medieval Centuries ° TB/1192

DAVID HERLIHY, Ed.: Medieval Culture and Socicety # HR/1340

4

J. M. HUSSEY: The Byzantine World TB/1057
ROBERT LATOUCHE: The Birth of Western Economy: *Economic Aspects of the Dark Ages* ° TB/1290
HENRY CHARLES LEA: The Inquisition of the Middle Ages. || *Introduction by Walter Ullmann* TB/1456
FERDINARD LOT: The End of the Ancient World and the Beginnings of the Middle Ages. *Introduction by Glanville Downey* TB/1044
H. R. LOYN: The Norman Conquest TB/1457
ACHILLE LUCHAIRE: Social France at the time of Philip Augustus. *Intro. by John W. Baldwin* TB/1314
GUIBERT DE NOGENT: Self and Society in Medieval France: *The Memoirs of Guibert de Nogent.* || Edited by John F. Benton TB/1471
MARSILIUS OF PADUA: The Defender of Peace. The Defensor Pacis. *Translated with an Introduction by Alan Gewirth* TB/1310
CHARLES PETET-DUTAILLIS: The Feudal Monarchy in France and England: *From the Tenth to the Thirteenth Century* ° TB/1165
STEVEN RUNCIMAN: A History of the Crusades Vol. I: *The First Crusade and the Foundation of the Kingdom of Jerusalem. Illus.* TB/1143
Vol. II: *The Kingdom of Jerusalem and the Frankish East 1100-1187. Illus.* TB/1243
Vol. III: *The Kingdom of Acre and the Later Crusades. Illus.* TB/1298
J. M. WALLACE-HADRILL: The Barbarian West: *The Early Middle Ages, A.D. 400-1000* TB/1061

History: Renaissance & Reformation

JACOB BURCKHARDT: The Civilization of the Renaissance in Italy. *Introduction by Benjamin Nelson and Charles Trinkaus. Illus.* Vol. I TB/40; Vol. II TB/41
JOHN CALVIN & JACOPO SADOLETO: A Reformation Debate. *Edited by John C. Olin* TB/1239
FEDERICO CHABOD: Machiavelli and the Renaissance TB/1193
THOMAS CROMWELL: Thomas Cromwell on Church and Commonwealth,: *Selected Letters 1523-1540.* ¶ Ed. with an Intro. by Arthur J. Slavin TB/1462
R. TREVOR DAVIES: The Golden Century of Spain, 1501-1621 ° TB/1194
J. H. ELLIOTT: Europe Divided, 1559-1598 *a* ° TB/1414
G. R. ELTON: Reformation Europe, 1517-1559 ° *a* TB/1270
DESIDERIUS ERASMUS: Christian Humanism and the Reformation: *Selected Writings. Edited and Translated by John C. Olin* TB/1166
DESIDERIUS ERASMUS: Erasmus and His Age: *Selected Letters. Edited with an Introduction by Hans J. Hillerbrand. Translated by Marcus A. Haworth* TB/1461
WALLACE K. FERGUSON et al.: Facets of the Renaissance TB/1098
WALLACE K. FERGUSON et al.: The Renaissance: *Six Essays. Illus.* TB/1084
FRANCESCO GUICCIARDINI: History of Florence. *Translated with an Introduction and Notes by Mario Domandi* TB/1470
WERNER L. GUNDERSHEIMER, Ed.: French Humanism, 1470-1600. * *Illus.* TB/1473
MARIE BOAS HALL, Ed.: Nature and Nature's Laws: *Documents of the Scientific Revolution* # HR/1420
HANS J. HILLERBRAND, Ed., The Protestant Reformation # HR/1342
JOHAN HUIZINGA: Erasmus and the Age of Reformation. *Illus.* TB/19

JOEL HURSTFIELD: The Elizabethan Nation TB/1312
JOEL HURSTFIELD, Ed.: The Reformation Crisis TB/1267
PAUL OSKAR KRISTELLER: Renaissance Thought: *The Classic, Scholastic, and Humanist Strains* TB/1048
PAUL OSKAR KRISTELLER: Renaissance Thought II: *Papers on Humanism and the Arts* TB/1163
PAUL O. KRISTELLER & PHILIP P. WIENER, Eds.: Renaissance Essays TB/1392
DAVID LITTLE: Religion, Order and Law: *A Study in Pre-Revolutionary England.* § *Preface by R. Bellah* TB/1418
NICCOLÒ MACHIAVELLI: History of Florence and of the Affairs of Italy: *From the Earliest Times to the Death of Lorenzo the Magnificent. Introduction by Felix Gilbert* TB/1027
ALFRED VON MARTIN: Sociology of the Renaissance. ° *Introduction by W. K. Ferguson* TB/1099
GARRETT MATTINGLY et al.: Renaissance Profiles. *Edited by J. H. Plumb* TB/1162
J. E. NEALE: The Age of Catherine de Medici ° TB/1085
J. H. PARRY: The Establishment of the European Hegemony: 1415-1715: *Trade and Exploration in the Age of the Renaissance* TB/1045
J. H. PARRY, Ed.: The European Reconnaissance: *Selected Documents* # HR/1345
BUONACCORSO PITTI & GREGORIO DATI: Two Memoirs of Renaissance Florence: *The Diaries of Buonaccorso Pitti and Gregorio Dati. Edited with Intro. by Gene Brucker. Trans. by Julia Martines* TB/1333
J. H. PLUMB: The Italian Renaissance: *A Concise Survey of Its History and Culture* TB/1161
A. F. POLLARD: Henry VIII. *Introduction by A. G. Dickens.* ° TB/1249
RICHARD H. POPKIN: The History of Scepticism from Erasmus to Descartes TB/139
PAOLO ROSSI: Philosophy, Technology, and the Arts, in the Early Modern Era 1400-1700. || *Edited by Benjamin Nelson. Translated by Salvator Attanasio* TB/1458
FERDINAND SCHEVILL: The Medici. *Illus.* TB/1010
FERDINAND SCHEVILL: Medieval and Renaissance Florence. *Illus.* Vol. I: *Medieval Florence* TB/1090
Vol. II: *The Coming of Humanism and the Age of the Medici* TB/1091
R. H. TAWNEY: The Agrarian Problem in the Sixteenth Century. *Intro. by Lawrence Stone* TB/1315
H. R. TREVOR-ROPER: The European Witch-craze of the Sixteenth and Seventeenth Centuries and Other Essays ° TB/1416
VESPASIANO: Rennaissance Princes, Popes, and XVth Century: *The Vespasiano Memoirs. Introduction by Myron P. Gilmore. Illus.* TB/1111

History: Modern European

RENE ALBRECHT-CARRIE, Ed.: The Concert of Europe # HR/1341
MAX BELOFF: The Age of Absolutism, 1660-1815 TB/1062
OTTO VON BISMARCK: Reflections and Reminiscences. *Ed. with Intro. by Theodore S. Hamerow* ¶ TB/1357
EUGENE C. BLACK, Ed.: British Politics in the Nineteenth Century # HR/1427

5

EUGENE C. BLACK, Ed.: European Political History, 1815-1870: *Aspects of Liberalism* ¶
TB/1331

ASA BRIGGS: The Making of Modern England, 1783-1867: *The Age of Improvement* °
TB/1203

D. W. BROGAN: The Development of Modern France ° Vol. I: *From the Fall of the Empire to the Dreyfus Affair* TB/1184
Vol. II: *The Shadow of War, World War I, Between the Two Wars* TB/1185

ALAN BULLOCK: Hitler, A Study in Tyranny. ° *Revised Edition. Illus.* TB/1123

EDMUND BURKE: On Revolution. *Ed. by Robert A. Smith* TB/1401

E. R. CARR: International Relations Between the Two World Wars. 1919-1939 ° TB/1279

E. H. CARR: The Twenty Years' Crisis, 1919-1939: *An Introduction to the Study of International Relations* ° TB/1122

GORDON A. CRAIG: From Bismarck to Adenauer: *Aspects of German Statecraft. Revised Edition* TB/1171

LESTER G. CROCKER, Ed.: The Age of Enlightenment # HR/1423

DENIS DIDEROT: The Encyclopedia: *Selections. Edited and Translated with Introduction by Stephen Gendzier* TB/1299

JACQUES DROZ: Europe between Revolutions, 1815-1848. ° *a Trans. by Robert Baldick* TB/1346

JOHANN GOTTLIEB FICHTE: Addresses to the German Nation. *Ed. with Intro. by George A. Kelly* ¶ TB/1366

FRANKLIN L. FORD: Robe and Sword: *The Re-Louis XIV* TB/1217

ROBERT & ELBORG FORSTER, Eds.: European Society in the Eighteenth Century # HR/1404

C. C. GILLISPIE: Genesis and Geology: *The Decades before Darwin* § TB/51

ALBERT GOODWIN, Ed.: The European Nobility in the Enghteenth Century TB/1313

ALBERT GOODWIN: The French Revolution
TB/1064

ALBERT GUERARD: France in the Classical Age: *The Life and Death of an Ideal* TB/1183

JOHN B. HALSTED: Romanticism # HR/1387

J. H. HEXTER: Reappraisals in History: *New Views on History and Society in Early Modern Europe* ° TB/1100

STANLEY HOFFMANN et al.: In Search of France: *The Economy, Society and Political System In the Twentieth Century* TB/1219

H. STUART HUGHES: The Obstructed Path: *French Social Thought in the Years of Desperation* TB/1451

JOHAN HUIZINGA: Dutch Civilisation in the 17th Century and Other Essays TB/1453

LIONAL KOCHAN: The Struggle for Germany: *1914-45* TB/1304

HANS KOHN: The Mind of Germany: *The Education of a Nation* TB/1204

HANS KOHN, Ed.: The Mind of Modern Russia: *Historical and Political Thought of Russia's Great Age* TB/1065

WALTER LAQUEUR & GEORGE L. MOSSE, Eds.: Education and Social Structure in the 20th Century. ° *Volume 6 of the Journal of Contemporary History* TB/1339

WALTER LAQUEUR & GEORGE L. MOSSE, Eds.: International Fascism, 1920-1945. ° *Volume 1 of the Journal of Contemporary History*
TB/1276

WALTER LAQUEUR & GEORGE L. MOSSE, Eds.: Literature and Politics in the 20th Century. ° *Volume 5 of the Journal of Contemporary History.* TB/1328

WALTER LAQUEUR & GEORGE L. MOSSE, Eds.: The New History: *Trends in Historical Research and Writing Since World War II.* ° *Volume 4 of the Journal of Contemporary History*
TB/1327

WALTER LAQUEUR & GEORGE L. MOSSE, Eds.: 1914: *The Coming of the First World War.* ° *Volume3 of the Journal of Contemporary History* TB/1306

C. A. MACARTNEY, Ed.: The Habsburg and Hohenzollern Dynasties in the Seventeenth and Eighteenth Centuries # HR/1400

JOHN MCMANNERS: European History, 1789-1914: *Men, Machines and Freedom* TB/1419

PAUL MANTOUX: The Industrial Revolution in the Eighteenth Century: *An Outline of the Beginnings of the Modern Factory System in England* TB/1079

FRANK E. MANUEL: The Prophets of Paris: *Turgot, Condorcet, Saint-Simon, Fourier, and Comte* TB/1218

KINGSLEY MARTIN: French Liberal Thought in the Eighteenth Century: *A Study of Political Ideas from Bayle to Condorcet* TB/1114

NAPOLEON III: Napoleonic Ideas: *Des Idées Napoléoniennes, par le Prince Napoléon-Louis Bonaparte. Ed. by Brison D. Gooch* ¶
TB/1336

FRANZ NEUMANN: Behemoth: *The Structure and Practice of National Socialism, 1933-1944*
TB/1289

DAVID OGG: Europe of the Ancien Régime, 1715-1783 ° *a* TB/1271

GEORGE RUDE: Revolutionary Europe, 1783-1815 ° *a* TB/1272

MASSIMO SALVADORI, Ed.: Modern Socialism #
TB/1374

HUGH SETON-WATSON: Eastern Europe Between the Wars, 1918-1941 TB/1330

DENIS MACK SMITH, Ed.: The Making of Italy, 1796-1870 # HR/1356

ALBERT SOREL: Europe Under the Old Regime. *Translated by Francis H. Herrick* TB/1121

ROLAND N. STROMBERG, Ed.: Realism, Naturalism, and Symbolism: *Modes of Thought and Expression in Europe, 1848-1914* # HR/1355

A. J. P. TAYLOR: From Napoleon to Lenin: *Historical Essays* ° TB/1268

A. J. P. TAYLOR: The Habsburg Monarchy, 1809-1918: *A History of the Austrian Empire and Austria-Hungary* ° TB/1187

J. M. THOMPSON: European History, 1494-1789
TB/1431

DAVID THOMSON, Ed.: France: Empire and Republic, 1850-1940 # HR/1387

ALEXIS DE TOCQUEVILLE & GUSTAVE DE BEAUMONT: Tocqueville and Beaumont on Social Reform. *Ed. and trans. with Intro. by Seymour Drescher* TB/1343

G. M. TREVELYAN: British History in the Nineteenth Century and After: 1792-1919 °
TB/1251

H. R. TREVOR-ROPER: Historical Essays TB/1269

W. WARREN WAGAR, Ed.: Science, Faith, and MAN: *European Thought Since 1914* #
HR/1362

MACK WALKER, Ed.: Metternich's Europe, 1813-1848 # HR/1361

ELIZABETH WISKEMANN: Europe of the Dictators, 1919-1945 ° *a* TB/1273

JOHN B. WOLF: France: 1814-1919: *The Rise of a Liberal-Democratic Society* TB/3019

Literature & Literary Criticism

JACQUES BARZUN: The House of Intellect
TB/1051

6

W. J. BATE: From Classic to Romantic: *Premises of Taste in Eighteenth Century England* TB/1036

VAN WYCK BROOKS: Van Wyck Brooks: The Early Years: *A Selection from his Works, 1908-1921 Ed. with Intro. by Claire Sprague* TB/3082

ERNST R. CURTIUS: European Literature and the Latin Middle Ages. *Trans. by Willard Trask* TB/2015

RICHMOND LATTIMORE, Translator: The Odyssey of Homer TB/1389

JOHN STUART MILL: On Bentham and Coleridge. *Introduction by F. R. Leavis* TB/1070

SAMUEL PEPYS: The Diary of Samual Pepys. ° *Edited by O. F. Morshead. 60 illus. by Ernest Shepard* TB/1007

ROBERT PREYER, Ed.: Victorian Literature ** TB/1302

ALBION W. TOURGEE: A Fool's Errand: *A Novel of the South during Reconstruction. Intro. by George Fredrickson* TB/3074

BASIL WILEY: Nineteenth Century Studies: *Coleridge to Matthew Arnold* ° TB/1261

RAYMOND WILLIAMS: Culture and Society, 1780-1950 ° TB/1252

Philosophy

HENRI BERGSON: Time and Free Will: *An Essay on the Immediate Data of Consciousness* ° TB/1021

LUDWIG BINSWANGER: Being-in-the-World: *Selected Papers. Trans. with Intro. by Jacob Needleman* TB/1365

H. J. BLACKHAM: Six Existentialist Thinkers: *Kierkegaard, Nietzsche, Jaspers, Marcel, Heidegger, Sartre* ° TB/1002

J. M. BOCHENSKI: The Methods of Contemporary Thought. *Trans. by Peter Caws* TB/1377

CRANE BRINTON: Nietzsche. *Preface, Bibliography, and Epilogue by the Author* TB/1197

ERNST CASSIRER: Rousseau, Kant and Goethe. *Intro. by Peter Gay* TB/1092

FREDERICK COPLESTON, S. J.: Medieval Philosophy TB/376

F. M. CORNFORD: From Religion to Philosophy: *A Study in the Origins of Western Speculation* § TB/20

WILFRID DESAN: The Tragic Finale: *An Essay on the Philosophy of Jean-Paul Sartre* TB/1030

MARVIN FARBER: The Aims of Phenomenology: *The Motives, Methods, and Impact of Husserl's Thought* TB/1291

MARVIN FARBER: Basic Issues of Philosophy: *Experience, Reality, and Human Values* TB/1344

MARVIN FARBER: Phenomenology and Existence: *Towards a Philosophy within Nature* TB/1295

PAUL FRIEDLANDER: Plato: *An Introduction* TB/2017

MICHAEL GELVEN: A Commentary on Heidegger's "Being and Time" TB/1464

J. GLENN GRAY: Hegel and Greek Thought TB/1409

W. K. C. GUTHRIE: The Greek Philosophers: *From Thales to Aristotle* ° TB/1008

G. W. F. HEGEL: On Art, Religion Philosophy: *Introductory Lectures to the Realm of Absolute Spirit. || Edited with an Introduction by J. Glenn Gray* TB/1463

G. W. F. HEGEL: Phenomenology of Mind. ° || *Introduction by George Lichtheim* TB/1303

MARTIN HEIDEGGER: Discourse on Thinking. *Translated with a Preface by John M. Anderson and E. Hans Freund. Introduction by John M. Anderson* TB/1459

F. H. HEINEMANN: Existentialism and the Modern Predicament TB/28

WERER HEISENBERG: Physics and Philosophy: *The Revolution in Modern Science. Intro. by F. S. C. Northrop* TB/549

EDMUND HUSSERL: Phenomenology and the Crisis of Philosophy. § *Translated with an Introduction by Quentin Lauer* TB/1170

IMMANUEL KANT: Groundwork of the Metaphysic of Morals. *Translated and Analyzed by H. J. Paton* TB/1159

IMMANUEL KANT: Lectures on Ethics. § *Introduction by Lewis White Beck* TB/105

WALTER KAUFMANN, Ed.: Religion From Tolstoy to Camus: *Basic Writings on Religious Truth and Morals* TB/123

QUENTIN LAUER: Phenomenology: *Its Genesis and Prospect. Preface by Aron Gurwitsch* TB/1169

MAURICE MANDELBAUM: The Problem of Historical Knowledge: *An Answer to Relativism* TB/1338

GEORGE A. MORGAN: What Nietzsche Means TB/1198

H. J. PATON: The Categorical Imperative: *A Study in Kant's Moral Philosophy* TB/1325

MICHAEL POLANYI: Personal Knowledge: *Towards a Post-Critical Philosophy* TB/1158

KARL R. POPPER: Conjectures and Refutations: *The Growth of Scientific Knowledge* TB/1376

WILLARD VAN ORMAN QUINE: Elementary Logic *Revised Edition* TB/577

WILLARD VAN ORMAN QUINE: From a Logical Point of View: *Logico-Philosophical Essays* TB/566

JOHN E. SMITH: Themes in American Philosophy: *Purpose, Experience and Community* TB/1466

MORTON WHITE: Foundations of Historical Knowledge TB/1440

WILHELM WINDELBAND: A History of Philosophy *Vol. I: Greek, Roman, Medieval* TB/38 *Vol. II: Renaissance, Enlightenment, Modern* TB/39

LUDWIG WITTGENSTEIN: The Blue and Brown Books ° TB/1211

LUDWIG WITTGENSTEIN: Notebooks, 1914-1916 TB/1441

Political Science & Government

C. E. BLACK: The Dynamics of Modernization: *A Study in Comparative History* TB/1321

KENNETH E. BOULDING: Conflict and Defense: *A General Theory of Action* TB/3024

DENIS W. BROGAN: Politics in America. *New Introduction by the Author* TB/1469

CRANE BRINTON: English Political Thought in the Nineteenth Century TB/1071

ROBERT CONQUEST: Power and Policy in the USSR: *The Study of Soviet Dynastics* ° TB/1307

ROBERT A. DAHL & CHARLES E. LINDBLOM: Politics, Economics, and Welfare: *Planning and Politico-Economic Systems Resolved into Basic Social Processes* TB/3037

HANS KOHN: Political Ideologies of the 20th Century TB/1277

ROY C. MACRIDIS, Ed.: Political Parties: *Contemporary Trends and Ideas* ** TB/1322

ROBERT GREEN MC CLOSKEY: American Conservatism in the Age of Enterprise, 1865-1910 TB/1137

MARSILIUS OF PADUA: The Defender of Peace. *The Defensor Pacis. Translated with an Introduction by Alan Gewirth* TB/1310

KINGSLEY MARTIN: French Liberal Thought in the Eighteenth Century: *A Study of Political Ideas from Bayle to Condorcet* TB/1114

BARRINGTON MOORE, JR.: Political Power and Social Theory: *Seven Studies* || TB/1221

BARRINGTON MOORE, JR.: Soviet Politics—The Dilemma of Power: *The Role of Ideas in Social Change* || TB/1222

BARRINGTON MOORE, JR.: Terror and Progress—USSR: *Some Sources of Change and Stability*

JOHN B. MORRALL: Political Thought in Medieval Times TB/1076

KARL R. POPPER: The Open Society and Its Enemies *Vol. I: The Spell of Plato* TB/1101 *Vol. II: The High Tide of Prophecy: Hegel, Marx, and the Aftermath* TB/1102

CONYERS READ, Ed.: The Constitution Reconsidered. *Revised Edition, Preface by Richard B. Morris* TB/1384

JOHN P. ROCHE, Ed.: Origins of American Political Thought: *Selected Readings* TB/1301

JOHN P. ROCHE, Ed.: American Political Thought: *From Jefferson to Progressivism* TB/1332

HENRI DE SAINT-SIMON: Social Organization, The Science of Man, and Other Writings. || *Edited and Translated with an Introduction by Felix Markham* TB/1152

CHARLES SCHOTTLAND, Ed.: The Welfare State ** TB/1323

JOSEPH A. SCHUMPETER: Capitalism, Socialism and Democracy TB/3008

PETER WOLL, Ed.: Public Administration and Policy: *Selected Essays* TB/1284

Psychology

ALFRED ADLER: The Individual Psychology of Alfred Adler: *A Systematic Presentation in Selections from His Writings. Edited by Heinz L. & Rowena R. Ansbacher* TB/1154

ALFRED ADLER: Problems of Neurosis: *A Book of Case Histories. Introduction by Heinz L. Ansbacher* TB/1145

LUDWIG BINSWANGER: Being-in-the-World: *Selected Papers. || Trans. with Intro. by Jacob Needleman* TB/1365

ARTHUR BURTON & ROBERT E. HARRIS: Clinical Studies of Personality Vol. I TB/3075 Vol. II TB/3076

HADLEY CANTRIL: The Invasion from Mars: *A Study in the Psychology of Panic* || TB/1282

MIRCEA ELIADE: Cosmos and History: *The Myth of the Eternal Return* § TB/2050

MIRCEA ELIADE: Myth and Reality TB/1369

MIRCEA ELIADE: Myths, Dreams and Mysteries: *The Encounter Between Contemporary Faiths and Archaic Realities* § TB/1320

MIRCEA ELIADE: Rites and Symbols of Initiation: *The Mysteries of Birth and Rebirth* § TB/1236

HERBERT FINGARETTE: The Self in Transformation: *Psychoanalysis, Philosophy and the Life of the Spirit* || TB/1177

SIGMUND FREUD: On Creativity and the Unconscious: *Papers on the Psychology of Art, Literature, Love, Religion.* § *Intro. by Benjamin Nelson* TB/45

J. GLENN GRAY: The Warriors: *Reflections on Men in Battle. Introduction by Hannah Arendt* TB/1294

WILLIAM JAMES: Psychology: *The Briefer Course. Edited with an Intro. by Gordon Allport* TB/1034

C. G. JUNG: Psychological Reflections. *Ed. by J. Jacobi* TB/2001

KARL MENNINGER, M.D.: Theory of Psychoanalytic Technique TB/1144

JOHN H. SCHAAR: Escape from Authority: *The Perspectives of Erich Fromm* TB/1155

MUZAFER SHERIF: The Psychology of Social Norms. *Introduction by Gardner Murphy* TB/3072

HELLMUT WILHELM: Change: *Eight Lectures on the* I *Ching* TB/2019

Religion: Ancient and Classical, Biblical and Judaic Traditions

W. F. ALBRIGHT: The Biblical Period from Abraham to Ezra TB/102

SALO W. BARON: Modern Nationalism and Religion TB/818

C. K. BARRETT, Ed.: The New Testament Background: *Selected Documents* TB/86

MARTIN BUBER: Eclipse of God: *Studies in the Relation Between Religion and Philosophy* TB/12

MARTIN BUBER: Hasidism and Modern Man. *Edited and Translated by Maurice Friedman* TB/839

MARTIN BUBER: The Knowledge of Man. *Edited with an Introduction by Maurice Friedman. Translated by Maurice Friedman and Ronald Gregor Smith* TB/135

MARTIN BUBER: Moses. *The Revelation and the Covenant* TB/837

MARTIN BUBER: The Origin and Meaning of Hasidism. *Edited and Translated by Maurice Friedman* TB/835

MARTIN BUBER: The Prophetic Faith TB/73

MARTIN BUBER: Two Types of Faith: *Interpenetration of Judaism and Christianity* ° TB/75

MALCOLM L. DIAMOND: Martin Buber: *Jewish Existentialist* TB/840

M. S. ENSLIN: Christian Beginnings TB/5

M. S. ENSLIN: The Literature of the Christian Movement TB/6

ERNST LUDWIG EHRLICH: A Concise History of Israel: *From the Earliest Times to the Destruction of the Temple in A.D. 70* ° TB/128

HENRI FRANKFORT: Ancient Egyptian Religion: *An Interpretation* TB/77

MAURICE S. FRIEDMAN: Martin Buber: *The Life of Dialogue* TB/64

ABRAHAM HESCHEL: The Earth Is the Lord's & The Sabbath. *Two Essays* TB/828

ABRAHAM HESCHEL: God in Search of Man: *A Philosophy of Judaism* TB/807

ABRAHAM HESCHEL: Man Is not Alone: *A Philosophy of Religion* TB/838

ABRAHAM HESCHEL: The Prophets: *An Introduction* TB/1421

T. J. MEEK: Hebrew Origins TB/69

JAMES MUILENBURG: The Way of Israel: *Biblical Faith and Ethics* TB/133

H. J. ROSE: Religion in Greece and Rome TB/55

H. H. ROWLEY: The Growth of the Old Testament TB/107

D. WINTON THOMAS, Ed.: Documents from Old Testament Times TB/85

Religion: General Christianity

ROLAND H. BAINTON: Christendom: *A Short History of Christianity and Its Impact on Western Civilization. Illus.* Vol. I TB/131; Vol. II TB/132

JOHN T. MCNEILL: Modern Christian Movements. *Revised Edition* TB/1402

ERNST TROELTSCH: The Social Teaching of the Christian Churches. *Intro. by H. Richard Niebuhr* Vol. TB/71; Vol. II TB/72

Religion: Early Christianity Through Reformation

ANSELM OF CANTERBURY: Truth, Freedom, and Evil: *Three Philosophical Dialogues. Edited and Translated by Jasper Hopkins and Herbert Richardson* TB/317

MARSHALL W. BALDWIN, Ed.: Christianity through the 13th Century # HR/1468

W. D. DAVIES: Paul and Rabbinic Judaism: *Some Rabbinic Elements in Pauline Theology. Revised Edition* ° TB/146

ADOLF DEISSMANN: Paul: *A Study in Social and Religious History* TB/15

JOHANNES ECKHART: Meister Eckhart: *A Modern Translation by R. Blakney* TB/8

EDGAR J. GOODSPEED: A Life of Jesus TB/1

ROBERT M. GRANT: Gnosticism and Early Christianity TB/136

WILLIAM HALLER: The Rise of Puritanism TB/22

GERHART B. LADNER: The Idea of Reform: *Its Impact on the Christian Thought and Action in the Age of the Fathers* TB/149

ARTHUR DARBY NOCK: Early Gentile Christianity and Its Hellenistic Background TB/111

ARTHUR DARBY NOCK: St. Paul ° TR/104

ORIGEN: On First Principles. *Edited by G. W. Butterworth. Introduction by Henri de Lubac* TB/311

GORDON RUPP: Luther's Progress to the Diet of Worms ° TB/120

Religion: The Protestant Tradition

KARL BARTH: Church Dogmatics: *A Selection. Intro. by H. Gollwitzer. Ed. by G. W. Bromiley* TB/95

KARL BARTH: Dogmatics in Outline TB/56

KARL BARTH: The Word of God and the Word of Man TB/13

HERBERT BRAUN, et al.: God and Christ: *Existence and Province. Volume 5 of Journal for Theology and the Church, edited by Robert W. Funk and Gerhard Ebeling* TB/255

WHITNEY R. CROSS: The Burned-Over District: *The Social and Intellectual History of Enthusiastic Religion in Western New York, 1800-1850* TB/1242

NELS F. S. FERRE: Swedish Contributions to Modern Theology. *New Chapter by William A. Johnson* TB/147

WILLIAM R. HUTCHISON, Ed.: American Protestant Thought: *The Liberal Era* ‡ TB/1385

ERNST KASEMANN, et al.: Distinctive Protestant and Catholic Themes Reconsidered. *Volume 3 of Journal for Theology and the Church, edited by Robert W. Funk and Gerhard Ebeling* TB/253

SOREN KIERKEGAARD: On Authority and Revelation: *The Book on Adler, or a Cycle of Ethico-Religious Essays. Introduction by F. Sontag* TB/139

SOREN KIERKEGAARD: Crisis in the Life of an Actress, *and Other Essays on Drama. Translated with an Introduction by Stephen Crites* TB/145

SOREN KIERKEGAARD: Edifying Discourses. *Edited with an Intro. by Paul Holmer* TB/32

SOREN KIERKEGAARD: The Journals of Kierkegaard. ° *Edited with an Intro. by Alexander Dru* TB/52

SOREN KIERKEGAARD: The Point of View for My Work as an Author: *A Report to History.* § *Preface by Benjamin Nelson* TB/88

SOREN KIERKEGAARD: The Present Age. § *Translated and edited by Alexander Dru. Introduction by Walter Kaufmann* TB/94

SOREN KIERKEGAARD: Purity of Heart. *Trans. by Douglas Steere* TB/4

SOREN KIERKEGAARD: Repetition: *An Essay in Experimental Psychology* § TB/117

SOREN KIERKEGAARD: Works of Love: *Some Christian Reflections in the Form of Discourses* TB/122

WILLIAM G. MCLOUGHLIN, Ed.: The American Evangelicals: 1800-1900: *An Anthology* TB/1382

WOLFHART PANNENBERG, et al.: History and Hermeneutic. *Volume 4 of Journal for Theology and the Church, edited by Robert W. Funk and Gerhard Ebeling* TB/254

JAMES M. ROBINSON, et al.: The Bultmann School of Biblical Interpretation: New Directions? *Volume 1 of Journal for Theology and the Church, edited by Robert W. Funk and Gerhard Ebeling* TB/251

F. SCHLEIERMACHER: The Christian Faith. *Introduction by Richard R. Niebuhr.*
Vol. I TB/108; Vol. II TB/109

F. SCHLEIERMACHER: On Religion: *Speeches to Its Cultured Despisers. Intro. by Rudolf Otto* TB/36

TIMOTHY L. SMITH: Revivalism and Social Reform: *American Protestantism on the Eve of the Civil War* TB/1229

PAUL TILLICH: Dynamics of Faith TB/42

PAUL TILLICH: Morality and Beyond TB/142

EVELYN UNDERHILL: Worship TB/10

Religion: The Roman & Eastern Christian Traditions

A. ROBERT CAPONIGRI, Ed.: Modern Catholic Thinkers II: *The Church and the Political Order* TB/307

G. P. FEDOTOV: The Russian Religious Mind: *Kievan Christianity, the tenth to the thirteenth Centuries* TB/370

GABRIEL MARCEL: Being and Having: *An Existential Diary. Introduction by James Collins* TB/310

GABRIEL MARCEL: Homo Viator: *Introduction to a Metaphysic of Hope* TB/397

Religion: Oriental Religions

TOR ANDRAE: Mohammed: *The Man and His Faith* § TB/62

EDWARD CONZE: Buddhism: *Its Essence and Development.* ° *Foreword by Arthur Waley* TB/58

EDWARD CONZE: Buddhist Meditation TB/1442

EDWARD CONZE et al, Editors: Buddhist Texts through the Ages TB/113

ANANDA COOMARASWAMY: Buddha and the Gospel of Buddhism TB/119

H. G. CREEL: Confucius and the Chinese Way TB/63

FRANKLIN EDGERTON, Trans. & Ed.: The Bhagavad Gita TB/115

SWAMI NIKHILANANDA, Trans. & Ed.: The Upanishads TB/114

D. T. SUZUKI: On Indian Mahayana Buddhism. ° *Ed. with Intro. by Edward Conze.* TB/1403

Religion: Philosophy, Culture, and Society

NICOLAS BERDYAEV: The Destiny of Man TB/61

RUDOLF BULTMANN: History and Eschatology: *The Presence of Eternity* ° TB/91

RUDOLF BULTMANN AND FIVE CRITICS: Kerygma and Myth: *A Theological Debate* TB/80

RUDOLF BULTMANN and KARL KUNDSIN: Form Criticism: *Two Essays on New Testament Research. Trans. by F. C. Grant* TB/96
WILLIAM A. CLEBSCH & CHARLES R. JAEKLE: Pastoral Care in Historical Perspective: *An Essay with Exhibits* TB/148
FREDERICK FERRE: Language, Logic and God. *New Preface by the Author* TB/1407
LUDWIG FEUERBACH: The Essence of Christianity. § *Introduction by Karl Barth. Foreword by H. Richard Niebuhr* TB/11
C. C. GILLISPIE: Genesis and Geology: *The Decades before Darwin* § TB/51
ADOLF HARNACK: What Is Christianity? § *Introduction by Rudolf Bultmann* TB/17
KYLE HASELDEN: The Racial Problem in Christian Perspective TB/116
MARTIN HEIDEGGER: Discourse on Thinking. *Translated with a Preface by John M. Anderson and E. Hans Freund. Introduction by John M. Anderson* TB/1459
IMMANUEL KANT: Religion Within the Limits of Reason Alone. § *Introduction by Theodore M. Greene and John Silber* TB/FG
WALTER KAUFMANN, Ed.: Religion from Tolstoy to Camus: *Basic Writings on Religious Truth and Morals. Enlarged Edition* TB/123
JOHN MACQUARRIE: An Existentialist Theology: *A Comparison of Heidegger and Bultmann. ° Foreword by Rudolf Bultmann* TB/125
H. RICHARD NIERUHR: Christ and Culture TB/3
H. RICHARD NIEBUHR: The Kingdom of God in America TB/49
ANDERS NYGREN: Agape and Eros. *Translated by Philip S. Watson* ° TB/1430
JOHN H. RANDALL, JR.: The Meaning of Religion for Man. *Revised with New Intro. by the Author* TB/1379
WALTER RAUSCHENBUSCHS Christianity and the Social Crisis. ‡ *Edited by Robert D. Cross* TB/3059
JOACHIM WACH: Understanding and Believing. *Ed. with Intro. by Joseph M. Kitagawa* TB/1399

Science and Mathematics

JOHN TYLER BONNER: The Ideas of Biology. Σ *Illus.* TB/570
W. E. LE GROS CLARK: The Antecedents of Man: *An Introduction to the Evolution of the Primates.* ° *Illus.* TB/559
ROBERT E. COKER: Streams, Lakes, Ponds. *Illus.* TB/586
ROBERT E. COKER: This Great and Wide Sea: *An Introduction to Oceanography and Marine Biology. Illus.* TB/551
W. H. DOWDESWELL: Animal Ecology. 61 *illus.* TB/543
C. V. DURELL: Readable Relativity. *Foreword by Freeman J. Dyson* TB/530
GEORGE GAMOW: Biography of Physics. Σ *Illus.* TB/567
F. K. HARE: The Restless Atmosphere TB/560
S. KORNER: The Philosophy of Mathematics: *An Introduction* TB/547
J. R. PIERCE: Symbols, Signals and Noise: *The Nature and Process of Communication* Σ TB/574
WILLARD VAN ORMAN QUINE: Mathematical Logic TB/558

Science: History

MARIE BOAS: The Scientific Renaissance, 1450-1630 ° TB/583
W. DAMPIER, Ed.: Readings in the Literature of Science. *Illus.* TB/512

STEPHEN TOULMIN & JUNE GOODFIELD: The Architecture of Matter: *The Physics, Chemistry and Physiology of Matter, Both Animate and Inanimate, as it has Evolved since the Beginnings of Science* TB/584
STEPHEN TOULMIN & JUNE GOODFIELD: The Discovery of Time TB/585
STEPHEN TOULMIN & JUNE GOODFIELD: The Fabric of the Heavens: *The Development of Astronomy and Dynamics* TB/579

Science: Philosophy

J. M. BOCHENSKI: The Methods of Contemporary Thought. *Tr. by Peter Caws* TB/1377
J. BRONOWSKI: Science and Human Values. *Revised and Enlarged. Illus.* TB/505
WERNER HEISENBERG: Physics and Philosophy: *The Revolution in Modern Science. Introduction by F. S. C. Northrop* TB/549
KARL R. POPPER: Conjectures and Refutations: *The Growth of Scientific Knowledge* TB/1376
KARL R. POPPER: The Logic of Scientific Discovery TB/576
STEPHEN TOULMIN: Foresight and Understanding: *An Enquiry into the Aims of Science. Foreword by Jacques Barzun* TB/564
STEPHEN TOULMIN: The Philosophy of Science: *An Introduction* TB/513

Sociology and Anthropology

REINHARD BENDIX: Work and Authority in Industry: *Ideologies of Management in the Course of Industrialization* TB/3035
BERNARD BERELSON, Ed., The Behavioral Sciences Today TB/1127
JOSEPH B. CASAGRANDE, Ed.: In the Company of Man: *Twenty Portraits of Anthropological Informants. Illus.* TB/3047
KENNETH B. CLARK: Dark Ghetto: *Dilemmas of Social Power. Foreword by Gunnar Myrdal* TB/1317
KENNETH CLARK & JEANNETTE HOPKINS: A Relevant War Against Poverty: *A Study of Community Action Programs and Observable Social Change* TB/1480
W. E. LE GROS CLARK: The Antecedents of Man: *An Introduction to the Evolution of the Primates.* ° *Illus.* TB/559
LEWIS COSER, Ed.: Political Sociology TB/1293
ROSE L. COSER, Ed.: Life Cycle and Achievement in America ** TB/1434
ALLISON DAVIS & JOHN DOLLARD: Children of Bondage: *The Personality Development of Negro Youth in the Urban South* ‖ TB/3049
ST. CLAIR DRAKE & HORACE R. CAYTON: Black Metropolis: *A Study of Negro Life in a Northern City. Introduction by Everett C. Hughes. Tables, maps, charts, and graphs* Vol. I TB/1086; Vol. II TB/1087
PETER E. DRUCKER: The New Society: *The Anatomy of Industrial Order* TB/1082
CORA DU BOIS: The People of Alor. *With a Preface by the Author* Vol. I *Illus.* TB/1042; Vol. II TB/1043
EMILE DURKHEIM et al.: Essays on Sociology and Philosophy: *with Appraisals of Durkheim's Life and Thought.* ‖ *Edited by Kurt H. Wolff* TB/1151
LEON FESTINGER, HENRY W. RIECKEN, STANLEY SCHACHTER: When Prophecy Fails: *A Social and Psychological Study of a Modern Group that Predicted the Destruction of the World* ‖ TB/1132

11